The Theory of
International Relations

The Theory of International Relations

Selected Texts from Gentili to Treitschke

M.G. Forsyth, H.M.A Keens-Soper, and P. Savigear, editors

AldineTransaction
A Division of Transaction Publishers
New Brunswick (U.S.A.) and London (U.K.)

First paperback printing 2009
Copyright © 1970 George Allen and Unwin Ltd.

This book is printed on acid-free paper that meets the American National Standard for Permanence of Paper for Printed Library Materials.

Library of Congress Catalog Number: 2008027960
ISBN: 978-0-202-36300-4
Printed in the United States of America

Library of Congress Cataloging-in-Publication Data

The theory of international relations : selected texts from Gentili to
Treitschke / M.G. Forsyth, H.M.A. Keens-Soper, and P. Savigear, editors.
    p. cm.
    Originally published: London : Allen & Unwin, 1970.
    Includes bibliographical references and index.
    ISBN 978-0-202-36300-4 (alk. paper)
    1. International relations--Sources. I. Forsyth, Murray Greensmith. II.
Keens-Soper, H. M. A. III. Savigear, Peter.

JZ63.T44 1970
327.101--dc22

                                                                    2008027960

CONTENTS

INTRODUCTION

This volume contains selections from nine authors, arranged in chronological sequence from Alberico Gentili, writing in 1598, to Heinrich von Treitschke, lecturing in Berlin at the end of the nineteenth century. Some of the selections are complete in themselves, others have been extracted from larger works. All are concerned with the nature of international politics. Why has this anthology been made, and in what sense does it contribute towards the theory of international relations? These are the questions which this introduction will try to answer.

There can be little doubt that the great writers of the past are at present neglected by students of international relations. It is significant that Gentz's essay on the balance of power has not appeared in English since 1806, while Rousseau's writings on international politics have never been fully translated at all. The American series called 'The Classics of International Law' (New York: Oceana Publications, Inc.), to which the editors of this volume are heavily indebted, have provided a magnificent service in republishing and translating several major texts. The size and complexity of many of these texts can, however, act as a deterrent to the inexperienced.

There is then a *prima facie* case for presenting in a manageable form the writings of the classic authors; such a case can only be made convincing if the relevance of these writings is also demonstrated. Do they genuinely deepen our understanding, or are they merely curiosities, part of the pre-history of a subject which is only now entering into its truly scientific phase? This is not the place to examine the merits of the behavioural or 'systems' approach to international relations. Suffice it to say that the editors of this volume believe that the most fruitful theoretical approach to this particular subject does not lie in the construction of all-embracing systems, nor in the deduction of scientific laws from the empirical observation of facts. To theorize about international relations is, in their opinion, to reflect philosophically and historically about this area of human activity.

It is not intended at this point to give a full exposé of the philosophical and historical methods of study; such a task would require a book of its own. A brief definition may, however, be suggested. By philosophical reflection is meant the identification and clarification of the universal features, or concepts, implicit in experience. Experience for the philosopher is not a set of separate 'facts' to be weighed and measured in order to reveal regularities or laws. Nor is it a chaos which has to be reduced to order by heuristic constructions which exist solely in the mind of the observer. Experience for the philosopher is essentially thought, a rational, self-critical activity. The philosopher's task is to re-think experience, and to elicit the basic, universal assumptions which are contained within it. Such a task is, needless to say, enormously difficult. It is linked intimately to the historian's task. The emphasis of the two subjects is different – the philosopher strives to distinguish the universal in experience, while the historian strives to identify experience within its particular temporal context – but the two activities are complementary, not mutually exclusive, and they share a common notion of experience. Without accurately identifying experience in an historical sense, philosophy can take place but be grossly misleading; without philosophical questioning, historical research can take place but be merely trivial. It is interesting that it was Kant, seemingly the ' purest ' of philosophers, who stressed that the philosophical mind must *as such* be thoroughly versed in history (see page 191).

If it is accepted that theorizing about international relations takes the form of a philosophical-cum-historical investigation of the type sketched above, then the selections included in this volume are not peripheral, but central to it. Indeed, in studying them, the philosophical and historical components of theorizing are very nearly in equilibrium. On the one hand the selections consist of thought at a fairly high level of abstraction, which is the form of experience most congenial to philosophy; on the other hand they consist of thought most definitely 'in the past', and this is the experience relevant to historians.

Having examined very briefly the methodological starting-point, a further question remains to be answered. Why these particular texts? Why Gentili to Treitschke? Why not Thucydides to Lenin? And why have Pufendorf and Saint Simon been left out, while Cobden and Vattel are included?

Let it be said immediately that the editors do not consider this particular selection to be definitive. It is intended as a preliminary *tour d'horizon*, a set of stepping-stones to further study. A vast amount of exploration requires to be done in this field, and undoubtedly new perspectives will be developed and other writers emerge into prominence as it progresses. In starting with this particular selection the editors had three main considerations in mind.

The first was that the writers chosen spanned a vital period – and area – in the development of international relations. It was in Europe between the sixteenth and nineteenth centuries that many of the underlying features of modern international society were developed. Perhaps the main developments were the emergence of *interstate* relationships as the key feature of international politics and the realization that these new relationships had their own specific rules and imperatives. The writings of the period reflect these developments in two ways. On the one hand they show a negative process, a desire to strip away the old, mediaeval, and primarily religious rules for international behaviour. On the other hand they attempt to develop new secular concepts to keep war within bounds – for example, the law of nature, international law, the balance of power, the league of nations, and the policy of non-intervention. It is primarily in order to illustrate these two themes that the writings which follow have been selected. They do not form a smooth, unilinear progression; each writer contributes his own distinctive viewpoint.

A second criterion which influenced the choice of writers was accessibility. The editors have given preference wherever possible to works which were difficult to obtain. Extracts will therefore not be found from Hobbes' *Leviathan*, Machiavelli's *The Prince*, or Rousseau's *Social Contract*, which all contain relevant material, but are readily available.

A final criterion was length. The editors did not wish to make the book into merely a collection of snippets illustrative of their own ideas! Although, inevitably, there are some very short excerpts included, preference has been given to pieces in which the argument is sufficiently sustained for the reader to make up his own mind, and form his own judgment. Burke and Pufendorf have been omitted largely because of the difficulty of finding such passages in their writings on the themes in question. For the same reason the editors' introduction to each writer has also been kept short.

It should be emphasized that the editors by no means consider that constructive thought about international politics ended with Treitschke. They hope to carry the story forward to the present in a further collection at a later date.

NOTE. All insertions or summaries by the editors or translators have been indicated in the texts by square brackets.

ALBERICO GENTILI

Alberico Gentili was born in San Ginesio, Italy, in 1552. He studied at Perugia University, from which he received the degree of Doctor of Laws in 1572. Being Protestant, the Gentili family came under the scrutiny of the Inquisition and was eventually forced to flee Italy. After considerable wandering Alberico arrived in England in 1580 and, largely through the influence of the Earl of Leicester, he secured a position at St John's College, Oxford. In 1584 he achieved considerable fame through his part in the case of the Spanish ambassador, Mendoza, whom the Privy Council wished to punish for his complicity in a plot against Queen Elizabeth. Gentili argued strongly in favour of ambassadorial inviolability, and it was his viewpoint which eventually prevailed. In 1586 Gentili left England, but he returned to become Regius Professor of Law at Oxford (1587). After 1598 he became increasingly engaged in forensic practice and resided chiefly in London, dying there in 1608. Gentili wrote prolifically, his main works in the field of international law being the *De Legationibus* (1585), the *De Jure Belli* (1598), and the *Advocationes Hispanicae*, published posthumously in 1613.

Gentili's position as the founder of modern thought about international relations rests on his determination to examine the subject from a secular rather than a theological standpoint. His celebrated cry *'Silete theologi in munere alieno'* – Let theologians keep silence about matters outside their province! – marks Gentili sharply off from his scholastic predecessors and expresses the advent of a new era. Nowhere does Gentili's fresh approach find better expression than in his firm rejection of war for religion's sake (Extract 3). His discussion of the 'just war' also reveals his secular standpoint (Extract 2).

Gentili's ability to shake off the past must be ascribed partly to his Protestantism, but it is important to realize that he was a Protestant of a particular type, able to separate clearly the claims of the state from those of religious conscience. Perhaps he is best seen as the counterpart, in the international field, of the French 'Politiques' – it is significant that he was well acquainted with the writings of Jean Bodin.

Gentili did not merely adopt a secular standpoint, he also tried to distinguish the international sphere from the national. In the first chapter of *De Jure Belli* (Extract 1) one can sense him struggling to give international law its own standing alongside civil law. At the same time his sketch of the sources of international law in this chapter provide a useful starting-point for subsequent discussions by later writers.

Gentili exercised a considerable influence on Grotius, as Grotius himself acknowledged (p. 57). But it is wrong to see Gentili merely as a forerunner of the Dutch writer. In several respects Gentili is both clearer and more 'modern' than Grotius.

The extracts which follow are all taken from the Translation by John C. Rolfe of the 1612 edition of the *De Jure Belli Libri Tres*. This is published in the series 'The Classics of International Law' edited by James Brown Scott (reprinted 1964). The extracts comprise pp. 3-5, 7-8 and 9-11; pp. 31-3; and pp. 38-41 of the volume. Gentili's marginal references have been printed as footnotes.

Suggested Reading

Dr Gesina H. J. Van Der Molen, *Alberico Gentili and the Development of International Law*, 1968.

Book I

CHAPTER I

ON INTERNATIONAL LAW
AS APPLIED TO WAR

Great and difficult is the task that I essay in undertaking to write on the Law of War, a subject which is hidden in Nature's inmost heart, which has manifold aspects, and is widely diffused. For this form of law is not assembled and given expression in the books of Justinian; otherwise we could readily refer to those works, or masters wiser than ourselves could direct us to them with no great difficulty. But those books do not discuss the variety of law, nor do any others in existence. For the brief treatises of the philosophers, several of which some one might suggest to me, treat the subject merely in a general way and in some cases only in outline, not going into its various phases with the view of explaining them with more precision. Even Marcus Tullius, after a very few observations on the subject, remarks: 'I have said enough about the obligations connected with war'.[1]

In fact, it does not appear to be the function either of the moral or of the political philosopher to give an account of the laws which we have in common with our enemies and with foreigners. For the moralist, whether he treats of the private customs of individuals or aims at the highest good in some other way, always confines himself within the city-state, and rather limits himself to the foundations of the virtues than rears lofty structures. Neither is it the part of the political philosopher to set forth the Law of War, since this relates, not to a single community, but to all.[2] It is for this reason that Aristotle separates from political

[1] Cicero, *On Duties,* I [xiii, 41].
[2] Piccolomini, *Universa philosophia de moribus,* Introd., vii, viii, ix; *Libri ad scientias de natura attinentes,* Introd., iii.

17

philosophy the part which has to do with the pursuit of arms and with military training.[1] This philosophy of war belongs to that great community formed by the entire world and the whole human race. Aristotle also writes that the political philosopher is not concerned with the injustice of those who do not belong to the state. Nevertheless, in writing of war he discusses this subject, inasmuch as he gives directions for defence against others outside the state, as well as for the punishment of their injustice.

Plato, it is true, declares that military science and the theory of warfare form a part of the art of citizenship, referring here to skill in the use of arms.[2] Aristotle also makes this same statement and we accept it as thoroughly true.[3] But what we maintain is this, that those philosophers have given no account of the laws of war, or even of military exercises, except with reference to the needs of their own states; whereas military science and the law of war are not confined within the bounds of communities, but on the contrary always look outward and have special reference to foreigners.

In the same way, too, our own Justinian, who made laws for his countrymen, did not go beyond the boundaries of the state which he desired to furnish with those laws. And although he discussed the law of nature and of nations, as the philosophers also did, as well as the cause of wars, prisoners, slaves, and some other topics relating to the subject; he nevertheless considered them all from the standpoint of his own state and explained them with reference to its requirements; for example, the status of a prisoner in his relation to the citizens, his property rights, and other questions of the kind.

What pray, shall I say of the modern interpreters of Justinian's laws, whom Jean Bodin justly declares to be wholly ignorant of this law of war.[4] Personally, I have read nothing save a few passages of Lignano's treatise on this subject and some scattered references of others; and all these I have read with no little contempt. So unsuitable are they and so lacking in clearness, to say nothing of the fact that these books contain a great deal which relates, not to war and the laws of war with reference to an enemy, but to military science, and the laws relating to our own citizens and

---

[1] Aristotle, *Politics*, III [VII, ii, 7].   [2] Plato, *Protagoras* [xii=p. 322 B].
[3] Aristotle, *Ethics* [I, ii, 4 ff.].   [4] Jean Bodin, *De republica*, V, vi.

soldiers. I find no fault with those learned men for that reason; but I repeat the statement, that hardly any knowledge of military law can be gained from the law of Justinian alone. For the greatest students of Justinian, although thoroughly acquainted with all his law, were utterly ignorant of that subject.

I have no patience with the modern commentators, who in this particular criticize their predecessors, while they offer themselves as guides to be followed. I mean the above-mentioned Bodin and Peter Faber, most distinguished jurists of the land of France.[1] For if the earlier interpreters have gone astray in introducing into this subject a bald and often inappropriate discussion of civil law, surely these more modern commentators have likewise erred in giving us a bare recital of history. For because of the diversity and the contradictory nature of the examples, and also because of the weakness of the form of argument, which seems for the most part based on examples, one could not easily derive from this treatment any system of law, and certainly not one which is regarded as natural and definite. Examples and events must, so to speak, be weighed in their own balance and their just value determined by their own standard.

The older legal writers perhaps included in their works this subject of war and other topics of the same kind relating to nations; Mutius, for example, Pomponius and some others, whose surviving fragments in some cases lend no slight support to this hypothesis of ours. Those men, who actively participated in great events and in the affairs of a great empire, as well as always keeping up a wide acquaintance with the other arts and not confining themselves to law, were able to have a clear insight also into these matters; while we, on the contrary, engaged as we are in such petty employments and dependent on the slight information given us by the works of Justinian, make them out darkly through a mist.

In particular, the works on the laws of the Fetiales had an exposition and orderly treatment of these laws of war[2]; for as a matter of fact the fetial priests were in charge of treaties, peace, wars, embassies, and other matters connected with these foreign relations.[3] But of those works nothing has come down to us save

---

[1] Peter Faber, *Semestria*, II, iii. [2] Cicero, *On Duties*, I [xi, 36].
[3] Varro, *On the Latin Language*, IV [V, lxxxvi].

the desire for them. For since that branch of the law began to be neglected even as early as the close of the Roman republic, that is to say, from the time when the Romans ceased to manage affairs systematically and began to do everything according to caprice, therefore the books on the fetial law perished, and even their memory and their expounders ceased to exist.

That which is not kept up disappears, and what is not valued is not kept up. Therefore that branch of law is buried in obscurity, and even its very existence will be called in question by some, who stoutly maintain that all law has its origin, not in nature, but in human thought. Accordingly, they will be found to be at variance with us, since we hold the firm belief that questions of war ought to be settled in accordance with the law of nations, which is the law of nature. But I say no more of these foes of nature, whom the arguments of the better philosophers have already refuted,[1] and I regard it as established that some law of nature exists and in accordance with it this subject of war should be discussed.

It remains, however, to investigate the intricate question, what that law is and how we shall prove that it is this or that. For obviously we must not only teach it in the manner of Plato, but because of conflicting opinions we must also demonstrate it in the manner of Aristotle. . . .

[Gentili here attacks the ignorant, who cannot discern natural law, and the perverse, who deny its existence. He also criticizes those jurists who have made international law more uncertain by adopting different and conflicting views about its content.]

And although international law is a portion of the divine law, which God left with us after our sin, yet we behold that light amid great darkness; and hence through error, bad habits, obstinacy, and other affections due to darkness we often cannot recognize it. So the philosophers have stated,[2] and we ourselves have observed the mania for disagreement which the disciples of Sabinus and Proculus have.

But truth exists, even though it be hidden in a well, and when it is diligently and faithfully sought, it can be brought forth and

---

[1] Plato, *Statesman*, and *On Laws*, X [p. 890 D]; Cicero, *On Laws*, I [x-xvii]; *On Invention*, II [liii, 160].

[2] Thomas Aquinas, I, ii, qu. 94, art. 2; Gregorio de Valentia, *Theological Commentaries*, Disp. vii, qu. 4, no. 2.

as a rule is brought forth. Abundant light is afforded us by the definitions which the authors and founders of our laws are unanimous in giving to this law of nations, which we are investigating. For they say that the law of nations is that which is in use among all the nations of men, which native reason has established among all human beings, and which is equally observed by all mankind.[1] Such a law is a natural law. 'The agreement of all nations about a matter must be regarded as a law of nature.'[2]

This statement, however, must not be understood to mean that all nations actually came together at a given time, and that thus the law of nations was established. The writers to whom I have referred do not make any such statement, and it is not necessary to understand the word *omnes* in such a way that when one speaks of the usage of all nations it should be considered to mean absolutely every nation[3]; since countless numbers of these, in regions widely separated from us, utterly different in their customs, and of different tongues, remain unknown. Do not be misled by the great jurist Hughes Doneau, who takes the definitions in that sense and therefore finds fault with them also.[4] But that which has successively seemed acceptable to all men should be regarded as representing the intention and purpose of the entire world, as Ambrose once showed in a treatise of his, as did also St Jerome.[5] And in fact an unwritten law, such as this, is like a custom and is established in that same manner. Moreover, such unanimity cannot fail to be recognized, just as it is known that all nations and races of men are agreed as to the existence of God. . . .[6]

[Gentili here argues that the jurists use the phrase 'all nations' because the empires of the Romans, of Alexander and of the Parthians did in fact embrace or come into contact with all the peoples of the east.]

But there is another more elegant definition of the law of nations and it is to the same purpose as that which Xenophon has handed down,[7] namely, that there are everywhere certain

---

[1] *Digest*, I, i, 1, 9; *Institutes*, I, ii.
[2] Cicero, *Tusculan Disputations*, I [xiii, 30].
[3] Baldus, *On Code*, VI, xxi, 1.
[4] Doneau, *Commentaries*, I, vi [4].
[5] Ambrose, *On Ephesians* IV; St. Jerome, *To Titus* [1].
[6] Cicero, *On the Nature of the Gods*, I [xvii, 44].
[7] Xenophon, *Memorabilia*, IV [iv].

unwritten laws, not enacted by men (since men could not all assemble in one place, nor were they all of one speech), but given to them by God. For example, the one which takes first place with all men, that one should worship God; and the second, that one should honour Father and Mother. Such laws are not written, but inborn; we have not learned, received, and read them, but we have wrested, drawn, and forced them out of Nature herself. We have not received them through instruction but have acquired them at birth; we have gained them, not by training, but by instinct.[1]

Nevertheless, this definition also permits us to ask the question what this natural reason is, or how it is made manifest. To this question the following reply must be made; that natural reason is evident of itself and therefore those who rely upon it are content merely to say: 'This is perfectly clear from nature itself', 'It is evident from natural reason', 'He has a knowledge derived from nature', 'Nature shows'; and there are many remarks of the same kind.[2] So also 'Just by nature', 'Nothing is so completely in harmony with natural justice', 'It is contrary to nature', 'Nature does not allow', and hundreds of other phrases.[3] Moreover, Aristotle says: 'By nature all men desire knowledge', 'All men seem to seek the good', etc.[4]

These things are so well known, that if you should try to prove them, you would render them obscure.[5] At any rate, it would be useless to prove what is already manifest.[6] Thus all the interpreters of the law say that things which are well known ought to be stated, but not demonstrated.[7] It has been made sufficiently clear that natural law does exist, and that if you should transgress it in any particular you would desire to conceal the act through very shame.[8] Or if you should go so far in shamelessness as to confess and try to justify the action, you would have the same feeling that one has towards those statements which are called

---

[1] Cicero, *For Milo* [iv, 10].
[2] *Digest*, XLV, i, 75; XLIV, vii, i; XVIII, vii, 5; L, xvi, 220.
[3] *Digest*, XLIII, xxvi, 2; XLI, i, 9; XLI, ii, 3 and 23.
[4] Aristotle, *Metaphysics*, pref. [I, i], and *Ethics*, pref. [I, i, 2].
[5] Aristotle, *Rhetoric*, III [xvii].
[6] Cardanus, *On Wisdom*, I.
[7] *Digest*, XXXIII, iv, i, §§ 8, 9.
[8] *Decretals*, II, xxi, v, 31; *Constitutions of Clement*, II, xii, 5.

axioms, namely, you would instinctively feel that the act could not be justified.

'This is the greatest gift of nature, that virtue sheds her light into the minds of all men',[1] 'We feel this by a kind of inner consciousness', says Augustine.[2] 'What is truly evil', says Tertullian. 'Not even those who are carried away by it will attempt to defend as good, for nature fills every evil thing either with shame, or with fear.'[3] Not only justice but shame as well, are said to have been sent from heaven, to govern men and hold them to their duty.[4] 'Although they may deny this, yet they cannot fail to blush for it', says Ambrose.[5]

In the same way the jurists say that nothing is to be regarded as just which cannot be desired honourably, without shame, with modesty and with reverence.[6]

In this way the law of nations is defended. But it will also be supported in many cases by the utterances of great authorities, which will find a place in our treatise, as they do in all the other arts and disciplines. In fact, it is the habit of philosophers and other wise men to speak according to the promptings of nature. And hence there will be found here the examples of those who are regarded as honourable and of good repute. For they too appear to have acted in accordance with nature. For although one ought not to judge from examples, and that principle is called Justinian's golden rule, yet it is clear that a plausible conjecture may be deducted from examples.[7] Indeed, in cases of doubt one is obliged to judge from examples, and also when anything has become a custom.[8] For it is not fitting to change things which have always had a fixed observance, and a decision has greater weight which is supported by the opinion of a large number of men.[9]

What I am to say of the actions of great and good men? These

---

[1] Seneca, *On Benefits* [IV, xvii, 4].
[2] Augustine, *On the Unity of Belief* [xvi].
[3] Tertullian, *Apology* [1].
[4] Plato, *Protagoras* [p. 322 C].
[5] Ambrose, *On Duties*, III, xiv.
[6] *Digest*, XXII, i, 3, 19; XII, vi, 15; XX, vi, 8; XXIII, ii, 14.
[7] *Code*, VII, xlv, 13; Alciati, *Consilia*, V, xxxiii, VI.
[8] Decianus, *Consilia*, III, c.
[9] Socinus, *Fallentiae regularum*, cclxxx; Cephalus, *Consilia*, XXV [16]; XCVI [24]; CXX [13]; CCCVII [17].

are always to be emulated; for it is foolish and treasonable not to desire to imitate those who were rated so high, again to quote Justinian.[1] 'What the world approves, I do not venture to disapprove', declares Baldus.[2]

Arguments too and reasoning will play a part here, as we have observed them to do elsewhere. And why not? 'Reason too is an imitation of nature.'[3] I shall not give you demonstrations, such as you may get from a mathematician, but the persuasive arguments which this kind of treatise allows. For as Aristotle writes at the beginning of his *Ethics*, 'It is the part of a philosopher to seek an exact explanation in each case, so far as the nature of the subject itself permits'.

There will be not a few things from the civil law of Justinian which it will be possible to adapt to our uses, or scattered references found there to this military law of nations. And most properly; for natural reason varies constantly according to men's intelligence and many are led not so much by the reason as by fantasy. But the laws which were laid down by the philosophers and approved by the judgment of every age undoubtedly possess natural reason, as the wise Alciati declares.[4]

The words which are written in the Sacred Books of God will properly be given special weight; since it is evident that they were uttered not merely for the Hebrews, but for all men, for all nations and for all times. For that these words are of a true nature, that is to say, one which is blameless and just, is most certain. 'These testimonies are forthwith divine; they do not need the successive step which the rest require. They are as simple as they are true, as widespread as they are simple, as popular as they are widespread, as natural as they are popular, as divine as they are natural.'[5]

Come then, since we do not lack material for formulating definitions of this law of war, let us at once begin the discussion itself.

[1] Alciati, *Consilia*, II, xiii; IX, xliv; Justinian, Edict xiii. [De Concept. Dig. I, 3.].
[2] Baldus, *Consilia*, IV, ccccxcvi [3].
[3] Seneca, *Letters*, lxvii [lxvi, 39].
[4] Alciati, *Consilia*, V, xxxviii.
[5] Tertullian, *De testimonio animae* [v].

Book I

CHAPTER VI

THAT WAR MAY BE WAGED
JUSTLY BY BOTH SIDES

But may a war be waged with justice on both sides? The learned Piccolomini raises this question somewhere, but does not answer it.[1] Among our jurists Fulgosius maintained the affirmative against the opinion of the others. Alciati has followed Fulgosius in more than one place.[2] I too follow him, but with the proviso that there may be reasonable doubt as to the justice of the cause. This same point has been made by our other jurists and by our theologians, who declare that there is justice on one side in reality, but on the other and on both through justifiable ignorance.[3] Thus, led by the voice of God, the Jews justly made war upon the Canaanites, and the Canaanites also justly resisted the Jews through ignorance of the divine utterance, acting in self-defence. And so Pius II wisely replied to the Hungarian envoys, who spoke against the Emperor, that he thought that the King of Hungary was not departing from what was honourable; while he also knew that the Emperor was a lover of justice, however much the two might differ as to the sovereignty.[4] For neither of them thought that he had an unjust cause.

It is the nature of wars for both sides to maintain that they are supporting a just cause.[5] In general, it may be true in nearly every kind of dispute, that neither of the two disputants is unjust. Aristotle makes an exception only when the enquiry is 'whether

---

[1] Piccolomini, *Universa philosophia de moribus*, VI, xxi.
[2] Alciati, *Paradoxa*, II, xxi, *On Digest*, I, i, 5.
[3] Conn, [Covarruvias], *in c. peccatum* § 10; Soto, *De iustitia et iure*, V, qu. 1, art, 7; Victoria, *Relectiones* [V, xx].
[4] Pius II, *Commentaries* III.   [5] Alciati, *Consilia*, VIII, xciii.

25

the act took place'.[1] And indeed in the case of one's own act our jurists are not in the habit of admitting ignorance as a defence. But they do admit it in the case of another's act, because that happens under different conditions. We are driven to this distinction by the weakness of our human nature, because of which we see everything dimly, and are not cognizant of that purest and truest form of justice, which cannot conceive of both parties to a dispute being in the right. For why, says Maximus of Tyre in this connexion,[2] should those whose purposes are just engage in strife with one another? And in fact it is either the unjust who fight with one another or the unjust with the just.

But we for the most part are unacquainted with that truth. Therefore we aim at justice as it appears from man's standpoint. In this way we avoid the objection of Baldus, that when war arises among contending parties, it is absolutely inevitable that one side or the other is in the wrong.[3] Accordingly we say that if it is evident that one party is contending without any adequate reason, that party is surely practising brigandage and not waging war. All agree on this point, and rightly. And it is quite true that the cause of the party which is in the right receives additional justification from that fact. 'The injustice of an adversary makes wars just', writes Augustine, and referring to the Romans he says: 'The injustice of others furnished them with adversaries with whom they could wage just wars'.[4]

But if it is doubtful on which side justice is, and if each side aims at justice, neither can be called unjust. Thus Baldus himself maintains that war between kings is just, whenever the aim on both sides is to retain majesty and justice.[5] Those who contend in the litigation of the Forum justly, that is to say, on a plausible ground, either as defendants or plaintiffs, and lose their case and the verdict, are not judged guilty of injustice.[6] And yet the oath regarding false accusation is taken by both parties. Why should the decision be different in this kind of dispute and in a contest of arms?

[1] Aristotle, *Rhetoric*, III [xv, 2].
[2] Maximus of Tyre, *Sermones*, xiv.
[3] Baldus, *On Digest*, I, i, 5.
[4] Augustine, *On the City of God*, IV [xv]; XIX [vii].
[5] Baldus, *Consilia*, II, ccclviii.
[6] Decio, *On Digest*, L, xvii, 42; Baldus, *Consilia*, V, ccxcix.

In particular Bartolus, Baldus, and some others apply arguments derived from those bloodless contests of the Forum to the strife of arms and the duel.[1] For example, some point is obscure and it is not clear whether a thing belongs to Titius or Sempronius; and since each lays claim to it, each tries to take it from the other. Will you find one of them guilty of injustice?

Baldus says, and it is perfectly evident, that no one ought to surrender his rights without a struggle, but that every possible effort should be made to maintain them.[2] Cicero appropriately says of the two factions of Julius Caesar and of Pompey: 'There was an element of uncertainty and a contest between leaders of distinction. Many were in doubt as to what was best, many wondered what would be to their advantage, many what was proper, some even what was lawful.'[3] And when the struggle is between expediency and honour, there is no slight degree of uncertainty as to which we ought to follow. We may add to the above the words of Severus to Albinus: 'When we fought against Niger, we did not have such specious reasons for our hostilities; for the empire was the prize of victory, and each of us with equal eagerness strove to win it, even while its lawful possession was still a matter of dispute'.[4]

I add here the cases in which one renders aid to allies, friends, kindred, neighbours and others whom one is under obligations to assist, and yet in so doing justly rouses against himself the arms of the adversary whom he is attacking. Thus Livy relates of the people of Caere that they espoused the cause of the men of Tarquinii against the Romans through compassion for their kinsfolk, and as the historian makes their own envoys say, not through design, but through the compulsion of necessity.[5]

This will, moreover, give rise to a third variety of the question, when the war is just on one side, but on the other is still more just. Such a case is of course possible, inasmuch as one man does not cease to be in the right because his opponent has a juster cause. The virtues admit of greater or less degrees, and the middle

---

[1] Alciati, *On Digest*, I, i, 5; *Consilia*, V, lxiii.
[2] Baldus, *Consilia*, I, cccxxvi.
[3] Cicero, *For Marcellus* [x, 30].
[4] Herodian, [*Histories*] III [VI, iv].
[5] Livy, VII [xix, 6, xx, 2 ff.].

ground of a virtue has length and breadth and is not limited to a point.[1]

I shall add other instances and other causes for war from time to time and take note of them. Of all our laws, however, that one seems to me the clearest which grants the rights of war to both contestants, makes what is taken on each side the property of the captors, and regards the prisoners of both parties as slaves. While others are endeavouring to evade this law, in opposition to Fulgosius, they are unquestionably indulging in a pleasurable madness[2]; as was demonstrated by Alciati, who also insists on that equality among enemies of which we made note before.[3]

But although it may sometimes happen (it will not occur very often, as you will learn forthwith) that injustice is clearly evident on one of the two sides, nevertheless this ought not to affect the general principle, and prevent the laws of war from applying to both parties. For laws are not based upon rare instances and adapted to them[4]; that is to say, on events which are rare in their own class, and which take place only occasionally, contrary to the general nature of the case. This is the doctrine of many of our learned men, and they maintain that the general rule (as I say) is not affected.[5] 'No law is altogether adapted to every one', said Marcus Cato.[6] Therefore no change must be made in this law of the enemy and of war; for it is impartial to both sides, just as in the contests of the Forum the law is impartial towards each of the litigants, until sentence has been pronounced in favour of one or the other of them. And then the defeated party, who contended unjustly, will suffer severe punishment at the hands of the victor because of his injustice.

But if the unjust man gain the victory, neither in a contention in arms nor in the strife carried on in the garb of peace is there any help for it. Yet it is not the law which is at fault, but the execution of the law. As Paulus says: 'The law is not to blame, but its application'.[7]

---

[1] Piccolomini, *Universa philosophia de moribus*, IX, liii.

[2] [Horace, *Odes*, III, iv, 6].

[3] Alciati, *On Digest*, I, i, 5 and L, xxxi, 23.

[4] *Digest*, I, iii, 3-6.

[5] Azo, *Sumina*; *On Dig.*, L, xvii, 64; Wesenbeck, *On Iustit.*, I, xix; Doneau, *Com.* I, xv; Alciati, *Paradoxa*, V, vii.

[6] Livy, xxxiv [iii, 5].   [7] *Digest*, XXV, ii, 30.

Perhaps you may console yourself by saying with the theologians and the philosophers that there is no sin without retribution, since every wicked deed is its own punishment.[1] As Seneca puts it: 'The first and greatest penalty for sinners is to have sinned'. Fear too is a chastisement, as the same philosopher points out, when he says: 'Fortune exempts many from punishment, but none from fear'. Besides, there is ill repute in the eyes of others and remorse in one's own heart, as the philosophers have made clear. There is also Hell, of which the philosophers have told us by induction, and the theologians from knowledge.

[1] Piccolomini, *Universa philosophia de moribus*, IX, liii.

Book I

CHAPTER IX

WHETHER IT IS JUST TO WAGE WAR
FOR THE SAKE OF RELIGION

Now if religion is of such a nature that it ought to be forced
upon no one against his will, and if a propaganda which exacts
faith by blows is called a strange and unheard-of thing, it follows
that force in connexion with religion is unjust.[1] 'To deprive
religion of its freedom and to forbid one to believe as one chooses,
so that I am not allowed to worship whom I wish, but am compelled
to honour one whom I could not desire to honour, this is a
justification of irreligion. And therefore even the Egyptians were
allowed the privilege of following their vain superstition, which
led them to deify birds and beasts and to condemn to death
whoever slew any god of that kind', says Tertullian.[2] And in
another passage he declares that religion has a natural power,
which Pomponius also asserts,[3] as well as that the religion of one
man does not injure or benefit another.

'Faith must be recommended, not forced upon one', says
Bernard,[4] and Hilarion declares that it is a new thing for men to
be compelled to believe, meanwhile admitting to Constantius
Caesar that Arianism, to which Constantius was trying to force
him, was the true faith.[5] 'We cannot command religious belief,
since no man is forced to believe against his will', was a decision
of the wise King Theodoric,[6] and King Theodatus also said that
sacrifice to the Lord must be voluntary, not made at the command

---

[1] *Decretum*, II, xxiii, qu. 5, c. 35; *Decretum*, I, xlv, 3; *Decretals*, III, xlii, 3.
[2] Tertullian, *Apology* [xxiv]; *To Scapula*.   [3] *Digest*, I, i, 2.
[4] St. Bernard, *Sermo in Cantica*, lxvi [12].
[5] Erasmus, *Hilarion*, preface.
[6] Cassiodorus, *Variae*, II, xxvii, X, xxvi.

of some one who compelled it. Lactantius declared that religion is not a matter of compulsion; that it is established by words, not by blows; that nothing should be so voluntary as religion; and that the Christians should not be worse than the Egyptians.[1]

Josephus expresses the opinion that every man ought to worship God of his own free will, and not at the bidding of another.[2] 'Religion', says Arnobius, 'is content with its own powers', and speaking against violence and arms he says: 'Because you are mighty with the sword and with the power of the steel, do you think therefore that you are superior in knowledge of the truth?'[3] The great L'Hôpital thus expresses himself in a bitter satire: 'We contend with words and with arms to decide which has the truer conviction as to religion, meanwhile scorning the laws and traditions of Moses',[4] etc.

You have heard the authorities; now listen to argument. Whatever is contrary to the nature of a thing does not tend to establish that thing, but rather to destroy it. To attempt by force what cannot be done by force is madness. A thing which is a matter of choice should not be made a necessity. It is folly to try to support by adventitious oaths a thing which can stand by its own weight. A thing which has its own standard should not be measured by that of another. Every innovation is unjust; what time has approved has almost the force of a law, as the worthy Duaren writes in his *Anniversary Disputations*. So much for the arguments.

Religion is a matter of the mind and of the will, which is always accompanied by freedom, as was brilliantly demonstrated both by philosophers and by others, and by Bernard in his book *On Free Will*. Our mind and whatever belongs to our mind are not affected by any external power or potentate, and the soul has no master save God only, who alone can destroy the soul. Do you understand? Yet hear still one more thing. Religion ought to be free. Religion is a kind of marriage of God with man. And so, as liberty of the flesh is resolutely maintained in the other wedlock, so in this one freedom of the spirit is granted.

But the learned Victoria declares that this principle of not

[1] Lactantius, *Divine Institutes*, V, xx, xxi[xix].
[2] Josephus, *Life* [23].
[3] Arnobius, *Against the Heathen*, III, IV.
[4] M. de L'Hôpital, *Letters*, IV.

making war from religious motives is approved by all without exception, and that religion was not a just reason for the war of his Spanish countrymen against the Indians.[1] Diego de Covarruvias, also a Spaniard and a learned jurist, names several canonists and theologians who preach this same doctrine[2]; and Baldus also declared with reference to Innocent that war is not lawful against infidels who live at peace with us and do us no harm.[3] Covarruvias himself too holds this opinion, yet does not deny that some take the opposite side, including Aquinas. But he also refutes the views of the others and their reasoning.

It is true that the fathers of Toledo made a decree that heretics should be punished by war, and that their decree was embodied in the canonical law.[4] And Baldus says that it is undoubtedly lawful to plunder the enemies of the Faith, that is to say of the Church.[5] Yet he does not support his conviction by a good argument, and in fact his interpretation rests on very doubtful grounds. Therefore it surely cannot be stated as a general principle that one is an enemy to the Faith who is an enemy of the Church, because the Church often wages war, not in behalf of religion and the Faith, but for those things which are called temporal. Elsewhere Baldus allows war against heretics, and (contradicting himself) against infidels, on this ground: that they are without realms of their own because of their heresy and infidelity, since a heretic and an infidel has no true jurisdiction, and it is impossible to live without a magistrate and jurisdiction, inasmuch as these are essentials of the law of nations.[6] But this argument is utterly inane; for it is God who confers jurisdiction upon them.[7]

There are indeed some things which have been said on this subject which are at variance with the teachers first mentioned and with their general principles; but I do not yet own myself defeated in the argument. 'Against the barbarian religion we waged war to the death', say the Christians, referring to the Saracenic faith; and Bernard, when arousing Louis King of the

---

[1] Victoria, *Relectiones theologicae* [V, x].
[2] Covarruvias, in *c. peccatum* [2] § 10.
[3] Baldus, *On Digest*, I, i, 5.
[4] *On Sext*, V, ii, 13; *Decretum*, I, xlv, 5.
[5] Baldus, *Consilia*, IV, cxl [cl].
[6] Baldus, *Consilia*, V, ccccxxxix.
[7] *I Peter*, ii; *Romans*, xiii; St Bernard, *Sermo de adventu Domini*, III.

French against Asia, asks: 'Have you any more just cause for war than this holy one?' The Lacedaemonians too, among other charges against the Athenians, alleged that there were violators of religion at Athens; and the Athenians retorted that the Lacedaemonians dragged forth suppliants from the temples and slew them, along with other charges of the same kind.

It is true, however, that these principles are said to be the invention of the most greedy of men and to be cloaks for their dishonesty; and that there is no religion so wicked as to order an attack upon men of a different belief.[1] In this way King Ferdinand, who was called the Catholic, covered almost all his excesses with a respectable mantle of religion, as Guicciardini remarks.[2] And it was under a similar pretext that the Emperor Charles, the grandson of Ferdinand, veiled his desire for dominion, as Giovio has written.[3]

Let no one at this point confront me with our own Justinian, who says somewhere that he undertook wars because of a religious motive.[4] Let no one cite Pepin, who like a dutiful magistrate burned and laid waste everything, since he did it to gratify the Pope.[5] Let no one cite others.

'Each man declares his own war a holy one. Each one insists that his enemies are godless men. Each names his own cause righteous. Every one has upon his lips the words "sacred" and "pious", but in purpose, aim, and intention he is otherwise affected. This dispute is about human justice. Remove that ground and there will be no cause for war. At present there is no abominable crime which is not shielded under the name of piety. The name of sacred warfare is given (alas!) to this strife', referring to that with which the King of Naples was assailed by the Pope. Thus at length and often does that great writer express himself.[6]

The acts of Justinian too were for the purpose of defending his subjects either from Persian idolaters or from Gothic or Vandal heretics, who now seized a part of the Roman Empire

---

[1] Comes, Natalis, *Universae historiae sui temporis*, I.
[2] Guicciardini, *History of Italy*, XII.
[3] Paolo Giovio, *Historiae sui temporis*, XXX [= II, p. 153].
[4] [Justinian] *Novels*, lxxviii.
[5] Paolo Emilio, *History of France*, II [xxxii].
[6] *Ibid.*, VI, VII, VIII.

and now attempted to oppress the subjects of Justinian who dwelt within the Empire. Besides, if Justinian made war to defend the Christians who were subjects of the Persians and were ill-treated by the Persians because of their religion, I tell you on the authority of Covarruvias that those causes were just.[1] So also the wars of the Franks and of the other peoples of Europe are approved, since their motive was to aid those who were harassed by the Turks and to avenge the wrongs of Christ.

But all this is another problem, namely that of defence, which I shall investigate later. Now the question before us is, whether it is lawful to wage war with religion as the sole motive. This I deny and I give as my reason the following: since the laws of religion do not properly exist between man and man, therefore no man's rights are violated by a difference in religion, nor is it lawful to make war because of religion. Religion is a relationship with God. Its laws are divine, that is between God and man; they are not human, namely, between man and man. Therefore a man cannot complain of being wronged because others differ from him in religion.

Other authorities declare that if religion is violated, all men are wronged.[2] And Marcus Tullius says that if piety towards the gods is abolished, faith is destroyed at the same time, as well as human society, and that most excellent of the virtues, justice.[3]

But we are not now speaking of those who, living rather like beasts than like men, are wholly without religious belief; for I should hold that such men, being the common foes of all mankind, as pirates are, ought to be assailed in war and forced to adopt the usages of humanity. For of a truth those seem to be dangerous to all men, who, wearing the human form, live the life of the most brutal of beasts; for it is reported and believed that certain even of the brutes have a kind of religion.[4] These are the men who war with God after the fashion of the giants; 'For what else than resistance to Nature can be called warring with the gods as the giants did?' [5]

---

[1] Covarruvias, *in c. peccatum*, [p. 2] § 10.
[2] *Code*, I, v, 4.
[3] Cicero, *On the Nature of the Gods*, I [ii, 4].
[4] Chassaneux, *Catalogus gloriae mundi*, Pr. XII, consid. 78.
[5] Cicero, *Laelius* [Cato Maior, ii, 5].

Religion is a part of the law of nature and therefore that law will not protect those who have no share in it. And yet I will add this: that no nation exists which is wholly destitute of religion.[1] Name me such a nation, if you can. Those are not without the pale of this law of nature who are victims of human liability to error and who, although led by the desire for what it is good, adopt a religion that is evil. Thus Agathias says that the Alemanni, who are idolaters, are deserving of pity.[2] Hence they ought to be instructed and patiently dealt with, not constrained nor exterminated. Many interpreters of the law, when consulted in special cases, have also decided that the Jews ought not to be molested or forced to adopt our faith, although since the coming of Christ they do not differ from idolaters.[3]

But those who separate themselves from the rest of the body politic and arouse one part of the state against the other are disturbers of the public peace, and an injury to the rest of the citizens. These it is who were referred to by the authorities cited above. But if men in another state live in a manner different from that which we follow in our own state, they surely do us no wrong. Therefore, since war against them will be either vindictive or punitive, it can in neither event be just; for we have not been injured, so that we can justly take vengeance, nor are they our subjects, so that it is our part to chastise them, as Covarruvias says. To punish a guilty person whom you have no right to punish is equivalent to chastising an innocent person.[4]

---

[1] Cicero, *On the Nature of the Gods*, I [xvi, 43].
[2] Agathias, *Histories*, I.
[3] Baldus, *Consilia*, I, cccxvi.
[4] Alexander of Imola, *Consilia*, VI, ccxxv.

HUGO GROTIUS

The style of Grotius (1583-1645) is not to modern liking. Endless reference to ancient authorities is burdensome. Yet in Grotius method and argument are closely linked.

As a child of wealthy, educated and well-connected parents he was a prodigy of learning. Before the age of twenty he had gained a European reputation. Although his lasting fame rests on the *De Jure Belli Ac Pacis Libri Tres*, Grotius wrote poetry, drama and criticism as well as works on law and theology. For political reasons, Grotius was obliged to leave Holland and it was in Paris in the diplomatic service of Sweden that he published in 1625 his major work. It is dedicated to Louis XIII.

Grotius' significance lies in the manner of his determination to meet the consequences of two important facts which by the seventeenth century and on the eve of the Thirty Years War had become prominent features of European life. The first was the determined claims by territorial and secular states to assert their complete independence from the traditional and often rival claims of the Holy Roman Empire and the Papacy. This process had been under way for centuries, but in the early seventeenth century the full implications had still to be drawn. The question was what, if anything, could stand between the remnants of a united and Christian Europe and an international anarchy of sovereign states.

The second fact which prompted Grotius was the incidence and havoc of war. He responded by positing a 'great society of states'. The character of this international society in which states are subject to restraint through law is according to Grotius a combination of rules, some of which, the laws of nature, derive from man's rational and social nature which demands order and justice, while others, like the laws of nations, are based on the will and consent of states. One implication of this conception is that states, members of an international society and mutually concerned with its preservation, are subject to restraints both in respect to the morality of war—the distinction between just and unjust wars—and in the conduct of any war declared by the highest public authorities.

Machiavelli argued that 'that war is just which is necessary' and Hobbes that 'Where there is no common power, there is no law; where no law, no injustice. Force, and fraud, are in war the two cardinal virtues.' Grotius combined—and confused—'is' and 'ought' in an attempt to assert some order into the facts of international life.

The extracts from *On the Law of War and Peace* are taken from the translation of the Latin edition of 1646 by Francis W. Kelsey. This translation forms part of the series, 'The Classics of International Law', published for the Carnegie Endowment for International Peace. Kelsey's translation of Grotius was published in 1925.

Extracts

I. *Prolegomena to the three books* on *The Law of War and Peace*, pp. 9-30.

II. *Book II Chapter I, Section I. What causes of war may be called justifiable*, pp. 169-171.

III. *Book II Chapter XX, Section XL. A discussion whether kings and peoples may rightly wage war on account of things done contrary to the law of nature, although not against them or their subjects*, pp. 504-506 and *Book II Chapter XX, Section XLIII* Paragraph 3, p. 508.

IV. *Book III Chapter X. Cautions in regard to things which are done in an unlawful war. Section I and Section III*, pp. 716-719.

V. *Book III Chapter XII, Section VIII. The advantages which follow from such moderation are pointed out*, pp. 754-756.

VI. *Book III Chapter XXV. Conclusion, with admonition on behalf of good faith and peace*, pp. 860-862.

Suggested Reading

W. S. M. Knight, *The Life and Works of Hugo Grotius*, 1925.

H. Lauterpacht, 'The Grotian Tradition in International Law', *British Yearbook of International Law*, 1946.

Hedley Bull, 'The Grotian Conception of International Society', *Diplomatic Investigations*, ed. H. Butterfield and Martin Wight, 1966.

C. van Vollenhoven, Grotius and Geneva, *Bibliotecha Visseriana*, Vol. VI, 1926.

Prolegomena

1. The municipal law of Rome and of other states has been treated by many, who have undertaken to elucidate it by means of commentaries or to reduce it to a convenient digest. That body of law, however, which is concerned with the mutual relations among states or rulers of states, whether derived from nature, or established by divine ordinances, or having its origin in custom and tacit agreement, few have touched upon. Up to the present time no one has treated it in a comprehensive and systematic manner; yet the welfare of mankind demands that this task be accomplished.

2. Cicero justly characterized as of surpassing worth a knowledge *For Balbus,* of treaties of alliance, conventions, and understandings of peoples, vi.15 kings and foreign nations; a knowledge, in short, of the whole law of war and peace. And to this knowledge Euripides gives the preference over an understanding of things divine and human; for he represents Theoclymenus as being thus addressed:

> For you, who know the fate of men and gods,   *Helena,*
> What is, what shall be, shameful would it be   928 f.
> To know not what is just.

3. Such a work is all the more necessary because in our day, as in former times, there is no lack of men who view this branch of law with contempt, as having no reality outside of an empty name. On the lips of men quite generally is the saying of Euphemus, which Thucydides quotes,[1] that in the case of a king or imperial

---

[1] (xix). The words are in Book VI (VI, lxxxv). The same thought is found in Book V (V, lxxxix), where the Athenians, who at the time of speaking were very powerful, thus address the Melians: 'According to human standards those arrangements are accounted just which are settled when the necessity on both sides is equal; as for the rest, the more powerful do all they can, the more weak endure'.

city nothing is unjust which is expedient. Of like implication is the statement that for those whom fortune favours might makes right, and that the administration of a state cannot be carried on without injustice.

Furthermore, the controversies which arise between peoples or kings generally have Mars as their arbiter. That war is irreconcilable with all law is a view held not alone by the ignorant populace; expressions are often let slip by well-informed and thoughtful men which lend countenance to such a view. Nothing is more common than the assertion of antagonism between law and arms. Thus Ennius says:

In Gellius,
xx, 10

> Not on grounds of right is battle joined,
> But rather with the sword do men
> Seek to enforce their claims.

Horace, too, describes the savage temper of Achilles in this wise:

Art of
Poetry, 122

> Laws, he declares, were not for him ordained;
> By dint of arms, he claims all for himself.

Lucan, I,
225

Another poet depicts another military leader as commencing war with the words:

> Here peace and violated laws I leave behind.

Plutarch,
Fort, of
Alex.,
330 E
Apoth.,
202 D

Antigonus when advanced in years ridiculed a man who brought to him a treatise on justice when he was engaged in besieging cities that did not belong to him. Marius declared that the din of arms made it impossible for him to hear the voice of the laws.[1] Even Pompey, whose expression of countenance was so mild, dared to say: 'When I am in arms, am I to think of laws?'[2]

---

[1] In Plutarch Lysander displaying his sword says (*Apophthegms, Lysander,* iii = 190 E): 'He who is master of this is in the best position to discuss questions relating to boundaries between countries'. In the same author Caesar declares (*Caesar,* xxxv = 725 B): 'The time for arms is not the time for laws'. Similarly Seneca, *On Benefits,* IV, xxxviii (IV, xxxvii): 'At times, especially in time of war, kings make many grants with their eyes shut. One just man cannot satisfy so many passionate desires of men in arms; no one can at the same time act the part of a good man and good commander.'

[2] This viewpoint of Pompey in relation to the Mamertines Plutarch expresses thus (*Pompey,* x = 623 D): 'Will you not stop quoting laws to us who are girt with swords?' Curtius says in Book IX (IX, iv, 7): 'Even to such a degree does war reverse the laws of nature'.

4. Among Christian writers a similar thought finds frequent ex- *Marius,*
pression. A single quotation from Tertullian may serve in place xxviii =
of many: 'Deception, harshness, and justice are the regular business 421 E
An Answer
of battles'. They who so think will no doubt wish to confront us *to the Jews,*
with this passage in Comedy: vii
Terence,
Eunuch,
I, i, 16 ff.

> These things uncertain should you, by reason's aid,
> Try to make certain, no more would you gain
> Than if you tried by reason to go mad.

5. Since our discussion concerning law will have been undertaken
in vain if there is no law, in order to open the way for a favourable
reception of our work and at the same time to fortify it against
attacks, this very serious error must be briefly refuted. In order
that we may not be obliged to deal with a crowd of opponents,
let us assign to them a pleader. And whom should we choose in
preference to Carneades? For he had attained to so perfect a
mastery of the peculiar tenet of his Academy that he was able to
devote the power of his eloquence to the service of falsehood not
less readily than to that of truth.

Carneades, then, having undertaken to hold a brief against
justice, in particular against that phase of justice with which we
are concerned, was able to muster no argument stronger than this,
that, for reasons of expediency, men imposed upon themselves
laws, which vary according to customs, and among the same
people often undergo changes as times change; moreover that
there is no law of nature, because all creatures, men as well as
animals, are impelled by nature towards ends advantageous to
themselves; that, consequently, there is no justice, or, if such
there be, it is supreme folly, since one does violence to his own
interests if he consults the advantage of others.

6. What the philosopher here says, and the poet reaffirms in Horace
Satires, I,
iii, 113
verse,

> And just from unjust cause Nature cannot know,

must not for one moment be admitted. Man is, to be sure, an
animal, but an animal of a superior kind, much farther removed
from all other animals than the different kinds of animals are
from one another; evidence on this point may be found in the

many traits peculiar to the human species. But among the traits characteristic of man is an impelling desire for society, that is, for the social life – not of any and every sort, but peaceful, and organized according to the measure of his intelligence, with those who are of his own kind; this social trend the Stoics called 'sociableness'.[1] Stated as a universal truth, therefore, the assertion that every animal is impelled by nature to seek only its own good cannot be conceded.

7. Some of the other animals, in fact, do in a way restrain the appetency for that which is good for themselves alone, to the advantage, now of their offspring, now of other animals of the same species.[2] This aspect of their behaviour has its origins, we

---

[1] Chrysostom, *On Romans*, Homily XXXI (Homily V, i, on chap, i, verse 31): 'We men have by nature a kind of fellowship with men; why not, when even wild beasts in their relation to one another have something similar?' See also the same author, *On Ephesians*, chap. i (Homily I), where he explains that the seeds of virtue have been implanted in us by nature. The Emperor Marcus Aurelius, a philosopher of parts, said (V, xvi): 'It was long ago made clear that we were born for fellowship. Is it not evident that the lower exist for the sake of the higher for one another's sake?'

[2] There is an old proverb, 'Dogs do not eat the flesh of dogs'. Says Juvenal (*Sat.* xv, 163, 159):

> Tigress with ravening tigress keeps the peace;
> The wild beast spares its spotted kin.

There is a fine passage of Philo, in his commentary on the Fifth Commandment, which he who will may read in Greek. As it is somewhat long, I shall here quote it only once and in Latin (Philo, *On the Ten Commandments*, xxiii, in English as follows):

'Men, be ye at last imitators of dumb brutes. They, trained through kindness, know how to repay in turn. Dogs defend our homes; they even suffer death for their masters, if danger has suddenly come upon them. It is said that shepherd dogs go in advance of their flocks, fighting till death, if need be, that they protect the shepherds from hurt. Of things disgraceful is not the most disgraceful this, that in return of kindness man should be outdone by a dog, the gentlest creature by the most fierce?

'But if we fail to draw our proper lesson from the things of earth, let us pass to the realm of winged creatures that make voyage through the air, that from them we may learn our duty. Aged storks, unable to fly, stay in their nests. Their offspring fly, so to say, over all lands and seas, seeking sustenance in all places for their parents; these, in consideration of their age, deservedly enjoy quiet, abundance, even comforts. And the younger storks console themselves for the irksomeness of their voyaging (xx) with the consciousness of their discharge of filial duty and the expectation of similar treatment on the part of their offspring, when they too have grown old. Thus they pay back, at the time

believe, in some extrinsic intelligent principle, because with regard to other actions, which involve no more difficulty than those referred to, a like degree of intelligence is not manifest in them. The same thing must be said of children. In children, even before their training has begun, some disposition to do good to others appears, as Plutarch sagely observed; thus sympathy for others comes out spontaneously at that age. The mature man in fact has knowledge which prompts him to similar actions under similar conditions,[1] together with an impelling desire for society, for the gratification of which he alone among animals possesses a special instrument, speech. He has also been endowed with the faculty of knowing and of action in accordance with general principles. Whatever accords with that faculty is not common to all animals, but peculiar to the nature of man.

Consolation, 608 D

8. This maintenance of the social order,[2] which we have roughly sketched, and which is consonant with human intelligence, is the

when needed, the debt they owe, returning what they have received; or from others they cannot obtain sustenance either at the beginning of life, when they are small, or, when they have become old, at life's end. From no other teacher than nature herself have they learned to care for the aged, just as they themselves were cared for when they were young.

'Should not they who do not take care of their parents have reason to hide themselves for very shame when they hear this – they that neglect those whom alone, or above all others, they ought to help, especially when by so doing they are not really called upon to give, but merely to return what they owe? Children have as their own nothing to which their parents do not possess a prior claim; their parents have either given them what they have, or have furnished to them the means of acquisition.'

In regard to the extraordinary care of doves for their young, see Porphyry, *On Abstaining from Animal Food*, Book III; concerning the regard of the parrot-fish and lizard-fish for their kind, see Cassiodorus (Variae), XI, xl.

[1] Marcus Aurelius, Book IX (IX, xiii): 'Man was born to benefit others'; also (IX, ix): 'It would be easier to find a thing of earth out of relation with the earth than a human being wholly cut off from human kind'. The same author in Book X (X, ii): 'That which has the use of reason necessarily also craves civic life'.

Nicetas of Chonae (*On Isaac Angelus*, III, ix): 'Nature has ingrained in us, and implanted in our souls, a feeling for our kin'. Add what Augustine says, *On Christian Doctrine*, III, xiv.

[2] Seneca, *On Benefits*, Book IV, chap. xviii: 'That the warm feeling of a kindly heart is in itself desirable you may know from this, that ingratitude is something which in itself men ought to flee from, since nothing so dismembers and destroys the harmonious union of the human race as does this fault. Upon what other resource, pray tell, can we rely for safety, than mutual aid through

source of law properly so called. To this sphere of law belong the abstaining from that which is another's,[1] the restoration to another of anything of his which we may have, together with any gain which we may have received from it; the obligation to fulfil promises, the making good of a loss incurred through our fault, and the inflicting of penalties upon men according to their deserts.

9. From this signification of the word law there has flowed another and more extended meaning. Since over other animals man has the advantage of possessing not only a strong bent towards social life, of which we have spoken, but also a power of discrimination which enables him to decide what things are agreeable or harmful (as to both things present and things to come), and what can lead to either alternative: in such things it is meet for the nature of man, within the limitations of human intelligence, to follow the direction of a well-tempered judgment, being neither led astray by fear or the allurement of immediate pleasure, nor carried away by rash impulse. Whatever is clearly at variance with such judgment is understood to be contrary also to the law of nature, that is, to the nature of man.

reciprocal services? This alone it is, this interchange of kindness, which makes our life well equipped, and well fortified against sudden attacks.

'Imagine ourselves as isolated individuals, what are we? The prey, the victims of brute beasts – blood most cheap, and easiest to ravage; for to all other animals strength sufficient for their own protection has been given. The beasts that are born to wander and to pass segregate lives are provided with weapons; man is girt round about with weakness. Him no strength of claws or teeth makes formidable to others. To man (deity) gave two resources, reason and society; exposed as he was to danger from all other creatures, these resources rendered him the most powerful of all. Thus he who in isolation could not be the equal of any creature, is become the master of the world.

'It was society which gave to man dominion over all other living creatures; man, born for the land, society transferred to a sovereignty of a different nature, bidding him exercise dominion over the sea also. Society has checked the violence of disease, has provided succour for old age, has given comfort against sorrows. It makes us brave because it can be invoked against Fortune. Take this away and you will destroy the sense of oneness in the human race, by which life is sustained. It is, in fact, taken away, if you shall cause that an ungrateful heart is not to be avoided on its own account.'

[1] Porphyry, *On Abstaining from Animal Food*, Book III (III, xxvi): 'Justice consists in the abstaining from what belongs to others, and in doing no harm to those who do no harm'.

10. To this exercise of judgment belongs moreover the rational allotment[1] to each man, or to each social group, of those things which are properly theirs, in such a way as to give the preference now to him who is more wise over the less wise, now to a kinsman rather than to a stranger, now to a poor man rather than to a man of means, as the conduct of each or the nature of the thing suggests. Long ago the view came to be held by many, that this discriminating allotment is a part of law, properly and strictly so called; nevertheless law, properly defined, has a far different nature, because its essence lies in leaving to another that which belongs to him, or in fulfilling our obligations to him.

11. What we have been saying would have a degree of validity even if we should concede that which cannot be conceded without the utmost wickedness, that there is no God, or that the affairs of men are of no concern to Him. The very opposite of this view has been implanted in us partly by reason, partly by unbroken tradition, and confirmed by many proofs as well as by miracles attested by all ages. Hence it follows that we must without exception render obedience to God as our Creator, to Whom we owe all that we are and have; especially since, in manifold ways, He has shown Himself supremely good and supremely powerful, so that to those who obey Him He is able to give supremely great rewards, even rewards that are eternal, since He Himself is eternal. We ought, moreover, to believe that He has willed to give rewards, and all the more should we cherish such a belief if He has so promised in plain words; that He has done this, we Christians believe, convinced by the indubitable assurance of testimonies.

12. Herein, then, is another source of law besides the source in nature, that is, the free will of God,[2] to which beyond all cavil our reason tells us we must render obedience. But the law of nature of which we have spoken, comprising alike that which relates to the social life of man and that which is so called in a larger sense, proceeding as it does from the essential trait

---

[1] Ambrose treats this subject in his first book *On Duties* (I, xxx).

[2] (xxi). Hence, in the judgment of Marcus Aurelius, Book IX (IX, i): 'He who commits injustice is guilty of impiety'.

implanted in man, can nevertheless rightly be attributed to God,[1] because of His having willed that such traits exist in us. In this sense, too, Chrysippus and the Stoics used to say that the origin of law should be sought in no other source than Jupiter himself; and from the name Jupiter[2] the Latin word for 'law', *ius* was probably derived.

13. There is an additional consideration in that, by means of the laws which He has given, God has made those fundamental traits more manifest, even to those who possess feebler reasoning powers; and He has forbidden us to yield to impulses drawing us in opposite directions – affecting now our own interest, now the interest of others – in an effort to control more effectively our more violent impulses and to restrain them within proper limits.

14. But sacred history, besides enjoining rules of conduct, in no slight degree reinforces man's inclination towards sociableness by teaching that all men are sprung from the same first parents. In this sense we can rightly affirm also that which Florentinus asserted from another point of view, that a blood-relationship has been established among us by nature; consequently it is wrong for a man to set a snare for a fellow-man. Among mankind generally one's parents are as it were divinities,[3] and to them is

Dig., I, i, 3.

---

[1] Chrysostom, *On First Corinthians*, xi, 3 (Homily XXVI, iii): 'When I say nature I mean God, for He is the creator of nature'. Chrysippus in his third book *On the Gods* (Plutarch, *On the Contradictions of the Stoics*, ix = Morals, 1035 c): 'No other beginning or origin of justice can be found than in Jupiter and common nature; from that source must the beginning be traced when men undertake to treat of good and evil'.

[2] Unless perhaps it would be more true to say that the Latin word for 'right', *ius*, is derived, by process of cutting down, from the word for 'command', *iussum*, forming *ius*, genitive *iusis*, just as the word for 'bone', *os*, was shortened from *ossum; iusis* afterwards becoming *iuris*, as *Papirii* was formed from *Papisii*, in regard to which see Cicero, *Letters*, Book IX, xxi (*Ad Fam.*, IX, xxi, 2).

[3] Hierocles, in his commentary on the *Golden Verse* (rather *How parents should be treated*, quoted by Stobaeus, *Anthology*, tit. lxxix, 53), calls parents 'gods upon earth'; Philo, *On the Ten Commandments* (chap. xxiii), 'Visible gods, who imitate the Unbegotten God in giving life'. Next after the relationship between God and man comes the relationship between parent and child; Jerome, *Letters*, xcii (cxvii, 2). Parents are the likenesses of gods; Plato, *Laws*, Book XI (XI, ii). Honour is due to parents as to gods; Aristotle, *Nicomachean Ethics*, Book IX, chap. ii.

owed an obedience which, if not unlimited, is nevertheless of an altogether special kind.

15. Again, since it is a rule of the law of nature to abide by pacts (for it is necessary that among men there be some method of obligating themselves one to another, and no other natural method can be imagined), out of this source the bodies of municipal law have arisen. For those who had associated themselves with some group, or had subjected themselves to a man or to men, had either expressly promised, or from the nature of the transaction must be understood impliedly to have promised, that they would conform to that which should have been determined, in the one case by the majority, in the other by those upon whom authority had been conferred.

16. What is said, therefore, in accordance with the view not only of Carneades but also of others, that

> Expediency is, as it were, the mother
> Of what is just and fair,[1]

is not true, if we wish to speak accurately. For the very nature of man, which even if we had no lack of anything would lead us into the mutual relations of society, is the mother of the law of nature. But the mother of municipal law is that obligation which arises from mutual consent; and since this obligation derives its force from the law of nature, nature may be considered, so to say, the great-grandmother of municipal law.

The law of nature nevertheless had the reinforcement of expediency; for the Author of nature willed that as individuals we should be weak and should lack many things needed in order to live properly, to the end that we might be the more constrained to cultivate the social life. But expediency afforded an opportunity also for municipal law, since that kind of association of which we have spoken, and subjection to authority, have their roots in

---

[1] In regard to this passage Acron, or some other ancient interpreter of Horace (*Sat.* I, iii, 98): 'The poet is writing in opposition to the teachings of the Stoics. He wishes to show that justice does not have its origin in nature, but is born of expediency.' For the opposite view see Augustine's argument, *On Christian Doctrine*, Book III, chap. xiv.

expediency. From this it follows that those who prescribe laws for others in so doing are accustomed to have, or ought to have, some advantage in view.

17. But just as the laws of each state have in view the advantage of that state, so by mutual consent it has become possible that certain laws should originate as between all states, or a great many states; and it is apparent that the laws thus originating had in view the advantage, not of particular states, but of the great society of states. And this is what is called the law of nations, whenever we distinguish that term from the law of nature.

This division of law Carneades passed over altogether. For he divided all law into the law of nature and the law of particular countries. Nevertheless if undertaking to treat of the body of law which is maintained between states – for he added a statement in regard to war and things acquired by means of war – he would surely have been obliged to make mention of this law.

18. Wrongly, moreover, does Carneades ridicule justice as folly. For since, by his own admission, the national who in his own country obeys its laws is not foolish, even though, out of regard for that law, he may be obliged to forgo certain things advantageous for himself, so that nation is not foolish which does not press its own advantage to the point of disregarding the laws common to nations. The reason in either case is the same. For just as the national, who violates the law of his country in order to obtain an immediate advantage,[1] breaks down that by which the advantages of himself and his posterity are for all future time assured, so the state which transgresses the laws of nature and of nations cuts away also the bulwarks which safeguard its own future peace. Even if no advantage were to be contemplated from the keeping of the law, it would be a mark of wisdom, not of folly, to allow

---

[1] This comparison Marcus Aurelius pertinently uses in Book IX (IX, xxiii): Every act of thine that has no relation, direct or indirect, to the common interest, rends thy life and does not suffer it to be one; such an act is not less productive of disintegration than he is who creates a dissension among a people'. The same author, Book XI (XI, viii): 'A man cut off from a single fellow-man cannot but be considered as out of fellowship with the whole human race'. In effect, as the same Antoninus says (VI, liv): 'What is advantageous to the swarm is advantageous to the bee'.

ourselves to be drawn towards that to which we feel that our nature leads.

19. Wherefore, in general, it is by no means true that

> You must confess that laws were framed
> From fear of the unjust,[1]

a thought which in Plato someone explains thus, that laws were invented from fear of receiving injury, and that men are constrained by a kind of force to cultivate justice. For that relates only to the institutions and laws which have been devised to facilitate the enforcement of right; as when many persons in themselves weak, in order that they might not be overwhelmed by the more powerful, leagued themselves together to establish tribunals and by combined force to maintain these, that as a united whole they might prevail against those with whom as individuals they could not cope.

And in this sense we may readily admit also the truth of the saying that right is that which is acceptable to the stronger; so that we may understand that law fails of its outward effect unless it has a sanction behind it. In this way Solon accomplished very great results, as he himself used to declare, *Plutarch, Solon, xv*

> By joining force and law together,
> Under a like bond.

20. Nevertheless law, even though without a sanction, is not entirely devoid of effect. For justice brings peace of conscience, *Gorgias, xxx* while injustice causes torments and anguish, such as Plato describes, in the breasts of tyrants. Justice is approved, and injustice condemned, by the common agreement of good men. But, most important of all, in God injustice finds an enemy, justice a protector. He reserves His judgments for the life after this, yet in such a way that He often causes their effects to become manifest even in this life, as history teaches by numerous examples.

21. Many hold, in fact, that the standard of justice which they insist upon in the case of individuals within the state is inapplicable

---

[1] As Ovid says (*Metamorphoses*, VIII, 59):
  Strong is the cause when arms the cause maintain

to a nation or the ruler of a nation. The reason for the error lies in this, first of all, that in respect to law they have in view nothing except the advantage which accrues from it, such advantage being apparent in the case of citizens who, taken singly, are powerless to protect themselves. But great states, since they seem to contain in themselves all things required for the adequate protection of life, seem not to have need of that virtue which looks toward the outside, and is called justice.

22. But, not to repeat what I have said, that law is not founded on expediency alone, there is no state so powerful, that it may not some time need the help of others outside itself, either for purposes of trade, or even to ward off the forces of many foreign nations united against it. In consequence we see that even the most powerful peoples and sovereigns seek alliances, which are quite devoid of significance according to the point of view of those who confine law within the boundaries of states. Most true is the saying, that all things are uncertain the moment men depart from law.

Stobaeus, x, 50 23. If no association of men can be maintained without law, as Aristotle showed by his remarkable illustration drawn from brigands,[1] surely also that association which binds together the human race, or binds many nations together, has need of law; this was perceived by him who said that shameful deeds ought

---

[1] Chrysostom, *On Ephesians*, chap. iv (Homily IX, iii): 'But how does it happen, someone will say, that brigands live on terms of peace? And when? Tell me, I pray. This happens, in fact, when they are not acting as brigands; for if, in dividing up their loot, they did not observe the precepts of justice and make an equitable apportionment, you would see them engaged in strifes and battles among themselves.'

Plutarch (*Pyrrhus*, ix = 388 A) quotes the saying of Pyrrhus, that he would leave his kingdom to that one of his children who should have the sharpest (xxii) sword, declaring that this has the same implication as the verse of Euripides in the *Phoenician Maidens* (line 68):

That they with gory steel the house divide.

He adds, moreover, the noble sentiment: 'So inimical to the social order, and ruthless, is the determination to possess more than is one's own!'

Cicero, *Letters*, XI, xvi (*Ad Fam.*, IX, xvi, 3): 'All things are uncertain when one departs from law.' Polybius, Book IV (IV, xxix, 4): 'This above all other causes breaks up the private organizations of criminals and thieves, that they cease to deal fairly with one another; in fine, that good faith among them has perished'.

not to be committed even for the sake of one's country. Aristotle takes sharply to task[1] those who, while unwilling to allow any one to exercise authority over themselves except in accordance with law, yet are quite indifferent as to whether foreigners are treated according to law or not.

Cicero,
On Duties,
I, xiv, 159
Politics,
VII, ii

24. That same Pompey, whom I just now quoted for the opposite view, corrected the statement which a king of Sparta had made, that the state is the most fortunate whose boundaries are fixed by spear and sword; he declared that that state is truly fortunate which has justice for its boundary line. On this point he might have invoked the authority of another king of Sparta, who gave the preference to justice over bravery in war,[2] using this argument, that bravery ought to be directed by a kind of justice, but if all men were just they would have no need for bravery in war.

Bravery itself the Stoics defined as virtue fighting on behalf of equity. Themistius in his address to Valens argues with eloquence that kings who measure up to the rule of wisdom make account not only of the nation which has been committed to them, but of the whole human race, and that they are, as he himself says, not 'friends of the Macedonians' alone, or 'friends of the Romans',[3] but 'friends of mankind'. The name of Minos[4] became odious to

x = p. 132 BC.

---

[1] Plutarch, *Agesilaus* (xxxvii = 617 D): 'In their conception of honour the Lacedaemonians assign the first place to the advantage of their country; they neither know nor learn any other kind of right than that which they think will advance the interests of Sparta'.

In regard to the same Lacedaemonians the Athenians declared, in Thucydides, Book V (V, cv): 'In relations with one another and according to their conception of civil rights they are most strict in their practice of virtue. But with respect to others, though many considerations bearing upon the subject might be brought forward, he will state the fact in a word who will say that in their view what is agreeable is honourable, what is advantageous is just.'

[2] Hearing that the king of the Persians was called great, Agesilaus remarked: 'Wherein is he greater than I, if he is not more just?' The saying is quoted by Plutarch (*Apophthegms, Agesilaus*, lxiii = *Morals*, 213 C).

[3] Marcus Aurelius exceedingly well remarks (VI, xliv): 'As Antoninus, my city and country are Rome; as a man, the world'. Porphyry, *On Abstaining from Animal Food*, Book III (III, xxvii): 'He who is guided by reason keeps himself blameless in relation to his fellow-citizens, likewise also in relation to strangers and men in general; the more submissive to reason, the more godlike a man is'.

[4] In regard to Minos there is a verse of an ancient poet:

Under the yoke of Minos all the island groaned.

On this point see Cyril, *Against Julian*, Book VI.

51

future ages for no other reason than this, that he limited his fair-dealing to the boundaries of his realm.

25. Least of all should that be admitted which some people imagine, that in war all laws are in abeyance. On the contrary war ought not to be undertaken except for the enforcement of rights; when once undertaken, it should be carried on only within the bounds of law and good faith. Demosthenes well said that war is directed against those who cannot be held in check by judicial processes. For judgments are efficacious against those who feel that they are too weak to resist; against those who are equally strong, or think that they are, wars are undertaken. But in order that wars may be justified, they must be carried on with not less scrupulousness than judicial processes are wont to be.

On the Affairs in the Chersonese viii, 29

26. Let the laws be silent, then, in the midst of arms, but only the laws of the state, those that the courts are concerned with, that are adapted only to a state of peace; not those other laws, which are of perpetual validity and suited to all times. It was exceedingly well said by Dio of Prusa, that between enemies written laws, that is, laws of particular states, are not in force, but that unwritten laws[1] are in force, that is, those which nature prescribes, or the agreement of nations has established. This is set forth by that ancient formula of the Romans, 'I think that those things ought to be sought by means of a war that is blameless and righteous'.

Orations, lxxvi

Livy, I, xxxii, 12

The ancient Romans, as Varro noted, were slow in undertaking war, and permitted themselves no licence in that matter, because they held the view that a war ought not to be waged except when free from reproach. Camillus said that wars should be carried on justly no less than bravely; Scipio Africanus, that the Roman people commenced and ended wars justly. In another passage you may read: 'War has its laws no less than peace'. Still another writer admires Fabricius as a great man who maintained his

Livy, V, xxvii, 6; XXX, xvi, 9
V, xxvii, 6
Seneca, *Letters*, cxx, 6

---

[1] Thus King Alphonse, being asked whether he owed a greater debt to books or to arms, said that from books he had learned both the practice and laws of arms. Plutarch (*Camillus*, x = 123 B): 'Among good men certain laws even of war are recognized, and a victory ought not to be striven for in such a way as not to spurn an advantage arising from wicked and impious actions'.

probity in war – a thing most difficult – and believed that even in relation to an enemy there is such a thing as wrongdoing.

27. The historians in many a passage reveal how great in war is the influence of the consciousness that one has justice on his side[1]; they often attribute victory chiefly to this cause. Hence the proverbs, that a soldier's strength is broken or increased by his cause; that he who has taken up arms unjustly rarely comes back in safety; that hope is the comrade of a good cause; and others of the same purport.

No one ought to be disturbed, furthermore, by the successful outcome of unjust enterprises. For it is enough that the fairness

---

[1] Pompey well says in Appian (*Civil Wars*, II, viii, 51): 'We ought to trust in the gods and in the cause of a war which has been undertaken with the honourable and just (xxiii) purpose of defending the institutions of our country'. In the same author Cassius (*Civil Wars*, IV, xii, 97): 'In wars the greatest hope lies in the justice of the cause'. Josephus, *Antiquities of the Jews*, Book XV (XV, v, 3): 'God is with those who have right on their side'.

Procopius has a number of passages of similar import. One is in the speech of Belisarius, after he had started on his expedition to Africa (*Vandalic War*, I, xii, 21): 'Bravery is not going to give the victory, unless it has justice as a fellow soldier'. Another is in the speech of the same general before the battle not far from Carthage (I, xii, 19). A third is in the address of the Lombards to the Herulians, where the following words, as corrected by me, are found (*Gothic War*, II, xiv): 'We call to witness God, the slightest manifestation of whose power is equal to all human strength. He, as may well be believed, making account of the causes of war, will give to each side the outcome of battle which each deserves!' This saying was soon afterward confirmed by a wonderful occurrence.

In the same author Totila thus addresses the Goths (*Gothic War*, III, viii): 'It cannot, it cannot happen, I say, that they who resort to violence and injustice can win renown in fighting; but as the life of each is, such the fortune of war that falls to his lot'. Soon after the taking of Rome Totila made another speech bearing on the same point (*Gothic War*, III, xxi).

Agathias, Book II (*Histories*, II, i): 'Injustice and forgetfulness of God are to be shunned always, and are harmful, above all in war and in time of battle'. This statement he elsewhere proves by the notable illustrations of Darius, Xerxes, and the Athenians in Sicily (*Histories*, II, x). See also the speech of Crispinus to the people of Aquileia, in Herodian, Book VIII (*Histories* VIII, iii, 5, 6).

In Thucydides, Book VII (VII, xviii), we find the Lacedaemonians reckoning the disasters which they had suffered in Pylus and elsewhere as due to themselves, because they had refused a settlement by arbitration which has been offered them. But as afterwards the Athenians, having committed many wicked deeds, refused arbitration, a hope of greater success in their operations revived in the Lacedaemonians.

of the cause exerts a certain influence, even a strong influence upon actions, although the effect of that influence, as happens in human affairs, is often nullified by the interference of other causes. Even for winning friendships, of which for many reasons nations as well as individuals have need, a reputation for having undertaken war not rashly nor unjustly, and of having waged it in a manner above reproach, is exceedingly efficacious. No one readily allies himself with those in whom he believes that there is only a slight regard for law, for the right, and for good faith.

28. Fully convinced, by the considerations which I have advanced, that there is a common law among nations, which is valid alike for war and in war, I have had many and weighty reasons for undertaking to write upon this subject. Throughout the Christian world I observed a lack of restraint in relation to war, such as even barbarous races should be ashamed of; I observed that men rush to arms for slight causes, or no cause at all, and that when arms have once been taken up there is no longer any respect for law, divine or human; it is as if, in accordance with a general decree, frenzy had openly been let loose for the committing of all crimes.

29. Confronted with such utter ruthlessness many men, who are the very furthest from being bad men, have come to the point of forbidding all use of arms to the Christian,[1] whose rule of conduct Johann Wild above everything else comprises the duty of loving all men. To this opinion sometimes John Ferus and my fellow-countryman Erasmus seem to incline, men who have the utmost devotion to peace in both Church and State; but their purpose, as I take it, is, when things have gone in one direction, to force them in the opposite direction, as we are accustomed to do, that they may come back to a true middle ground. But the very effort of pressing too hard in the opposite direction is often so far from being helpful that it does harm, because in such arguments the detection of what is extreme is easy, and results in weakening the influence of other statements which are well within the bounds of truth.

---

[1] Tertullian, *On the Resurrection of the Flesh* (chap. xvi): 'The sword which has become bloodstained in war, and has thus been employed in man-killing of a better sort'.

For both extremes therefore a remedy must be found, that men may not believe either that nothing is allowable or that everything is.

30. At the same time through devotion to study in private life I have wished – as the only course now open to me, undeservedly forced out from my native land, which had been graced by so many of my labours – to contribute somewhat to the philosophy of the law, which previously, in public service, I practised with the utmost degree of probity of which I was capable. Many heretofore have purposed to give to this subject a well-ordered presentation; no one has succeeded. And in fact such a result cannot be accomplished unless – a point which until now has not been sufficiently kept in view – those elements which come from positive law are properly separated from those which arise from nature. For the principles of the law of nature, since they are always the same, can easily be brought into a systematic form; but the elements of positive law, since they often undergo change and are different in different places, are outside the domain of systematic treatment, just as other notions of particular things are.

31. If now those who have consecrated themselves to true justice should undertake to treat the parts of the natural and unchangeable philosophy of law, after having removed all that has its origin in the free will of man; if one, for example, should treat legislation, another taxation, another the administration of justice, another the determination of motives, another the proving of facts, then by assembling all these parts a body of jurisprudence could be made up.

32. What procedure we think should be followed we have shown by deed rather than by words in this work, which treats by far the noblest part of jurisprudence.

33. In the first book, having by way of introduction spoken of the origin of law, we have examined the general question, whether there is any such thing as a just war; then, in order to determine the differences between public war and private war, we found it necessary to explain the nature of sovereignty – what nations,

what kings possess complete sovereignty; who possess sovereignty only in part, who with right of alienation, who otherwise; then it was necessary to speak also concerning the duty of subjects to their superiors.

34. The second book, having for its object to set forth all the causes from which war can arise, undertakes to explain fully what things are held in common, what may be owned in severalty; what rights persons have over persons, what obligation arises from ownership; what is the rule governing royal succession; what right is established by a pact or a contract; what is the force of treaties of alliance; what of an oath private or public, and how it is necessary to interpret these; what is due in reparation for damage done; in what the inviolability of ambassadors consists; what law controls the burial of the dead, and what is the nature of punishments.

35. The third book has for its subject, first, what is permissible in war. Having distinguished that which is done with impunity, or even that which among foreign peoples is defended as lawful, from that which actually is free from fault, it proceeds to the different kinds of peace, and all compacts relating to war.

36. The undertaking seemed to me all the more worth while because, as I have said, no one has dealt with the subject-matter as a whole, and those who have treated portions of it have done so in a way to leave much to the labours of others. Of the ancient philosophers nothing in this field remains; either of the Greeks, among whom Aristotle had composed a book with the title *Rights of War*, or – what was especially to be desired – of those who gave their allegiance to the young Christianity. Even the books of the ancient Romans on fetial law have transmitted to us nothing of themselves except the title. Those who have made collections of the cases which are called 'cases of conscience' have merely written chapters on war, promises, oaths, and reprisals, just as on other subjects.

37. I have seen also special books on the law of war, some by theologians, as Franciscus de Victoria, Henry of Gorkum, William

Matthaei[1]; others by doctors of law, as John Lupus, Franciscus Arias, Giovanni da Legnano, Martinus Laudensis. All of these, however, have said next to nothing upon a most fertile subject; most of them have done their work without system, and in such a way as to intermingle and utterly confuse what belongs to the law of nature, to divine law, to the law of nations, to civil law, and to the body of law which is found in the canons.

38. What all these writers especially lacked, the illumination of history, the very learned Faur undertook to supply in some chapters of his *Semestria,* but in a manner limited by the scope of his own work, and only through the citation of authorities. The same thing was attempted on a larger scale, and by referring a great number of examples to some general statements, by Balthazar Ayala; and still more fully, by Alberico Gentili. Knowing that others can derive profit from Gentili's painstaking, as I acknowledge that I have, I leave it to his readers to pass judgment, on the shortcomings of his work as regards method of exposition, arrangement of matter, delimitation of enquiries, and distinctions between the various kinds of law. This only I shall say, that in treating controversial questions it is his frequent practice to base his conclusions on a few examples, which are not in all cases worthy of approval, or even to follow the opinions of modern jurists, formulated in arguments of which not a few were accommodated to the special interests of clients, not to the nature of that which is equitable and upright.

The causes which determine the characterization of a war as lawful or unlawful Ayala did not touch upon. Gentili outlined certain general classes, in the manner which seemed to him best; but he did not so much as refer to many topics which have come up on notable and frequent controversies.

39. We have taken all pains that nothing of this sort escape us; and we have also indicated the sources from which conclusions are drawn, whence it would be an easy matter to verify them even if any point has been omitted by us. It remains to explain

---

[1] To these add the work of Joannes de Carthagena, published at Rome in 1609.

briefly with what helps, and with what care, I have attacked this task.

First of all, I have made it my concern to refer the proofs of things touching the law of nature to certain fundamental conceptions which are beyond question, so that no one can deny them without doing violence to himself. For the principles of that law, if only you pay strict heed to them, are in themselves manifest and clear, almost as evident as are those things which we perceive by the external senses; and the senses do not err if the organs of perception are present. Thus in his *Phoenician Maidens* Euripides represents Polynices, whose cause he makes out to have been manifestly just, as speaking thus:

494-6

> Mother, these words, that I have uttered, are not
> Inwrapped with indirection, but, firmly based
> On rules of justice and of good, are plain
> Alike to simple and to wise.[1]

The poet adds immediately a judgment of the chorus, made up of women, and barbarian women at that, approving these words.

40. In order to prove the existence of this law of nature, I have, furthermore, availed myself of the testimony of philosophers,[2] historians, poets and finally also of orators. Not that confidence is to be reposed in them without discrimination; for they were accustomed to serve the interests of their sect, their subject, or their cause. But when many at different times, and in different places, affirm the same thing as certain, that ought to be referred to a universal cause; and this cause, in the lines of enquiry which we are following, must be either a correct conclusion drawn from the principles of nature, or common consent. The former points to the law of nature; the latter, to the law of nations.

[1] The same Euripides represents Hermione as saying to Andromache (*Andromache*, 243):
> Not under laws barbaric do men live
> In this city:

and Andromache as answering (*ibid.*, 244):
> What there is base, here too not blameless is.

[2] Why should not one avail himself of the testimony of the philosophers, when Alexander Severus constantly read Cicero *On the Commonwealth* and *On Duties*? (Lampridius, *Alexander Severus*, xxx, 2).

The distinction between these kinds of law is not to be drawn from the testimonies themselves (for writers everywhere confuse the terms law of nature and law of nations), but from the character of the matter. For whatever cannot be deducted from certain principles by a sure process of reasoning, and yet is clearly observed everywhere, must have its origin in the free will of man.

41. These two kinds of law, therefore, I have always particularly sought to distinguish from each other and from municipal law. Furthermore, in the law of nations I have distinguished between that which is truly and in all respects law, and that which produces merely a kind of outward effect simulating that primitive law, as, for example, the prohibition to resist by force, or even the duty of defence in any place by public force, in order to secure some advantage, or for the avoidance of serious disadvantages. How necessary it is, in many cases, to observe this distinction, will become apparent in the course of our work.

With not less pains we have separated those things which are strictly and properly legal, out of which the obligation of restitution arises, from those things which are called legal because any other classification of them conflicts with some other stated rule of right reason. In regard to this distinction of law we have already said something above.

42. Among the philosophers Aristotle deservedly holds the foremost place, whether you take into account his order of treatment, or the subtlety of his distinctions, or the weight of his reasons. Would that this pre-eminence had not, for some centuries back, been turned into a tyranny, so that Truth, to whom Aristotle devoted faithful service, was by no instrumentality more repressed than by Aristotle's name!

For my part, both here and elsewhere I avail myself of the liberty of the early Christians, who had sworn allegiance to the sect of no one of the philosophers, not because they were in agreement with those who said that nothing can be known – than which nothing is more foolish – but because they thought that there was no philosophic sect whose vision had compassed all truth, and none which had not perceived some aspect of truth. Thus they believed that to gather up into a whole the truth which was

59

scattered among the different philosophers[1] and dispersed among the sects, was in reality to establish a body of teaching truly Christian.

43. Among other things – to mention in passing a point not foreign to my subject – it seems to me that not without reason some of the Platonists and early Christians[2] departed from the teachings of Aristotle in this, that he considered the very nature of virtue as a mean in passions and actions. That principle, once adopted, led him to unite distinct virtues, as generosity and frugality, into one; to assign to truth extremes between which, on any fair premiss, there is no possible co-ordination, boastfulness, and dissimulation; and to apply the designation of vice to certain things which either do not exist, or are not in themselves vices, such as contempt for pleasure and for honours, and freedom from anger against men.

44. That this basic principle, when broadly stated, is unsound, becomes clear even from the case of justice. For, being unable to find in passions and acts resulting therefrom the too much and the too little opposed to that virtue, Aristotle sought each extreme in the things themselves with which justice is concerned. Now in

---

[1] The words are those of Lactantius, Divine Institutes, Book VI, chap. ix (VII, vii, 4). Justin, First Apology (Second Apology, chap. xiii): 'Not because the teachings of Plato are altogether different from the teachings of Christ, but because they do not completely harmonize, as the teachings of others do not (xxiv) – for example, those of the Stoics, the poets, and the writers of history. For each one of these spoke rightly in part, in accordance with the reason which had been implanted in him, perceiving what was consistent therewith.'

Tertullian (On the Soul, xx): 'Seneca often on our side'; but the same writer also warns us (An Answer to the Jews, ix) that the entire body of spiritual teachings was to be found in no man save Christ alone.

Augustine, Letters, ccii (xci, 3): 'The rules of conduct which Cicero and other philosophers recommend, are being taught and learned in the churches that are increasing all over the world'. On this point, if time is available, consult the same Augustine in regard to the Platonists, who, he says, with changes in regard to a few matters can be Christians; Letters, liv (cxviii, 21). On the True Religion, chap. iii, and Confessions, Book VII, chap. ix, and Book VIII, chap. ii.

[2] Lactantius treats this subject at length in the Institutes, VI, xv, xvi. Says Cassiodorus (Peter of Blois, On Friendship, chap. Quod effectus sine consensu non multum prosit vel obsit): 'It is advantageous or harmful to be moved not by feelings, but in accordance with feelings'.

the first place this is simply to leap from one class of things over into another class, a fault which he rightly censures in others; then, for a person to accept less than belongs to him may in fact under unusual conditions constitute a fault, in view of that which, according to the circumstances, he owes to himself and to those dependent on him; but in any case the act cannot be at variance with justice, the essence of which lies in abstaining from that which belongs to another.

By equally faulty reasoning Aristotle tries to make out that adultery committed in a burst of passion, or a murder due to anger, is not properly an injustice. Whereas nevertheless injustice has no other essential quality than the unlawful seizure of that which belongs to another; and it does not matter whether injustice arises from avarice, from lust, from anger, or from ill-advised compassion; or from an overmastering desire to achieve eminence, out of which instances of the gravest injustice constantly arise. For to disparage such incitements, with the sole purpose in view that human society may not receive injury, is in truth the concern of justice.

45. To return to the point whence I started, the truth is that some virtues do tend to keep passions under control, but that is not because such control is a proper and essential characteristic of every virtue. Rather it is because right reason, which virtue everywhere follows, in some things prescribes the pursuing of a middle course,[1] in other stimulates to the utmost degree. We cannot, for example, worship God too much, for superstition errs not by worshipping God too much, but by worshipping in a perverse way. Neither can we too much seek after the blessings that shall abide for ever, nor fear too much the everlasting evils, nor have too great hatred for sin.

With truth therefore was it said by Aulus Gellius, that there IV, ix, 14 are some things of which the extent is limited by no boundaries –

---

[1] *Agathias*, Book V, in a speech of Belisarius (*Histories*, V, xviii): 'Of the emotions of the soul those ought in every case to be seized in which there is found, pure and unmixed, an impulse in harmony with the requirements of duty and worthy to be chosen. Those emotions, however, which have a trend and inclination toward evil, are not to be utilized in all cases, but only so far as they are contribute to our advantage. That good judgment is a blessing pure and unmixed no one would deny. In anger the element of energy is praiseworthy, but what exceeds the proper limit is to be avoided, as involving disadvantage.'

the greater, the more ample they are, the more excellent. Lactantius, having discussed the passion at great length, says:

Divine Institutes, VI, xvi, 7

'The method of wisdom consists in controlling not the passions, but their causes, since they are stirred from without. And putting a check upon the passions themselves ought not to be the chief concern, because they may be feeble in the greatest crime, and very violent without leading to crime.'

Our purpose is to make much account of Aristotle, but reserving in regard to him the same liberty which he, in his devotion to truth, allowed himself with respect to his teachers.

46. History in relation to our subject is useful in two ways: it supplies both illustrations and judgments. The illustrations have greater weight in proportion as they are taken from better times and better peoples; thus we have preferred ancient examples, Greek and Roman, to the rest. And judgments are not to be slighted, especially when they are in agreement with one another; for by such statements the existence of the law of nature, as we have said, is in a measure proved, and by no other means, in fact, is it possible to establish the law of nations.

47. The views of poets and of orators do not have so great weight; and we make frequent use of them not so much for the purpose of gaining acceptance by that means for our argument, as of adding, from their words, some embellishment to that which we wished to say.

48. I frequently appeal to the authority of the books which men inspired by God have either written or approved, nevertheless with a distinction between the Old Testament and the New. There are some who urge that the Old Testament sets forth the law of nature. Without doubt they are in error, for many of its rules come from the free will of God. And yet this is never in conflict with the true law of nature; and up to this point the Old Testament can be used as a source of the law of nature, provided we carefully distinguish between the law of God, which God sometimes executes through men, and the law of men in their relations with one another.

This error we have, so far as possible, avoided, and also another opposed to it, which supposes that after the coming of the New Testament the Old Testament in this respect was no longer of use. We believe the contrary partly because the character of the New Testament is such that in its teachings respecting the moral virtues it enjoins the same as the Old Testament or even enjoins greater precepts. In this way we see that the early Christian writers used the witnesses of the Old Testament.

49. The Hebrew writers,[1] moreover, most of all those who have thoroughly understood the speech and customs of their people are able to contribute not a little to our understanding of the thought of the books which belong to the Old Testament.

50. The New Testament I use in order to explain – and this cannot be learned from any other source – what is permissible to Christians. This, however – contrary to the practice of most men – I have distinguished from the law of nature, considering it as certain that in that most holy law a greater degree of moral perfection is enjoined upon us than the law of nature, alone and by itself, would require. And nevertheless I have not omitted to note the things that are recommended to us rather than enjoined, that we may know that, while the turning aside from what has been enjoined is wrong and involves the risk of punishment, a striving for the highest excellence implies a noble purpose and will not fail of its reward.

51. The authentic synodical canons are collections embodying the general principles of divine law as applied to cases which come up; they either show what the divine law enjoins, or urge us to that which God would fain persuade. And this truly is the mission of the Christian Church, to transmit those things which were transmitted to it by God, and in the way in which they were transmitted.

Furthermore, customs which were current, or were considered praiseworthy, among the early Christians and those who rose to the measure of so great a name, deservedly have the force of canons.

---

[1] This was perceived by Cassian (Cassiodorus) as shown by his *Institute of Holy Writ* (Preface).

Next after these comes the authority of those who, each in his own time, have been distinguished among Christians for their piety and learning, and have not been charged with any serious error; for what these declare with great positiveness, and as if definitely ascertained, ought to have no slight weight for the interpretation of passages in Holy Writ which seem obscure. Their authority is the greater the more there are of them in agreement, and as we approach nearer to the times of pristine purity, then neither desire for domination nor any conspiracy of interests had as yet been able to corrupt the primitive truth.

52. The Schoolmen, who succeeded these writers, often show how strong they are in natural ability. But their lot was cast in an unhappy age, which was ignorant of the liberal arts; wherefore it is less to be wondered at if among many things worthy of praise there are also some things which we should receive with indulgence. Nevertheless when the Schoolmen agree on a point of morals, it rarely happens that they are wrong, since they are especially keen in seeing what may be open to criticism in the statements of others. And yet in the very ardour of their defence of themselves against opposing views, they furnish a praiseworthy example of moderation; they contend with one another by means of arguments – not, in accordance with the practice which has lately begun to disgrace the calling of letters, with personal abuse, base offspring of a spirit lacking self-mastery.

53. Of those who profess knowledge of the Roman law there are three classes.

The first consists of those whose work appears in the Pandects, the Codes of Theodosius and Justinian, and the Imperial Constitutions called Novellae.

To the second class belong the successors of Irnerius, that is Accursius, Bartolus, and so many other names of those who long ruled the bar.

The third class comprises those who have combined the study of classical literature with that of law.

To the first class I attribute great weight. For they frequently give the very best reasons in order to establish what belongs to the law of nature, and they often furnish evidence in favour of this law and of the law of nations. Nevertheless, they, no less than the others, often confuse these terms, frequently calling that the law of nations which is only the law of certain peoples, and that, too, not as established by assent, but perchance taken over through imitation of others or by pure accident. But those provisions which really belong to the law of nations they often treat, without distinction or discrimination, along with those which belong to the Roman law, as may be seen by reference to the title *On Captives and Postliminy*. We have therefore endeavoured to distinguish these two types from each other.

54. The second class, paying no heed to the divine law or to ancient history, sought to adjust all controversies of kings and peoples by application of the laws of the Romans, with occasional use of the canons. But in the case of these men also the unfortunate condition of their times was frequently a handicap which prevented their complete understanding of those laws, though, for the rest, they were skilful enough in tracing out the nature of that which is fair and good. The result is that while they are often very successful in establishing the basis of law, they are at the same time bad interpreters of existing law. But they are to be listened to with the utmost attention when they bear witness to the existence of the usage which constitutes the law of nations in our day.

55. The masters of the third class, who confine themselves within the limits of the Roman law and deal either not at all, or only slightly, with the common law of nations, are of hardly any use in relation to our subject. They combine the subtlety of the Schoolmen with a knowledge of laws and of canons; and in fact two of them, the Spaniards Covarruvias and Vázquez, did not refrain from treating the controversies of peoples and kings, the latter with great freedom, the former with more restraint and not without precision of judgment.

The French have tried rather to introduce history into their study of laws. Among them Bodin and Hotman have gained a great name, the former by an extensive treatise, the latter by separate questions; their statements and lines of reasoning will frequently supply us with material in searching out the truth.

56. In my work as a whole I have, above all else, aimed at three things: to make the reasons for my conclusions as evident as possible; to set forth in a definite order the matters which needed to be treated; and to distinguish clearly between things which seemed to be the same and were not.

57. I have refrained from discussing topics which belong to another subject, such as those that teach what may be advantageous in practice. For such topics have their own special field, that of politics, which Aristotle rightly treats by itself, without introducing extraneous matter into it. Bodin, on the contrary, mixed up politics with the body of law with which we are concerned. In some places nevertheless I have made mention of that which is expedient, but only in passing, and in order to distinguish it more clearly from what is lawful.

58. If any one thinks that I have had in view any controversies of our own times, either those that have arisen or those which can be foreseen as likely to arise, he will do me an injustice. With all truthfulness I aver that, just as mathematicians treat their figures as abstracted from bodies, so in treating law I have withdrawn my mind from every particular fact.

59. As regards manner of expression, I wished not to disgust the reader, whose interest I continually had in mind, by adding prolixity of words to the multiplicity of matters needing to be treated. I have therefore followed, so far as I could, a mode of speaking at the same time concise and suitable for exposition, in order that those who deal with public affairs may have, as it were, in a single view both the kinds of controversies which are wont to arise and the principles by reference to which they may be decided. These points being known, it will be easy to adapt one's argument to the matter at issue, and expand it at one's pleasure.

60. I have now and then quoted the very words of ancient writers, where they seemed to carry weight or to have unusual charm of expression. This I have occasionally done even in the case of Greek writers, but as a rule only when the passage was brief, or

such that I dared not hope that I could bring out the beauty of it in a Latin version. Nevertheless, in all cases I have added a Latin translation for the convenience of those who have not learned Greek.[1]

61. I beg and adjure all those into whose hands this work shall come, that they assume towards me the same liberty which I have assumed in passing upon the opinions and writings of others. They who shall find me in error will not be more quick to advise me than I to avail myself of their advice.

And now if anything has here been said by me inconsistent with piety, with good morals, with Holy Writ, with the concord of the Christian Church, or with any aspect of truth, let it be as if unsaid.

---

[1] The English translation, of course, follows Grotius' Latin Version, which sometimes differs from the original Greek.

Book II

CHAPTER I

THE CAUSES OF WAR: FIRST, DEFENCE OF SELF AND PROPERTY

Section I. *What causes of war may be called justifiable*

1. Let us proceed to the causes of war – I mean justifiable causes; for there are also other causes which influence men through regard for what is expedient and differ from those that influence men through regard for what is right.

The two kinds of causes Polybius accurately distinguishes from each other and from beginnings of war,[1] such as the (wounding of the) stag was in the war between Aeneas and Turnus. Although the distinction between these matters is clear, nevertheless the words applied to them are often confused. For what we call justifiable causes Livy, in the speech of the Rhodians, called beginnings: 'You certainly are Romans[2] who claim that your wars are so fortunate because they are just, and pride yourselves not

---

[1] (109) Virgil (Aeneid, VII, 40) calls these 'the beginnings of battle' (*exordia pugnae*).

[2] Certainly, hardly any race has remained for so long a time scrupulous in examining into the causes of war. Thus in Suidas, under the word ἐμβαίνειν, Polybius says: 'The Romans have striven earnestly for this, that they be not the first to lay violent hands upon their neighbours, but that it should always be believed that they proceeded against an enemy in order to ward off injuries'. Dio Cassius, *Excerpta Peiresciana* (Diodorus Siculus, pp. 314, 316), manifests the same point of view in an excellent comparison of the Romans with Philip of Macedon and King Antiochus; and again in the *Selections on Embassies* he says: 'The ancients thus did nothing in haste, to the end that they might begin their wars justly'. And again, *Excerpta Peiresciana*, p. 341 (also Diodorus), the same author says: 'The Romans desire earnestly that the wars which they undertake be just and that they decree nothing of that sort without cause or rashly'.

so much on their outcome, in that you gain the victory, as upon their beginnings, because you do not undertake wars without cause'.

In the same sense also Aelian (in Book XII, chapter liii) speaks of the beginnings of wars, and Diodorus Siculus (Book XIV), giving an account of the war of the Lacedaemonians against the Eleans, expresses the same idea by using the words 'pretexts' and 'beginnings'.[1]

2. These justifiable causes are the special subject of our discussion. Pertinent thereto is the famous saying of Coriolanus quoted by Dionysius of Halicarnassus: 'This, I think, ought to be your first concern, that you have a cause for war which is free from reproach and just'. Similarly Demosthenes says: 'As the substructures of houses, the framework of ships, and similar things ought to be most firm, so, in the case of actions, the causes and fundamental reasons[2] ought to be in accord with justice and truth'. Equally pertinent is the statement of Dio Cassius: 'We must give the fullest consideration to justice. With justice on our side, military prowess warrants good hope; without it, we have nothing sure, even if the first successes equal our desires.' Cicero also says, 'Those wars are unjust which have been undertaken without cause'; and in another passage he criticizes Crassus because Crassus had determined to cross the Euphrates without any cause[3] for war.

3. What has been said is no less true of public than of private wars. Hence the complaint of Seneca:

We try to restrain murders and the killing of individuals. Why are wars and the crime of slaughtering nations full of glory? Avarice and cruelty know no bounds. In accordance with decrees of the Senate and orders of the people atrocities are committed,

---

[1] Procopius, *Gothic War*, III (III, xxxiv) calls these 'just occasions'. See also below, beginning of chap. xxii of this book.

[2] So also Julian said 'excuse' for war in his oration *On the Praises of Constantius* (ii = p. 95 B Spen.).

[3] Appian (*Civil Wars*, II, iii, 18) says that the same Crassus was forbidden by the tribunes 'to make war on the Parthians, who had been found guilty of no wrong-doing'. And Plutarch (*Crassus*, xvi = 552 E) of the same man: 'A large party arose which was displeased that any one should go to make war on men who were not only not guilty of any injustice but were protected by treaty relations'.

and actions forbidden to private citizens are commanded in the name of the state.[1]

Wars that are undertaken by public authority have, it is true, in some respects a legal effect, as do judicial decisions, which we shall need to discuss later; but they are not on that account more free from wrong if they are undertaken without cause. Thus Alexander, if he commenced war on the Persians and other peoples without cause, was deservedly called a brigand by the Scythians, according to Curtius, as also by Seneca[2]; likewise by Lucan he was styled a robber, and by the sages of India 'a man given over to wickedness', while a pirate once put Alexander in the same class with himself. Similarly, Justin tells how two kings of Thrace were deprived of their royal power by Alexander's father, Philip, who exemplified the deceit and wickedness of a brigand. In this connection belongs the saying of Augustine: 'If you take away justice, what are empires if not vast robberies?' In full accord with such expressions is the statement of Lactantius: 'Ensnared by the appearance of empty glory, men give to their crimes the name of virtue'.

4. No other just cause for undertaking war can there be excepting injury received. 'Unfairness of the opposing side occasions just wars', said the same Augustine, using 'unfairness' when he meant 'injury', as if he had confused the Greek words for these two concepts. In the formula used by the Roman fetial are the words, 'I call you to witness that that people is unjust and does not do what is right in making restitution'.

---

[1] Also Seneca, *On Anger*, II, viii (II, ix, 3): 'Some actions are considered as glorious which, so long as they can be restrained, are held to be crimes'. See other passages from Seneca and Cyprian cited below, III, iv, 5, near the end.

[2] The citation is from *On Benefits*, I, xiii (I, xiii, 3). Justin Martyr in his *Second Apology* (I, xii) well says: 'Rulers who place their own opinions above the truth are just as powerful as robbers in a desert'. Philo *On the Ten Commandments*, xxvi): 'Those who commit great thefts, who under the honourable name of government cover up actions that in reality are nothing else than robberies'.

Book II

CHAPTER XX

ON PUNISHMENTS

Section XL. *A discussion whether kings and peoples may rightly wage war on account of things done contrary to the law of nature, although not against them or their subjects; with a refutation of the view that the law of nature requires right of jurisdiction for the exaction of punishment.*

1. The fact must also be recognized that kings, and those who possess rights equal to those kings, have the right of demanding punishments not only on account of injuries committed, against themselves or their subjects, but also on account of injuries which do not directly affect them but excessively violate the law of nature or of nations in regard to any persons whatsoever. For liberty to serve the interests of human society through punishments, which originally, as we have said, rested with individuals, now after the organization of states and courts of law is in the hands of the highest authorities, not, properly speaking, in so far as they rule over others but in so far as they are themselves subject to no one. For subjection has taken this right away from others.

Truly it is more honourable to avenge the wrongs of others rather than one's own, in the degree that in the case of one's own wrongs it is more to be feared that through a sense of personal suffering one may exceed the proper limit or at least prejudice his mind.

2. And for this cause Hercules was famed by the ancients because he freed from Antaeus, Busiris, Diomedes and like tyrants the lands[1] which, as Seneca says, he traversed, not from a desire

[1] And seas. Philo, *On the Embassy to Gaius* (xi): (360) 'Hercules cleansed land and sea, undertaking contests most necessary and most beneficial to all

to acquire but to protect, becoming, as Lysius points out, the bestower of the greatest benefits upon men through his punishment of the unjust. Diodorus Siculus speaks of him thus: 'By slaying lawless men and arrogant despots he made the cities happy'. In another passage Diodorus said: 'He traversed the world chastising the unjust'. Of the same hero Dio of Prusa said: 'He punished wicked men and overthrew the power of the haughty or transferred it to others'. Aristides in his *Panathenaic Oration* declares that Hercules deserved to be elevated among the gods because of his espousal of the common interest of the human race.

In like manner Theseus is praised because he removed the robbers Sciron, Sinis, and Procrustes. Euripides in the *Suppliants* represents him as speaking thus about himself:

> Already throughout Greece my deeds to me
> This name have given; scourge of the wicked I am called.[1]

Of him Valerius Maximus wrote: 'All that was anywhere monstrous or criminal, he suppressed by the courage of his heart and the strength of his right hand'.

3. So we do not doubt that wars are justly waged against those who act with impiety towards their parents, like the Sogdianians before Alexander taught them to abandon this form of barbarity; against those who feed on human flesh[2] from which custom, according to Diodorus, Hercules compelled the ancient Gauls to abstain[3]; and against those who practise piracy. Says Seneca:

men, for the purpose of doing away with injurious or harmful being, among men and among animals'.

[1] And there to the herald who says (line 574):

> Did thy father then beget thee as a match for all?

Theseus replies:

> For the insolent at least; good deeds we do not punish.

Plutarch, in his *Life of Theseus* (Comparison of Theseus and Romulus, i = 37): 'He freed Greece of cruel tyrants', and 'Although having suffered no wrong himself he assailed wicked men on behalf of others'.

[2] Alexander taught the Scythians to give up this custom also (Plutarch, *loc. cit.*)

[3] See the statement of Dionysius of Halicarnassus (I, xxxviii) that Hercules abolished this and many other customs, making no distinction in his benefits between Greeks and barbarians. The equally great benefits of the Romans towards mankind are lauded by Pliny (*Natural History*), XXX, i: 'One cannot adequately compute what a debt is owed to the Romans, who have done away

'If a man does not attack my country, but yet is a heavy burden to his own, and although separated from my people he afflicts his own, such debasement of mind nevertheless cuts him off from us'. Augustine says: 'They think that they should decree the commission of crimes of such sort that if any state upon earth should decree them, or had decreed them, it would deserve to be overthrown by a decree of the human race'.

Regarding such barbarians, wild beasts rather than men, one may rightly say what Aristotle wrongly said of the Persians, who were in no way worse than the Greeks, that war against them was sanctioned by nature; and what Isocrates said, in his *Panathenaic Oration*, that the most just war is against savage beasts, the next against men who are like beasts.

4. Thus far we follow the opinion of Innocent, and others who say that war may be waged upon those who sin against nature.[1]

The contrary view is held by Victoria, Vázquez, Azor, Molina, and others, who in justification of war seem to demand that he who undertakes it should have suffered injury either in his person or his state, or that he should have jurisdiction over him who is attacked. For they claim that the power of punishing is the proper effect of civil jurisdiction, while we hold that it also is derived from the law of nature; this point we discussed at the beginning of the first book. And in truth, if we accept the view of those from whom we differ, no enemy will have the right to punish another, even after a war that has been undertaken for another reason than that of inflicting punishment. Nevertheless, many persons admit this right, which is confirmed also by usage of all nations, not only after the conclusion of a war but also while the war is still going on; and not on the basis of any civil jurisdiction, but of that law of nature which existed before states were organized,

with those monstrous practices in which the slaughter of a man was considered a most sacred act, and to devour him most healthful'. Add also what will be said in section 47 of this chapter.

Thus Justinian forbade the rulers of the Abasgi to castrate the male children of their subjects, as Procopius, *Gothic War*, IV (IV, iii), and Zonaras, in the history of Leo, the Isaurian (XV, i), record. The Incas, Kings of Peru, forcibly compelled the neighbouring peoples, who did not listen to a warning, to abstain from incest, from the intercourse of male persons, from the eating of human flesh, and from other crimes of that kind. And in this way they won for themselves an empire, the most just of all that we have read of, except in its religion.

[1] See Joseph Acosta, *De Procuranda Indorum Salute*, II, iv.

and is even now enforced, in places where men live in family groups and not in states.

Section XLIII. *In the law of nature we must distinguish between what is evident and what is not evident*

3. Finally, to avoid repeating often what I have said, we must add this word of warning, that wars which are undertaken to inflict punishment are under suspicion of being unjust, unless the crimes are very atrocious and very evident, or there is some other coincident reason. Perhaps Mithridates was not far wrong in saying of the Romans: 'They assail not the faults of kings but the power and authority of kings'.

Book III

CHAPTER X

CAUTIONS IN REGARD TO THINGS WHICH ARE DONE IN AN UNLAWFUL WAR

Section I. *With what meaning a sense of honour may be said to forbid what the law permits*

1. I must retrace my steps, and must deprive those who wage war of nearly all the privileges which I seemed to grant, yet did not grant to them. For when I first set out to explain this part of the law of nations I bore witness that many things are said to be 'lawful' or 'permissible' for the reason that they are done with impunity, in part also because coactive tribunals lend to them their authority; things which, nevertheless, either deviate from the rule of right (whether this has its basis in law strictly so called, or in the admonition of other virtues), or at any rate may be omitted on higher grounds and with greater praise among good men.

2. In the *Trojan Women* of Seneca, when Pyrrhus says:

No law the captive spares, nor punishment restrains,

Agamemnon makes answer:

What law permits, this sense of shame forbids to do.

In this passage the sense of shame signifies not so much a regard for men and reputation as a regard for what is just and good, or at any rate for that which is more just and better.

So in the *Institutes* of Justinian we read: 'Bequests in trust (*fideicommissa*) were so called, because they rested not upon a legal obligation, but only upon the sense of honour in those who were asked to take charge of them'. In Quintilian the Father, again:

'The creditor goes to the surety, without violating his sense of honour, only in case he is unable to recover from the debtor'. With this meaning you may often see justice associated with the sense of honour. (Thus Ovid):

> Not yet had justice fled before men's guilt;
> Last of divinities she left the earth,
> And sense of honour in the place of fear
> Ruled o'er the people without force.

Hesiod sang:

> Nowhere a sense of honour, nowhere golden Justice;
> The base assail the better wantonly.

The sentence of Plato, in the twelfth book of his *Laws*, 'For Justice is called, and truly called, the virgin daughter of Honour' (παρθένος γὰρ αἰδοῦς Δίκη λέγεταί τε καὶ ὄντως εἴρηται), I would amend by πάρεδδος so that the sense would be: 'Justice is called the councillor of honour, and this has been said with truth'. For in another place Plato also speaks thus: 'The deity, fearing for the human race, lest it should utterly perish, endowed men with a sense of honour and justice, in order that there might be adornments of cities and bonds of friendship'.

In like manner Plutarch calls 'justice' a 'house-companion of the sense of honour', and elsewhere he connects 'sense of honour' and 'justice'. In Dionysius of Halicarnassus, 'sense of honour and justice' are mentioned together. Likewise Josephus also links 'sense of honour and equity'. Paul the jurist, too, associates the law of nature and the sense of honour. Moreover Cicero draws the boundary line between justice and a sense of reverence (*verecundia*) in this way, that it is the function of justice not to do violence to men, that of the sense of reverence not to offend them.

3. The verse which we quoted from Seneca is in complete agreement with a statement in his philosophical works: 'How limited the innocence to be innocent merely according to the letter of the law?[1] How must more widely extend the rules of

---

[1] Seneca, *On Benefits*, V, xxi, says also: 'Many good things are not covered by any law, and find no form of procedure in court, but yet they are protected by the practice of human society, which is more potent than any law'.
Quintilian, *Institutes of Oratory*, III, viii (III, vi, 84), declares: 'For there are

duty than the rules of law? How many things are demanded by devotion to gods, country and kin, by kindness, generosity, justice, and good faith? Yet all these requirements are outside the statutes of the law.' Here you see 'law' distinguished from 'justice', because he considers as law that which is in force in external judgments.

The same writer elsewhere well illustrates this by taking as an example the right of the master over slaves: 'In the case of a slave you must consider, not how much he may be made to suffer with impunity, but how far such treatment is permitted by the nature of justice and goodness, which bids us to spare even captives and those bought for a price'. Then: 'Although all things are permissible against a slave, yet there is something which the common law of living things forbids to be permissible against a human being'. In this passage we must again note the different interpretations of the term 'to be permissible', the one external, the other internal.

Section III. *What is done by reason of an unjust war is unjust from the point of view of moral injustice*

In the first place, then, we say that if the cause of a war should be unjust, even if the war should have been undertaken in a lawful way, all acts which arise therefrom are unjust from the point of view of moral injustice (*interna iniustitia*). In consequence the persons who knowingly perform such acts, or co-operate in them, are to be considered of the number of those who cannot reach the Kingdom of Heaven without repentance. True repentance, again, if time and means are adequate, absolutely requires that he who inflicted the wrong, whether by killing, by destroying property, or by taking booty, should make good the wrong done.[1]

certain things which are not naturally praiseworthy, but are permitted by law, as the provision in the Twelve Tables that the body of a debtor could be divided among his creditors, a law which public practice repudiates'.

Cicero, *On Duties*, III (III, xvii, 68), writes: 'For the laws dispose of sharp practices in one way, and philosophers in another; the laws in so far as they can apply physical force, but philosophers in so far as they can apply reason and intelligence'.

[1] *Numbers*, v. 6 (and 7). Jerome, *To Rusticus*, says: 'The pronouncement of vengeance is not cancelled unless the whole is restored'. Augustine, in a letter

Thus God says He is not pleased with the fasting of those who held prisoners that had been wrongfully captured[1]; and the king of Nineveh, in proclaiming a public mourning, ordered that men should cleanse their hands of plunder, being led by nature to recognize the fact that, without such restitution, repentance would be false and in vain. We see that this is the opinion not merely of Jews[2] and Christians, but also of Mohammedans.[3]

to Macedonius, which is liv (*Letters*, cliii, 20), writes: 'If the property of another, for the sake of which the sin was committed, can be returned, and it is not returned, repentance is not felt but pretended'. This is cited by Gratian, in the *Decretum*, II, xi, 6 (LL, xiv, 6.1).

[1] There is a significant passage in *Isaiah*, lviii. 5, 6 and 7. You find it in Greek in Justin Martyr, *Dialogue with Trypho* (xv).

[2] See the penitential canons of Moses Maimonides, ii, 2. Also Moses de Kotzi, *Precepts Bidding*, 16.

[3] See Leunclavius, *Turkish History*, V and XVII.

Book III

CHAPTER XII

MODERATION IN LAYING WASTE AND SIMILAR THINGS

Section VIII. *The advantages which follow from such moderation are pointed out*

I. It is, in truth, not strictly a part of our purpose to enquire at this point what is advantageous; we desire rather to restrict the unrestrained licence of war to that which is permitted by nature, or to the choice of the better among the things permitted. Nevertheless, virtue itself, in low esteem in the present age, ought to forgive me if, when of itself it is despised, I cause it to be valued on account of its advantages.

In the first place, then, such moderation, by preserving things which do not delay the war, deprives the enemy of a great weapon, despair. There is a saying of Archidamus in Thucydides: 'Think of the enemy's land as nothing else than a hostage, the better the more it is cultivated; therefore it must be spared, so far as is possible, that despair may not make the enemy harder to conquer'. The same policy was followed by Agesilaus[1] when, contrary to the view of the Achaeans, he let the Acarnanians sow their crops in freedom, saying that the more they sowed the more desirous of peace they would be. This is what the satire says: 'For those, who have been plundered of everything, weapons still remain'. Livy, in relating the capture of the city of Rome by the Gauls, says: 'The chiefs of the Gauls had decided that all the houses should not be burned down, in order that what remained of the city might serve them as a pledge to break the morale of the foe'.

[1] This is recorded also by Plutarch, *Agesilaus* (xxii = p. 608 B).

79

2. There is the further consideration that, in the course of a war, such moderation gives the appearance of great assurance of victory, and that clemency is of itself suited to weaken and to conciliate the spirit. According to Livy, Hannibal did no damage in the territory of Tarentum: 'It appeared', he says, 'that this course was pursued not because of the moderation of the soldiers or their general, but (536) in order to conciliate the feelings of the Tarentines'.

For a similar cause Augustus Caesar refrained from pillaging the Pannonians. Dio gives the reason: 'He hoped that in this way he would win them over to him without compulsion'. Polybius (Polyaenus) says that Timotheus, with that care of which we have already spoken, above all else 'sought to win great goodwill from the enemy themselves'. Regarding Quintius[1] and those Romans who were under his orders, Plutarch, having narrated what we have said above, adds: 'Not long afterwards he received the fruit of this moderation; for, when he arrived in Thessaly, the cities went over to him. Then in fact the Greeks who dwelt within Thermopylae also ardently longed for Quintius; and the Achaeans, renouncing the friendship of Philip, entered with the Romans into an alliance against him'.

The state of the Lingones escaped the devastation which they had dreaded in the war waged by the general Cerealis, under the authority of Domitian, against Civilis the Batavian and his allies; regarding it, Frontinus narrates the following: 'Because the state had not lost any of its possessions, owing to the fact that contrary to expectation it had not been laid waste, when brought back to its allegiance it furnished to him seventy thousand armed men'.

3. Opposite results have attended the opposite policy. Livy gives an example in the case of Hannibal: 'His spirit, inclined to avarice and cruelty, was prone to despoil what he could not protect. This policy was destructive both in its inception and in its result. For it alienated the minds not only of those who suffered undeserved wrong, but of others also, since more persons were affected by the example than by the disaster.'

4. Moreover, that which has been observed by certain theologians I hold to be true, that it is the duty of the highest authorities and commanders, who wish themselves to be regarded as Christians

[1] Naturally Titus Quintius Flaminius (Flamininus).

both by God and by men, to forbid the violent sack of cities and other similar actions. Such actions cannot take place without very serious harm to many innocent persons, and often are of little consequence for the result of the war; so that Christian goodness almost always, and bare justice very often, shrinks from them.

Surely the bond which unites Christians is greater than that which united the Greeks of old, in whose wars a decree of the Amphictyons provided against the blotting out of a Greek city. And the ancients relate that Alexander of Macedon repented of nothing that he had done more than that he had completely destroyed Thebes.

Book III

CHAPTER XXV

CONCLUSION, WITH ADMONITIONS ON BEHALF OF GOOD FAITH AND PEACE

Section I. *Admonitions to preserve peace*

At this point I think that I can bring my work to an end, not because all has been said that could be said, but because sufficient has been said to lay the foundations. Whoever may wish to build on these foundations a more imposing structure will not only find me free from envy, but will have my sincere gratitude.

Yet before I dismiss the reader I shall add a few admonitions which may be of value in war, and after war, for the preservation of good faith and of peace; just as in treating of the commencement of war I added certain admonitions regarding the avoidance of wars, so far as this can be accomplished.

And good faith should be preserved, not only for other reasons but also in order that the hope of peace may not be done away with. For not only is every state sustained by good faith, as Cicero declares, but also that greater society of states. Aristotle truly says that, if good faith has been taken away, 'all intercourse among men ceases to exist'.

Rightly the same Cicero says that 'it is an impious act to destroy the good faith which holds life together'. To use Seneca's phrase, it is 'the most exalted good of the human heart'. And this good faith the supreme rulers of men ought so much the more earnestly than others to maintain as they violate it with greater impunity; if good faith shall be done away with, they will be like wild beasts,[1] whose violence all men fear. Justice, it is true, in its other aspects often contains elements of obscurity; but the bond of good faith is in itself plain to see, nay more, it is brought into use to so great an extent that it removes all obscurity from business transactions.

It is, then, all the more the duty of kings to cherish good faith scrupulously, first for conscience's sake, and then also for the sake of the reputation by which the authority of the royal power is supported. Therefore let them not doubt that those who instil in them the arts of deception are doing the very thing which they teach. For that teaching cannot long prosper which makes a man antisocial with his kind and also hateful in the sight of God.

Section II. *In war peace should always be kept in view*

Again, during the entire period of administration of a war the soul cannot be kept serene and trusting in God unless it is always looking forward to peace. Sallust most truly said, 'The wise wage war for the sake of peace'. With this the opinion of Augustine agrees: 'Peace is not sought that war may be followed, but war is waged that peace may be secured'. Aristotle himself more than once condemns those nations which made warlike pursuits, as it were, their end and aim. Violence is characteristic of wild beasts, and effort should be put forth that it be tempered with humanity, lest by imitating wild beasts too much we forget to be human.

[1] According to Procopius, *Persian War*, II (II, x), the ambassadors of Justinian thus address Chosroes:

'Unless, O king, this address were being made to you in person, we should never have believed that Chosroes, son of Cabades, would have entered Roman territory in arms after first scorning the sworn oaths, which are believed to be the highest and strongest pledge of truth and good faith among men; and besides, after breaking the treaty, in which rests the only hope left for those who are not living in safety on account of the evils of war.

What else should we say that this is, than to exchange the life of men for the life of wild beasts? For when treaties have been done away with it will follow that all peoples will wage unending wars with one another. But unending wars have the effect, that they keep men continuously estranged from their own nature.'

Section III. *And peace should also be accepted even at a loss, especially by Christians*

If, then, it is possible to have peace with sufficient safety, it is well established by condonation of offences, damages, and expenses; this holds especially among Christians, on whom the Lord has bestowed His peace. And His best interpreter wishes us, so far as it is possible and within our power, to seek peace with all men. It is characteristic of a good man, as we read in Sallust, to be unwilling to begin war, not gladly to pursue it to the bitter end.

Section IV. *The consideration stated is useful to the conquered*

This one consideration ought to be sufficient. However, human advantage also often draws in the same direction, first, those who are weaker, because a long contest with a stronger opponent is dangerous, and, just as on a ship, a greater misfortune must be avoided at some loss, with complete disregard of anger and hope which, as Livy has rightly said, are deceitful advisers. The thought is expressed by Aristotle thus[1]: 'It is better to relinquish something of one's possessions to those who are stronger, than to be conquered in war and perish with the property'.

Section V. *The consideration stated is also useful to the conqueror*

Again, human advantage draws in the same direction also the stronger. The reason is, as the same Livy no less truly says, that peace is bounteous and creditable to those who grant it while their affairs are prosperous; and it is better and safer than a victory that is hoped for. It must be kept in mind that Mars is on both sides. As Aristotle says, 'In war men ought to consider how many and how unexpected changes are wont to occur'. In a certain oration for peace in Diodorus Siculus those are censured who magnify the greatness of their exploits, as if it were not evidently customary for the fortune of war to bestow favours alternately.

[1] Philo, *De Constitutione Principis* (*On Justice*, xiii), says: 'Peace, even though with great loss, is better than war'.

84

And especially must the boldness of the desperate be feared;[1] wild beasts bite most fiercely when dying.

Section VI. *The consideration stated is useful likewise to those whose fortunes are in doubt*

But, if both sides seem to be equal to each other, this in truth, as Caesar says, is the best time to treat of peace, while each has confidence in himself.

Section VII. *Peace, when made, must be kept with the utmost scruple*

Moreover peace, whatever the terms on which it is made, ought to be preserved absolutely, on account of the sacredness of good faith, which I have mentioned; and not only should treachery be anxiously avoided, but everything else that may arouse anger. What Cicero said about private friendships you may apply to public friendships no less correctly: not only should all friendships be safeguarded with the greatest devotion and good faith, but especially those which have been restored to goodwill after enmity.

Section VIII. *A prayer, and the end of the work*

May God, who alone hath the power, inscribe these teachings on the hearts of those who hold sway over the Christian world. May He grant to them a mind possessing knowledge of divine and human law, and having ever before it the reflection that it hath been chosen as a servant for the rule of man,[2] the living thing most dear to God.

---

[1] (Plutarch, *Marius*, xiv = p. 432 C):

   We even have to fear the dying lion's den.

[2] So Chrysostom in his sermon *On Alms* (beginning): 'Man is the being dearest to God'.

EMMERICH DE VATTEL

Emmerich de Vattel was born in Couvet in the principality of Neuchâtel
(now a Swiss canton, but at that time belonging to Prussia) in 1714.
He studied at Geneva and Basle, his first inclination being towards
literature and philosophy. In 1741 he published a defence of Leibniz's
philosophical system, and in the same year he went to Berlin, hoping in
vain for employment from Frederick II. Moving to Dresden in 1743, he
succeeded in obtaining patronage from Count Brühl, favourite of the
Elector of Saxony. The Elector appointed him councillor of embassy
(1746), and a year later he became minister plenipotentiary at Berne. It
was during his appointment at Berne that Vattel completed his major
work *The Law of Nations*, which was published in 1758. The book
proved an immediate success; it was translated and reissued frequently
and became a standard handbook for governments and diplomats. Vattel
was recalled to Dresden in 1758 and was appointed privy councillor.
From that time forward he was occupied with the most important
affairs of Saxony. His health suffered as a result of overwork, and he
died at Neuchâtel in 1767.

In *The Law of Nations* Vattel blends together the abstract, *a priori*
theories of the German philosopher Christian Wolff (1679-1754) with
his own more practical ideas. The blend is not always successful,
and there is considerable ambivalence in the book. However, certain
concepts emerge with clarity, of which the most important is that of
the equality and independence of states. This concept, outlined in the
Introduction (Extract 2), finds further expression in Vattel's comparatively modern idea of neutrality, his advocacy of non-intervention,
and the high priority which he accords to treaties as methods of solving
international disputes. Occasionally it is obscured by Vattel's simul-
taneous insistence that states have a duty to promote justice in the
international world, but ultimately it is the principle of independence
which takes precedence. This marks a significant step beyond Grotius.

Methodologically Vattel is important in that he stresses that the
natural law appropriate for individuals cannot be directly applied to
states. Here again he shows a considerable advance over Grotius.
Finally Vattel introduces into his discussion of international law the
idea of the balance of power, an idea which he clearly favours, though
he has some difficulty in reconciling it with his belief in the independence of states and their duty to uphold justice.

Of the selections which follow, the first two indicate Vattel's overall approach to the subject; the third contains his discussion of the balance of power, and the fourth shows him adjusting the rival claims of independence and justice. The extracts have been taken from *The Law of Nations or the Principles of Natural Law applied to the Conduct and to the Affairs of Nations and of Sovereigns*, by E. de Vattel, Volume III; translated by Charles G. Fenwick from the edition of 1758, and published in the series 'The Classics of International Law' (reprinted 1964). The extracts comprise pp. 3a-13a, pp. 3-9, pp. 248-52, and pp. 304-6 of the volume. Vattel's paragraph headings, and cross-references to them, have been omitted.

Suggested Reading

P. P. Remec, *The Position of the Individual in International Law according to Grotius and Vattel*, 1960.

Preface

The Law of Nations, great and important a subject as it is, has thus far not received the attention which it merits. The majority of men, indeed, have but vague, superficial, and often even mistaken ideas regarding it. The great body of writers, including even authors of repute, understand by the term Law of Nations merely certain rules and certain customs which are accepted among Nations and have become binding upon them by reason of their mutual consent. Such a view restricts within very narrow limits a law of wide extent and of great importance to the human race, and at the same time degrades its position by misconceiving its true origin.

There is no doubt of the existence of a natural Law of Nations, inasmuch as the Law of Nature is no less binding upon States, where men are united in a political society, than it is upon the individuals themselves. Now an exact knowledge of this law cannot be had by a mere understanding of what the Law of Nature prescribes for individual persons. When a law is applied to different subjects it must be applied in a manner suited to the nature of each subject. Hence it follows that the natural Law of Nations is a special science which consists in a just and reasonable application of the Law of Nature to the affairs and the conduct of Nations and of sovereigns. All those treatises, therefore, which confuse the Law of Nations with the ordinary natural law must fail to convey a distinct idea and a thorough knowledge of the sacred Law of Nations.

The Romans often confused the Law of Nations with the Law of Nature, giving the term 'Law of Nations' (*ius gentium*) to the natural law, inasmuch as the latter was generally recognized and adopted by all civilized nations.[1] The Emperor Justinian's definitions of natural law, the Law of Nations, and civil law, are

---

[1] Neque vero hoc solum natura, id est, iure gentium', etc. Cicero, *De offic.*, Book III, c. 5.

well known. 'Natural law,' he says, 'is the law taught by nature to all animals.'[1] This is a definition of the Law of Nature in its widest extent, and not the natural law peculiar to man which is derived from his rational as well as from his animal nature. 'The civil law,' continues the Emperor, 'is that law which is established by each people for itself and which is peculiar to each State or civil society; whereas that law which is established among all men by natural reason, and which is equally observed by every people, is called the Law of Nations, since it is a law which all Nations follow.'[2] In the following paragraph the Emperor seems to come nearer to the sense which we give to the term today. 'The Law of Nations,' he says, 'is common to the whole human race. Nations have been led by the needs of their intercourse to set up for themselves certain rules of law. For wars have broken out and there has resulted a state of captivity and of servitude which is contrary to the natural law; since by the natural law all men from the beginning were born free.'[3] But his further remark that almost all contracts whether of purchase and sale, of hire of partnership, of trust, and numberless others owe their origin to this same Law of Nations – this, I say, shows us that Justinian's idea is merely that, in accordance with the condition and circumstances in which men happened to be, right reason has dictated to them certain rules of justice (*droit*), which, being based upon the very nature of things, have won recognition and acceptance on all sides. But that is nothing else than the natural law in its applicability to all men.

Nevertheless the Romans recognized the existence of a law having force between Nations as such, and to it they refer the right of embassies. They had likewise their *fetial* law, which was nothing more than the Law of Nations in its relation to public treaties and particularly to war. The *fetials* were the interpreters,

---

[1] 'Ius naturale est, quod natura omnia animalia docuit'. *Instit*, Book 1, tit. 2.

[2] 'Quod quisque populus ipse sibi jus constituit, id ipsius proprium civitatis est, vocaturque jus civile, quasi jus proprium ipsius civitatis: quod vero naturalis ratio inter omnes homines constituit, id apud omnes peræque custoditur, vocaturque jus gentium, quasi quo jure omnes gentes utantur.' *Ibid.*, 1.

[3] 'Ius autem gentium omni humano generi commune est; nam usu exigente et humanis necessitatibus, gentes humanae jura quædam sibi constituerunt. Bella etenim orta sunt, et captivitates sequutæ, et servitutes, quæ sunt naturali juri contrariæ. Jure enim naturali omnes ab initio liberi nascebantur.' *Ibid.*, 2.

the guardians, and in a manner the priests of the public good faith.[1]

Modern writers generally agree in restricting the term Law of Nations (*Droit des Gens*) to the law which should prevail between Nations or sovereign States. They differ only in the view they take of the origin of this law and of its foundations. The celebrated Grotius understands by the 'Law of Nations' a law established by the common consent of Nations, and he thus distinguishes it from the natural law. 'When a number of persons at different times and in different places maintain the same principle as true, their common opinion must be attributed to some general cause. Now in the matter before us this cause can only be one or the other of these two, either a just deduction from natural principles or a universal consent. In the former we see the *Law of Nature*, in the latter the *Law of Nations*.'[2]

From many passages of his excellent work it can be seen that this great writer had some conception of the true view. But as he was breaking ground, so to speak, in an important subject hitherto much neglected, it is not surprising that with his mind burdened by a large number of subjects and of quotations which formed part of his plan, he failed at times to arrive at those distinct ideas which are so essential to a science. With the conviction that Nations or sovereign powers are subject to the authority of the natural law, obedience to which he so often recommends to them, this learned man perceives that there is at bottom a natural Law of Nations (which he somewhere calls the 'internal' Law of Nations); and it may perhaps appear that he differs from us only in his terms. But we have already remarked that in constructing this Law of Nations it is not enough merely to apply to Nations the dictates of the natural law with regard to individuals. Moreover, Grotius, by the very distinction which he draws, and by his application of the term 'Law of Nations' merely to those principles established by the consent of Nations, apparently gives us to understand that it is only these latter principles which sovereigns

---

[1] '*Fetiales*, quod fidei publicæ inter populos præerant: nam per hos fiebat, ut justum conciperetur bellum (et inde desitum) et ut fœdere fides pacis constitueretur. Ex his mittebant, antequam conciperetur, qui res repeterent: et per hos etiam nunc fit fœdus,' Varro. de Ling, Lat., Book IV.

[2] *De Jure Belli et Pacis*, translated by Barbeyrac; Preliminary Discourse, 41.

can insist on being observed, the *internal* law remaining a guide for their consciences. If with his idea that political societies or Nations live together in a mutual interdependence in the state of nature, and that as political bodies they are subject to the Law of Nature, Grotius had considered, in addition, that the law ought to be applied to these new subjects according to their nature, this thoughtful writer would have easily perceived that the natural Law of Nations is a special science; that it gives rise among Nations even to an exterior obligation independent of their will, and that the consent of Nations is the foundation and the source only of that particular division of the Law of Nations which is called the 'arbitrary Law of Nations'.

Hobbes, whose work, in spite of its paradoxes and its detestable principles, shows us the hand of the master – Hobbes, I repeat, was the first, to my knowledge, to give us a distinct though imperfect idea of the Law of Nations. He divides the natural law into the 'natural law of man' and the 'natural law of States'. The latter, in his view, is what is ordinarily called the 'Law of Nations'. 'The principles,' he adds, 'of both of these laws are exactly the same; but as States acquire what are in a way the characteristics of persons, the same law which we call natural in speaking of the duties of individuals we call the Law of Nations when we apply it to the entire people of a State or Nation.'[1] His statement that the Law of Nations is the natural law as applied to States or Nations is sound. But in the course of this work we shall see that he was mistaken in thinking that the natural law did not necessarily undergo any change in being thus applied; a belief which led him to conclude that the principles of the natural law and those of the Law of Nations were exactly the same.

Pufendorf declares that this opinion of Hobbes meets with his unqualified approval.[2] Hence he did not give the Law of Nations

---

[1] 'Rursus (lex) *naturalis* dividi potest in naturalem hominum, quæ sola obtinuit dici *Lex Naturae* et naturalem *civitatum*, quæ dici potest Lex Gentium, vulgo autem *Jus Gentium* appellatur. Præcepta utriusque eadem sunt: sed quia civitates semel institutæ induunt proprietates hominum personales, lex quam loquentes de hominum singulorum officio *naturalem* dicimus, applicata totis civitatibus, nationibus sive gentibus, vocatur *Jus Gentium*', *De Cive*, Chap. XIV, 4. I make use of Barbeyrac's translation of Pufendorf's *Jus Naturae et Gentium*, Book II, Chap. II.
[2] Pufendorf, *Jus Naturae et Gentium*, Book II, Chap. III, 23.

a distinct treatment by itself, but included it in his treatment of the natural law in its proper sense.

Barbeyrac, as translator and commentator of Grotius and Pufendorf, came much nearer to the true conception of the Law of Nations. Although the work is in everyone's hands, I shall reproduce here, for the convenience of the reader, this learned translator's note upon Grotius's *De Jure Belli et Pacis*, Book I, Chap. I, 14, N.3. 'I grant,' he says, 'that there are laws common to all Nations, or principles which all Nations ought mutually to observe, and those who wish to may very well call them the Law of Nations. But apart from the fact that the consent of Nations is not the foundation of the obligation to observe these laws, and indeed could here have no place whatsoever, the principles and rules of such a law are fundamentally the same as those of the Law of Nature in its proper sense, the only distinction being in the application of those principles. This application will be somewhat different by reason of the different manner in which Nations sometimes settle their common affairs.'

The author we have just been quoting saw clearly that the rules and precepts of the natural law cannot be applied, pure and simple, to sovereign States, and that they ought necessarily to undergo some change according to the nature of the new subjects to which they are applied. But he does not appear to have perceived the full extent of that idea, since he seems to disapprove of giving a separate treatment to the Law of Nations from that of the natural law governing individuals. He merely praises the method of Buddeus, saying 'that this author did well in noting (in his *Elementa Philos. pract.*), after each article of the natural law the application which could be made of it to Nations in their mutual relations; as far at least as the matter in question would permit or require'.[1] This was taking a step in the right direction. But more profound thought and wider views were required to conceive the idea of a system of the natural Law of Nations which could act as a law for sovereigns and Nations, and to perceive the usefulness of such a work, and above all to be the first to carry it out.

---

[1] Note 2 on Pufendorf's *Jus Naturae et Gentium*, Book II, Chap. III, 23. I have not been able to procure the work of Buddeus, from which I suspect Barbeyrac drew this idea of the Law of Nations.

This honour was reserved for Baron de Wolff. This great philosopher saw that the application of the natural law to entire Nations, or to States, in a manner suited to the nature of the subjects, could only be made with precision, clearness, and thoroughness by the aid of certain general principles and leading ideas which should control it. He saw that it was only by means of this principle that it could be clearly shown that the precepts of the natural law with respect to individuals ought, by reason of the character of that very law, to be changed and modified when being applied to States or political societies, and so to form a natural and necessary Law of Nations.[1] Hence he concluded that the Law of Nations should be treated as a distinct system, a task which he has successfully performed. But we would prefer to hear Mr Wolff speak for himself in his preface.

'Since Nations[2] [he says] recognize in their mutual relations no other law than that established by nature it would seem superfluous to treat the Law of Nations as something distinct from the natural law. But persons of this opinion have not fully grasped the subject. It is true that Nations can only be considered as so many individual persons living together in a state of nature, and therefore all the duties and the rights which nature prescribes and imposes upon all men, in so far as they are by nature born free and are held together only by the ties of nature, should be applied to States as well. In thus applying them there arises a law and there result obligations, which are derived from that unchanging law founded on man's nature; and to this extent the Law of Nations is certainly connected with the Law of Nature. Hence we call it the *natural* Law of Nations, by reference to its origin; and by reference to its binding force we

---

[1] If it were not more desirable for the sake of brevity to avoid repetition and to take advantage of ideas already well formed and established; if, I say, it were not better for these reasons to suppose here a knowledge of the ordinary natural law and to proceed to apply it to sovereign States, instead of speaking of such an application, it would be more exact to say that as the natural law in its proper sense is the Law of Nature for individuals, being founded upon man's nature, so that natural Law of Nations is the Law of Nature for political societies, being founded on the nature of these societies. However, as both methods come to the same thing, I have chosen the briefer one. The natural law has already been sufficiently treated; it is shorter simply to make a logical application of it to Nations.

[2] A Nation here means a sovereign State, an independent political society.

call it the *necessary* Law of Nations. This law is common to all nations, and that nation which does not act according to it violates the common law of all mankind.

But as Nations or sovereign States are corporate persons and the subjects of obligations and rights which in virtue of the natural law result from the act of association by which political bodies are formed, the nature and essence of these moral persons will necessarily differ in many respects from the nature and essence of the physical units, or men, who compose them. Hence, since rights and duties must be consistent with the nature of their subjects, in applying to Nations the duties which the natural law imposes upon each individual and the rights it confers in order that he may fulfil those duties, they must necessarily be changed so as to suit the nature of the new subjects. Thus it is seen that the latter controls the actions of individuals. Why, therefore, should it not have a separate treatment as being a law peculiar to Nations.'

Under persuasion of the usefulness of such a work I impatiently waited for Mr Wolff's to appear; and on its appearance I resolved to facilitate for a wider circle of readers a knowledge of the brilliant ideas it contained in it. The treatise on the Law of Nations by the philosopher of Halle is connected with the same author's previous works upon philosophy and the natural law. Of these there are some sixteen volumes in quarto, and a study of them is necessary to an understanding of the work before us. Besides, it is written after the method and systematic form of treatises on geometry – all constituting obstacles which render the work almost useless to persons whose chief desire and interest is a knowledge of the true principles of the Law of Nations. I thought at first that I would only have to separate this treatise from the whole system, so that it would be independent of any of Mr Wolff's previous works, and then to make it accessible to cultured people in a more attractive form. I made several efforts to do so. But I soon saw that if I was to reach the circle of readers I had in mind I should have to compose a new work quite different from the one before me. Mr Wolff's method produced a very dry work and one incomplete in many respects. The subjects treated of are so scattered through the work as to weary the attention; and as the writer had already treated of universal public law in his *Law of Nature* he is frequently satisfied with mere reference to it when he speaks in his *Law of Nations* of the duties of a State towards itself.

I therefore limited myself to choosing from Mr Wolff's work what I found most valuable, especially his definitions and general principles. I was discriminating in my choice and I adapted to my design the materials I had collected. Those who are familiar with Mr Wolff's treatise on the natural law and the Law of Nations will see to what extent I have profited by them. Had I wished to indicate my indebtedness at all times, I should have burdened my pages with quotations both useless and wearisome to the reader. It is better to acknowledge here once for all my obligations to that great master. Although those who take the trouble to make a comparison will see how different my work is from his, I confess that I should never have had the courage to enter on so wide a field had not the noted philosopher of Halle gone before me and shown the way.

At times, however, I have ventured to leave my guide and to oppose his views, For example, Mr Wolff, influenced perhaps by the majority of writers, devotes several articles[1] to a consideration of the nature of *patrimonial* kingdoms, without either rejecting or correcting an idea so hurtful to mankind. I do not even acknowledge the term, which I consider at once revolting, untrue and dangerous in the effect it may produce upon the minds of sovereigns. In this dissent I am encouraged to think that I shall win the approval of every man of judgment and right feeling and every true citizen.

Mr Wolff concludes (*Jus Gentium*, 878) that the Law of Nature permits the use of poisoned weapons in warfare. This conclusion shocks me and I deeply regret finding it in the work of so great a man. Happily for the human race the contrary doctrine can easily be established, and this according to Mr Wolff's own principles. My remarks on this question will be found in Book III, 156.

From the outset it will be seen that I differ entirely from Mr Wolff in the foundation I lay for that division of the Law of Nations which we term *voluntary*. Mr Wolff deduces it from the idea of a sort of great republic (*Civitas Maxima*) set up by nature herself, of which all the Nations of the world are members. To

---

[1] In the eighth part of his *Law of Nature*, and in his *Law of Nations*.

his mind, the *voluntary* Law of Nations acts as the civil law of this great republic. This does not satisfy me, and I find the fiction of such a republic neither reasonable nor well enough founded to deduce therefrom the rules of a Law of Nations at once universal in character, and necessarily accepted by sovereign States. I recognize no other natural society among Nations than that which nature has set up among men in general. It is essential to every civil society (*Civitas*) that each member should yield certain of his rights to the general body, and that there should be some authority capable of giving commands, prescribing laws, and compelling those who refuse to obey. Such an idea is not to be thought of as between Nations. Each independent State claims to be, and actually is, independent of all the others. Even according to Mr Wolff's view, they ought to be regarded as so many free individuals who live together in a state of nature, and recognize no other laws than those of nature, or of its divine author. Now although nature has so constituted men that they absolutely require the assistance of their fellow-men if they are to live as it befits men to live, and has thus established a general society among them, yet nature cannot be said to have imposed upon men the precise obligation of uniting together in civil society; and if all men followed the laws of that good mother subjection to civil society would be needless. It is true that men, seeing that the Laws of Nature were not being voluntarily observed, have had recourse to political association as the one remedy against the degeneracy of the majority, as the one means of protecting the good and restraining the wicked; and the natural law itself approves of such a course. But it is clear that there is by no means the same necessity for a civil society among Nations as among individuals. It cannot be said, therefore, that nature recommends it to an equal degree, far less that it prescribes it. Individuals are so constituted that they could accomplish but little by themselves and could scarcely get on without the assistance of civil society and its laws. But as soon as a sufficient number have united under a government, they are able to provide for most of their needs, and they find the help of other political societies not so necessary to them as the State itself is to individuals.

But these individual societies have, it is true, strong motives for mutual communication and intercourse; they have even an obligation to this effect since without good reason no man may refuse his assistance to another. But this mutual intercourse can be sufficiently regulated by the natural law. States are not like individuals in the conduct of their affairs. Ordinarily their resolutions are not taken nor their public policy determined by the blind rashness or the whim of an individual. Advice is taken and more calmness and deliberation shown; and in delicate or important situations arrangements are made and agreements reached by means of treaties. Moreover, independence is necessary to a State, if it is to fulfil properly its duties towards itself and its citizens and to govern itself in the manner best suited to it. Hence, I repeat, it is enough that Nations conform to the demands made upon them by that natural and world-wide society established among all men.

But Mr Wolff says that in the intercourse of this society of Nations, the natural law is not always to be followed in all its strictness; changes must be made which can only be deduced from his idea of a sort of great republic of the Nations whose laws, dictated by right reason and founded upon necessity, will determine what changes must be made in the natural and necessary Law of Nations, just as the civil laws of a State determine with respect to individuals the changes to be made in the natural law. I do not perceive the force of this conclusion. I am confident that I shall be able to prove in this work that all the modifications, all the restrictions, in brief, all the changes which must be made in the strictness of the natural law when applied to the affairs of Nations, whence results the *voluntary* Law of Nations – may all be deduced from the natural liberty of Nations, from considerations of their common welfare, from the nature of their mutual intercourse, from their reciprocal duties, and from the distinction between *internal* and *external*, *perfect* and *imperfect* rights. I shall reason much as Mr Wolff has reasoned with respect to individuals in his treatise on the Law of Nature.

That treatise shows us that the rules which by reason of man's free nature may govern *external* right do not destroy the obligation which the *internal* right imposes upon the conscience of each individual. It is easy to apply this doctrine to Nations, and to teach them by careful distinctions between *internal* and *external* right, that is to say, between the *necessary* Law of Nations and the *voluntary* Law of Nations, not to feel free to do whatever can be done with impunity, when it is contrary to the immutable laws of justice and the voice of conscience.

Now since Nations must mutually recognize these exceptions and modifications in the strict application of the *necessary* law, whether we deduce them from the idea of a great republic of which all the peoples of the world are members, or whether they be drawn from the sources from which I propose to draw, there is no reason why the law which results therefrom should not be called the *voluntary* Law of Nations, in contradistinction to the *necessary* Law of Nations, which is the inner law of conscience. Terms count for little; what is really important is the careful distinction between those two kinds of law, so that we may never confuse what is just and good in itself with what is merely tolerated through necessity.

The *necessary* Law of Nations and the *voluntary* law have therefore both been established by nature, but each in its own way: the former as a sacred law to be respected and obeyed by Nations and sovereigns in all their actions; the latter as a rule of conduct which the common good and welfare oblige them to accept in their mutual intercourse. The *necessary* law is derived immediately from nature; while this common mother of men merely recommends the observance of the *voluntary* Law of Nations in view of the circumstances in which Nations happen to find themselves, and for their common good. This double law, based upon fixed and permanent principles, is susceptible of demonstration, and it will form the principal subject of my work.

There is another species of the Law of Nations called by authors *arbitrary* because its origin is in the will or the consent of Nations. States, like individuals, can acquire rights and contract obligations by express promises, by compacts and by treaties, from which there results a *conventional* Law of Nations peculiar to the contracting parties. Moreover, Nations may bind themselves by their tacit consent; this is the foundation of all those practices which have been introduced among Nations, and which form the *custom* of Nations or the Law of Nations founded upon custom. It is clear that this law can bind only those Nations which by long usage have adopted its principles. It is a special law, as *conventional* law is. Both draw their entire binding force from the natural law, which demands that Nations keep their compacts, whether express or tacit. The natural law should likewise regulate the conduct of States with respect to the treaties they conclude and the customs they adopt. On this subject I must limit myself to stating the general principles and the rules which the natural law furnishes for the conduct of sovereigns. Details of the different treaties and customs of Nations belong rather to history than to a systematic treatise on the Law of Nations.

Such a treatise, as we have remarked before, should consist principally in applying with judgment and discretion the principles of the natural law to the conduct and the affairs of Nations and of sovereigns. The study of the Law of Nations supposes, therefore, a previous knowledge of the Law of Nature; and in fact I shall presume, to a certain extent at least, such knowledge on the part of my readers. However, as recourse to other authorities in proof of a writer's statements is troublesome, I have been careful to state briefly the more important of those principles of the natural law which apply to Nations. But I was not of the opinion that the demonstration of those principles need always be carried back to their primary sources, and I have at times been content to rest them upon certain common truths accepted by every fair-minded reader, without carrying the analysis any further. My object is to persuade, and with that in view to advance as a principle no statement that will not readily be admitted by every reasonable man.

The Law of Nations is the law of sovereigns. It is for them especially and for their ministers that a treatise should be written. All men have a real interest in it, and every citizen of a free country would do well to study its principles. But the mere instruction of individuals, who have no share in the councils of Nations and in the determination of their policy, would be of little advantage. If the leaders of Nations, if all those who have charge of public affairs were to make a serious study of a science which ought to be their law and their guiding compass, what benefit could not be expected from a good treatise on the Law of Nations? The benefits in civil society from a good code of laws are daily felt; but the Law of Nations is as much superior to the civil law in point of importance as the acts of Nations and of sovereigns are more far-reaching in their consequences than those of individual persons.

But we know too well from sad experience how little regard those who are at the head of affairs pay to rights when they conflict with some plan by which they hope to profit. They adopt a line of policy which is often false, because often unjust; and the majority of them think that they have done enough in having mastered that. Nevertheless it can be said of States what has long been recognized as true of individuals, that the wisest and the safest policy is one that is founded upon justice. Cicero, who was no less a statesman than an orator and a philosopher, is not satisfied with rejecting the popular idea that 'a Republic cannot be successfully governed without committing certain unjust acts', but he goes so far as to assert the contrary principle as a permanent truth, maintaining that 'no one who has not the strictest regard for justice can administer public affairs to advantage'.[1]

From time to time Providence gives to the world kings and ministers who realize that great truth. Let us hope that the number of these wise rulers will increase some day; in the meantime let us endeavour, each in his own sphere, to hasten the advent of that happy time.

I have at times illustrated principles by examples, principally in the hope of making my work more acceptable to those who have most need to read and profit by it. In this design I have the approval of one of those ministers who, as enlightened friends of the human race, should alone be admitted to the councils of kings. But I have used such examples sparingly. Never seeking to make a vain show of learning, my sole object has been to afford a little relaxation to the reader at times, or to make the doctrine more evident by an example. I have sometimes shown how the practice of Nations has conformed to principle, and whenever the opportunity offered my first endeavour has been to inspire to a love of virtue by showing how beautiful and laudable it is as practised by some truly great men, and even its material advantages, as shown in some striking instance from history. The greater part of my examples have been taken from modern history, as being more interesting in themselves, and at the same time different

---

[1] 'Nihil est quod adhuc de republica putem dictum, et quo possim longius progredi, nisi sit confirmatum non modo falsum esse istud, sine injuria non posse, sed hoc verissimum, sine summa justitia rempublicam regi non posse.' Cicero, *Fragment*, from *De Republica*.

from those accumulated by Grotius, Pufendorf, and their commentators.

Finally, I have endeavoured, both in the examples I have cited and in my conclusions, to avoid giving offence to anyone, being very careful of the respect which is due to Nations and to sovereign powers. But I have made it a still more sacred rule to have regard for the truth and for the interests of the human race. If my principles are attacked by base flatterers of despotism, I shall have on my side men of virtue and courage, true citizens who are friends of the law.

I should prefer to remain entirely silent were I not at liberty to be guided in my writings by the light of my conscience. But there is nothing to restrain my pen, and I could never betray it to flattery. I was born in a country where freedom is the living spirit, the ideal, and the fundamental law. By birth, therefore, I am the friend of all Nations. Under such happy circumstances I an encouraged to be of some service to my fellow men by this work. I am conscious of my deficiencies in both knowledge and ability; I realize that I am undertaking a difficult task; but I shall rest content if those readers whose opinion I value recognize my work as that of an honest man and a good citizen.

Introduction

IDEA AND GENERAL PRINCIPLES OF
THE LAW OF NATIONS

Nations or States are political bodies, societies of men who have united together and combined their forces, in order to procure their mutual welfare and security.

Such a society has its own affairs and interests; it deliberates and takes resolutions in common, and it thus becomes a moral person having an understanding and a will peculiar to itself, and susceptible at once of obligations and of rights.

The object of this work is to establish on a firm basis the obligations and the rights of Nations. The *Law of Nations* is *the science of the rights which exist between Nations or States, and of the obligations corresponding to these rights.*

It will be seen from this treatise how States, as such, ought to regulate their actions. We shall examine the obligations of a Nation towards itself as well as towards other Nations, and in this way we shall determine the rights resulting from those obligations; for since a right is nothing else but the power of doing what is morally possible, that is to say, what is good in itself and conformable to duty, it is clear that right is derived from duty, or passive obligation, from the obligation of acting in this or that manner. A Nation must therefore understand the nature of its obligations, not only to avoid acting contrary to its duty, but also to obtain therefrom a clear knowledge of its rights, or what it can lawfully exact from other Nations.

Since Nations are composed of men who are by nature free and independent, and who before the establishment of civil society lived together in the state of nature, such Nations or sovereign States must be regarded as so many free persons living together in the state of nature.

Proof can be had from works on the *natural law* that liberty and independence belong to man by his very nature, and that they cannot be taken from him without his consent. Citizens of a State, having yielded them in part to the sovereign, do not enjoy them to their full and absolute extent. But the whole body of the Nation, the State, so long as it has not voluntarily submitted to other men or other Nations, remains absolutely free and independent.

As men are subject to the laws of nature, and as their union in civil society can not exempt them from the obligation of observing those laws, since in that union they remain none the less men, the whole Nation, whose common will is but the outcome of the united wills of the citizens, remains subject to the laws of nature and is bound to respect them in all its undertakings. And since *right* is derived from *obligation*, as we have just remarked a Nation has the same rights that nature gives to men for the fulfilment of their duties.

We must therefore apply to Nations the rules of the natural law to discover what are their obligations and their rights; hence the *Law of Nations* is in its origin merely the *Law of Nature applied to Nations.* Now the just and reasonable application of a rule requires that the application be made in a manner suited to the nature of the subject; but we must not conclude that the Law of Nations is everywhere and at all points the same as the natural law, except for a difference of subjects, so that no other change need be made than to substitute Nations for individuals. A civil society, or a State, is a very different subject from an individual person and therefore, by virtue of the natural law, very different obligations and rights belong to it in most cases. The same general rule, when applied to two different subjects, cannot result in similar principles, nor can a particular rule, however just for one subject, be applicable to a second of a totally different nature. Hence there are many cases in which the natural law does not regulate the relations of States as it would those of individuals. We must know how to apply it conformably to its subjects; and the art of so applying it, with a precision founded upon right reason, constitutes of the Law of Nations a distinct science.

We use the term *necessary Law of Nations* for that law which results from applying the natural law to Nations. It is *necessary,* because Nations are absolutely bound to observe it. It contains those precepts which the natural law dictates to States, and it is no less binding upon them than it is upon individuals. For States are composed of men, their policies are determined by men, and these men are subject to the natural law under whatever capacity they act. This same law is called by Grotius and his followers the *internal Law of Nations*, inasmuch as it is binding upon the conscience of Nations. Several writers call it the *natural Law of Nations*.

Since, therefore, the necessary Law of Nations consists in applying the natural law to States, and since the natural law is not subject to change, being founded on the nature of things and particularly upon the nature of man, it follows that the necessary Law of Nations is not subject to change.

Since this law is not subject to change and the obligations which it imposes are necessary and indispensable, Nations cannot alter it by agreement, nor individually or mutually release themselves from it.

It is by the application of this principle that a distinction can be made between lawful and unlawful treaties or conventions and between customs which are innocent and reasonable and those which are unjust and deserving of condemnation.

Things which are just in themselves and permitted by the necessary Law of Nations may form the subject of an agreement by Nations or may be given sacredness and force through practice and custom. Indifferent affairs may be settled either by treaty, if Nations so please, or by the introduction of some suitable custom or usage. But all treaties and customs contrary to the dictates of the necessary Law of Nations are unlawful. We shall see, however, that they are not always conformable to the *inner* law of conscience, and yet, for reasons to be given in their proper place, such conventions and treaties are often valid by the *external* law. Owing to the freedom and independence of Nations, the conduct of one Nation may be unlawful and censurable according to the laws of conscience, and yet other Nations must put up with it so long as it does not infringe upon their perfect rights. The liberty of a Nation would not remain complete if other Nations presumed to inspect and control its conduct; a presumption which would be contrary to the natural law, which declares every Nation free and independent of all other Nations.

Such is man's nature that he is not sufficient unto himself and necessarily stands in need of the assistance and intercourse of his fellows, whether to preserve his life or to perfect himself and live as befits a rational animal. Experience shows this clearly enough. We know of men brought up among bears, having neither the use of speech nor of reason, and limited like beasts to the use of the sensitive faculties. We observe, moreover, that nature has denied man the strength and the natural weapons with which it has provided other animals, and has given him instead the use of speech and of reason, or at least the ability to acquire them by intercourse with other men. Language is a means of communication, of mutual assistance, and of perfecting man's reason and knowledge; and, having thus become intelligent, he finds a thousand means of caring for his life and its wants. Moreover, every man realizes that he could not live happily or improve his condition without the help of intercourse with other men. Therefore, since nature has constituted men thus, it is a clear proof that it means them to live together and mutually to aid and assist one another.

From this source we deduce a natural society existing among all men. The general law of this society is that each member should assist the others in all their needs, as far as he can do so without neglecting his duties to himself – a law which all men must obey if they are to live conformably to their nature and to the designs of their common Creator; a law which our own welfare, our happiness, and our best interests should render sacred to each one of us. Such is the general obligations we are under of performing our duties; let us fulfill them with care if we would work wisely for our greatest good.

It is easy to see how happy the world would be if all men were willing to follow the rule we have just laid down. On the other hand, if each man thinks of himself first and foremost, if he does nothing for others, all will be alike miserable. Let us labour for the good of all men; they in turn will labour for ours, and we shall build our happiness upon the firmest foundations.

Since the universal society of the human race is an institution of nature itself, that is, a necessary result of man's nature, all men of whatever condition are bound to advance its interests and to fulfil its duties. No convention or special agreement can release them from the obligation. When, therefore, men unite in civil society and form a separate State or Nation they may, indeed, make particular agreements with others of the same State, but their duties towards the rest of the human race remain unchanged; but with this difference, that when men have agreed to act in common, and have given up their rights and submitted their will to the whole body as far as concerns their common good, it devolves thenceforth upon that body, the State, and upon its rulers, to fulfill the duties of humanity towards outsiders in all matters in which individuals are no longer at liberty to act, and it peculiarly rests with the State to fulfill these duties towards other States. We have already seen that men, when united in society, remain subject to the obligations of the Law of Nature. This society may be regarded as a moral person, since it has an understanding, a will, and a power peculiar to itself; and it is therefore obliged to live with other societies or States according to the laws of the natural society of the human race, just as individual men before the establishment of civil society lived according to them; with such exceptions, however, as are due to the difference of the subjects.

The end of the natural society established among men in general is that they should mutually assist one another to advance their own perfection and that of their condition; and Nations, too, since they may be regarded as so many free persons living together in a state of nature, are bound mutually to advance this human society. Hence the end of the great society established by nature among all nations is likewise that of mutual assistance in order to perfect themselves and their condition.

The first general law, which is to be found in the very end of the society of Nations, is that each Nation should contribute as far as it can to the happiness and advancement of other Nations.

But as its duties towards itself clearly prevail over its duties towards others, a Nation owes to itself, as a prime consideration, whatever it can do for its own happiness and advancement. (I say whatever it *can* do, not meaning *physically* only, but *morally* also, what it can do lawfully, justly, and honestly.) When, therefore, a Nation cannot contribute to the welfare of another without doing an essential wrong to itself, its obligation ceases in this particular instance, and the Nation is regarded as lying under a disability to perform the duty.

Since Nations are free and independent of one another as men are by nature, the second general law of their society is that each Nation should be left to the peaceable enjoyment of that liberty which belongs to it by nature. The natural society of nations cannot continue unless the rights which belong to each by nature are respected. No Nation is willing to give up its liberty; it will rather choose to break off all intercourse with those who attempt to encroach upon it.

In consequence of that liberty and independence it follows that it is for each Nation to decide what its conscience demands of it, what it can or cannot do; what it thinks well or does not think well to do; and therefore it is for each Nation to consider and determine what duties it can fulfill towards others without failing in its duty towards itself. Hence in all cases in which it belongs to a Nation to judge of the extent of its duty, no other Nation may force it to act one way or another. Any attempt to do so would be an encroachment upon the liberty of Nations. We may not use force against a free person, except in cases where this person is under obligation to us in a definite matter and for a definite reason not depending upon his judgment; briefly, in cases in which we have a perfect right against him.

To understand this properly we must note that obligations and the corresponding rights produced by them are distinguished into *internal* and *external*. Obligations are internal in so far as they bind the conscience and are deduced from the rules of our duty; they are external when considered relatively to other men as producing some right on their part. Internal obligations are always the same in nature, though they may vary in degree; external obligations, however, are divided into *perfect* and *imperfect*, and the rights they give rise to are likewise *perfect* and *imperfect*. *Perfect* rights are those which carry with them the right of compelling the fulfilment of the corresponding obligations; *imperfect* rights cannot so compel. *Perfect obligations* are those which give rise to the right of enforcing them; *imperfect obligations* give but the right to request.

It will now be easily understood why a right is always imperfect when the corresponding obligation depends upon the judgment of him who owes it; for if he could be constrained in such a case he would cease to have the right of deciding what are his obligations according to the law of conscience. Our obligations to others are always imperfect when the decision as to how we are to act rests with us, as it does in all matters where we ought to be free.

Since men are by nature equal, and their individual rights and obligations the same, as coming equally from nature, Nations, which are composed of men and may be regarded as so many free persons living together in a state of nature, are by nature equal and hold from nature the same obligations and the same rights. Strength or weakness, in this case, counts for nothing. A dwarf is as much a man as a giant is; a small Republic is no less a sovereign State than the most powerful Kingdom.

From this equality it necessarily follows that what is lawful or unlawful for one Nation is equally lawful or unlawful for every other Nation.

A Nation is therefore free to act as it pleases, so far as its acts do not affect the perfect rights of another Nation, and so far as the Nation is under merely *internal* obligations without any *perfect external* obligation. If it abuses its liberty it acts wrongfully; but other Nations cannot complain, since they have no right to dictate to it.

Since Nations are free, independent, and equal, and since each has the right to decide in its conscience what it must do to fulfill its duties the effect of this is to produce, before the world at least, a perfect equality of rights among Nations in their conduct of their affairs and in the pursuit of their policies. The intrinsic justice of their conduct is another matter which it is not for others to pass upon finally; so that what one may do another may do, and they must be regarded in the society of mankind as having equal rights.

When differences arise each Nation in fact claims to have justice on its side, and neither of the interested parties nor other Nations may decide the question. The one who is actually in the wrong sins against its conscience; but as it may possibly be in the right, it cannot be accused of violating the laws of the society of Nations.

It must happen, then, on many occasions that Nations put up with certain things although in themselves unjust and worthy of condemnation, because they cannot oppose them by force without transgressing the liberty of individual Nations and thus destroying the foundations of their natural society. And since they are bound to advance that society, we rightly presume that they have agreed to the principle just established. The rules resulting from it form what Wolf [sic] calls the *voluntary Law of Nations*; and there is no reason why we should not use the same expression although we have thought it our duty to differ from that learned man as to how the foundation of that law should be established.

The laws of the natural society of Nations are so important to the welfare of every State that if the habit should prevail of treading them under foot no Nation could hope to protect its existence or its domestic peace, whatever wise and just and temperate measures it might take. Now all men and all States have a perfect right to whatever is essential to their existence, since this right corresponds to an indispensable obligation. Hence all Nations may put down by force the open violation of the laws of the society which nature has established among them, or any direct attacks upon its welfare.

But care must be taken not to extend these rights so as to prejudice the liberty of Nations. They are all free and independent, though they are so far bound to observe the laws of nature that if one violates them the others may restrain it; hence the Nations as a body have no rights over the conduct of a single Nation, further than the natural society finds itself concerned therein. The general and common rights of Nations over the conduct of a sovereign State should be in keeping with the end of the society which exists among them.

The various agreements which Nations may enter into give rise to a new division of the Law of Nations which is called *conventional*, or the law *of treaties*. As it is clear that a treaty binds only the contracting parties *the conventional Law of Nations* is not universal, but restricted in character. All that can be said upon this subject in a treatise on the Law of Nations must be limited to a statement of the general rules which Nations must observe with respect to their treaties. The details of the various agreements between certain Nations, and of the resulting rights and obligations, are questions of fact, to be treated of in historical works.

Certain rules and customs, consecrated by long usage and observed by Nations as a sort of law, constitute the *customary*

Law of Nations, or *international custom.* This law is founded upon a tacit consent, or rather upon a tacit agreement of the Nations which observe it. Hence it evidently binds only those Nations which have adopted it and is no more universal than the *conventional law.* Hence we must also say of this *customary law* that its details do not come within a systematic treatise on the Law of Nations, and we must limit ourselves to stating the general theory of it, that is to say, the rules to be observed in it, both as regards its effects and its substance. On this latter point these rules will serve to distinguish lawful and innocent customs from unlawful and unjust ones.

When a custom or usage has become generally established either between all the civilized countries of the world or only between those of a given continent, Europe for example, or those which have more frequent intercourse with one another, if this custom be indifferent in nature, much more so if it be useful and reasonable, it becomes binding upon all those Nations which are regarded as having given their consent to it. They are bound to observe it towards one another so long as they have not expressly declared their unwillingness to follow it any longer. But if there be anything unjust or unlawful in such a custom it is of no force, and indeed every Nation is bound to abandon it, since there can be neither obligation nor authorization to violate the Law of Nature.

These three divisions of the Law of Nations, the *voluntary,* the *conventional,* and the *customary* law, form together the *positive Law of Nations,* for they all proceed from the agreement of Nations; the *voluntary* law from their presumed consent; the *conventional* law from their express consent; and the *customary* law from their tacit consent. And since there are no other modes of deducing a law from the agreement of Nations, there are but these three divisions of the positive Law of Nations.

We shall be careful to distinguish them from the *natural* or *necessary* Law of Nations, without, however, treating them separately. But after having established on each point what the necessary law prescribes, we shall then explain how and why these precepts must be modified by the *voluntary* law; or, to put it in another way, we shall show how, by reason of the liberty of nations and the rules of their natural society, the *external* law which they must observe towards one another differs on certain points from the principles of the *internal* law, which, however, are always binding upon the conscience. As for rights introduced by treaties or by custom, we need not fear that anyone will confuse them with the natural Law of Nations. They form that division of the Law of Nations which writers term the *arbitrary* law.

In order from the start to lay down broad lines for the distinction between the *necessary law* and the *voluntary law* we must note that since the *necessary law* is at all times obligatory upon the conscience, a Nation must never lose sight of it when deliberating upon the course it must pursue to fulfill its duty; but when there is question of what it can demand from other States, it must consult the *voluntary law*, whose rules are devoted to the welfare and advancement of the universal society.

Book III

CHAPTER III

THE JUST CAUSES OF WAR

We are here presented with a celebrated question which is of the greatest importance. It is asked whether the aggrandizement of a neighbouring State, in consequence of which a Nation fears that it will one day be oppressed, is a sufficient ground for making war upon it; whether a Nation can with justice take up arms to resist the growing power of that State, or to weaken the State, with the sole object of protecting itself from the dangers with which weak States are almost always threatened from an overpowerful one. The question presents no difficulties to the majority of statesmen; it is more perplexing for those who seek at all times to unite justice with prudence.

On the one hand, a State which increases its power by all the efforts of a good government does nothing but what is praiseworthy; it fulfills its duties towards itself and does not violate those which it owes to other Nations. The sovereign who by inheritance, by a free election, or by any other just and proper means, unites new provinces or entire kingdoms to his States, is merely acting on his right, and wrongs no one. How would it be right to attack a State which increases its power by lawful means? A Nation must have received an injury, or be clearly threatened with one before it is authorized to take up arms as having a just ground for war. On the other hand, we know only too well from sad and frequent experience that predominant States rarely fail to trouble their neighbours, to oppress them, and even to subjugate them completely, when they have an opportunity of doing so with impunity. Europe was on the point of being enslaved for lack of timely opposition to the growing power of Charles V. Must we await the danger? Must we let the storm gather strength when it might be scattered at its rising? Must we suffer a neighbouring State to grow in power and await quietly until it is ready to enslave us? Will it be time to defend ourselves when we are no longer able to? Prudence is a duty incumbent upon all men, and particularly upon the rulers of Nations, who are appointed to watch over the welfare of an entire people. Let us try to solve this important question conformably to the sacred principles of the Law of Nature and of Nations. It will be seen that they do not lead to weak scruples, and that it is always true to say that justice is inseparable from sound statesmanship.

First of all, let us observe that prudence, which is certainly a virtue very necessary in sovereigns, can never counsel the use of unlawful means in order to obtain a just and praiseworthy end. Do not object here that the welfare of the people is the supreme law of the State; for the welfare of the people, the common welfare of Nations, forbids the use of means that are contrary to justice and honour. Why are certain means unlawful? If we look at the matter closely, if we go back to first principles, we shall see that it is precisely because the introduction of such means would be hurtful to human society, a source of evil to all Nations. Note in particular what we said in treating of the observance of justice (Book II, chap. V). It is, therefore, to the interest and even to the welfare of all Nations that we must hold as a sacred principle that the end does not justify the means. And since war is only permissible in order to redress an injury received, or to protect ourselves from an injury with which we are threatened, it is a sacred rule of the Law of Nations that the aggrandizement of a State cannot alone and of itself give any one the right to take up arms to resist it.

Supposing, then, that no injury has been received from that State, we must have reason to think ourselves threatened with one before we may lawfully take up arms. Now, power alone does not constitute a threat of injury; the will to injure must accompany the power. It is unfortunate for the human race that the will to oppress can almost be believed to exist where there is found the power to do so with impunity. But the two are not necessarily inseparable; and the only right which results from the fact that they ordinarily or frequently go together is that first appearances may be taken as a sufficient proof. As soon as a State has given evidence of injustice, greed, pride, ambition, or a desire of domineering over its neighbours, it becomes an object of suspicion which they must guard against. They may hold it up at the moment it is about to receive a formidable addition to its power, and demand securities of it; and if it hesitates to give these, they may prevent its designs by force of arms. The interests of Nations have an importance quite different from the interests of individuals; the sovereign cannot be indolent in his guardianship over them; he cannot put aside his suspicions out of magnanimity and generosity. A Nation's whole existence is at stake when it has a neighbour that is at once powerful and ambitious. Since it is the lot of men to be guided in most cases by probabilities, these probabilities deserve their attention in proportion to the importance of the subject-matter; and if I may borrow a geometrical expression, one is justified in forestalling a danger in direct ratio to the degree of probability attending it, and to the seriousness of the evil with which one is threatened. If the evil in question be endurable, if the loss be of small account, prompt action need not be taken; there is no great danger in delaying measures of self-protection until we are certain that there is actual danger of the evil. But suppose the safety of the State is endangered; our foresight cannot extend too far. Are we to delay averting our destruction until it has become inevitable? If we trust too readily to appearances, it is the fault of our neighbour who has given evidence of his ambition in various ways. Had Charles II, King of Spain, instead of settling the succession upon the Duke of Anjou, appointed Louis XIV himself as heir, had he thus tamely suffered the union of the House of Spain to that of France, it would have meant, according to all the rules of human foresight, nothing less than delivering all Europe into servitude, or at least putting it in a most precarious condition. But if two independent Nations think fit to unite so as to form thenceforth but one Empire, have they not the right to do so? Who would be justified in opposing them? I answer, they have the right to unite, provided that in so doing they have no designs prejudicial to other Nations. Now, if each of these two Nations was able to govern and support itself unaided, and to protect itself from insult and oppression, it is reasonably presumed that their only object in uniting to form one State was to dominate over their neighbours; and on occasions where it is impossible or too dangerous to wait until we are fully certain, we can justly act upon a reasonable presumption. If an unknown man takes aim at me in the middle of a forest I am not yet certain that he wishes to kill me; must I allow him time to fire in order to be sure of his intent? Is there any reasonable casuist who would deny me the right to forestall the act? But presumption becomes almost equal to certitude if the Prince who is about to acquire enormous power has already given evidence of an unbridled pride and ambition. In the imaginary case mentioned above, who would have dared counsel the European States to allow Louis XIV to make such a formidable addition to his power? Too well convinced of the use he would have made of it, they would have united together in opposition to it, and the right of self-protection would have justified their action. To say that they should have allowed him time to strengthen his hold upon Spain and consolidate the union of the two monarchies, and that, from fear of doing him injustice, they should have quietly awaited until he had overwhelmed them – would not this be denying men the right to be guided according to the rules of prudence and to act on probabilities, and would it not be depriving them of the power of providing for their safety until they should have mathematical proof that it was in danger? It would be idle to preach such doctrines. The principal sovereigns of Europe, habituated, by the ministry of Louvois, to dread the power and the designs of Louis XIV, carried their mistrust so far that they were unwilling to permit a prince of the House of France to sit upon the throne of Spain, although he was called to it by the Nation, which approved of the will of its late King. He ascended the throne in spite of the efforts of those who feared so greatly his elevation; and events have proved that their policy was too suspicious.

It is still easier to prove that if this formidable sovereign should betray unjust and ambitious dispositions by doing the smallest wrong to another State, all Nations may profit by the opportunity, and together join forces with the injured State in order to put down the ambitious Prince and disable him from so easily oppressing his neighbours, or from giving them constant cause for fear. For a State which has received an injury has the right to provide for its future security by depriving the offender of the means of doing harm; and it is permissible, and even praise-worthy, to assist those who are oppressed or unjustly attacked. All this is sufficient to put statesmen at their ease, and to relieve them of any fear that in standing for strict justice in this matter they would be following the path to slavery. There is perhaps no case in which a State has received a notable increase of power without giving other States just grounds of complaint. Let all Nations be on their guard to check such a State, and they will have nothing to fear from it. The Emperor Charles V made of religion a pretext for oppressing the Princes of the Empire and subjecting them to his absolute authority. If he had taken advantage of his victory over the Elector of Saxony and brought that great plan to completion, the liberties of all Europe would have been in danger. Hence it was with good reason that France assisted the Protestants of Germany; justice permitted her to do so, and the care for her own safety required it. When the same Prince took possession of the Duchy of Milan, the sovereigns of Europe should have aided France in disputing his right to it, and should have taken advantage of the opportunity to reduce his power to proper limits. If they had made use of the just grounds which he soon gave them to unite against him, they would not afterwards have had to fear for their liberties.

But suppose that this powerful State is both just and prudent in its conduct and gives no ground of complaint; are we to regard its progress with an indifferent eye? Are we idly to look upon its rapid increase of power and imprudently lay ourselves open to the designs which its power may inspire in it? Certainly not. Careless indifference would be unpardonable in a matter of such great importance. The example of the Romans is a good lesson for all sovereigns. If the most powerful States of that day had united together to watch over the movements of Rome, to set limits to her progress, they would not have successively become subject to her. But force of arms is not the only means of guarding against a formidable State. There are gentler means, which are always lawful. The most efficacious of these is an alliance of other less powerful sovereigns, who, by uniting their forces, are enabled to counterbalance the sovereign who excites their alarm. Let them be faithful and steadfast in their alliance, and their union will insure the safety of each.

They also have the right mutually to favour one another, to the exclusion of the sovereign whom they fear; and by the privileges of every sort, and especially by the commercial privileges which they will mutually grant to one another's subjects, and which they will refuse to the subjects of that dangerous sovereign, they will add to their strength, and at the same time lessen his, without giving him reason for complaint, since every one may dispose freely of his favours.

Europe forms a political system in which the Nations inhabiting this part of the world are bound together by their relations and various interests into a single body. It is no longer, as in former times, a confused heap of detached parts, each of which had but little concern for the lot of the others, and rarely troubled itself over what did not immediately affect it. The constant attention of sovereigns to all that goes on, the custom of resident ministers, the continual negotiations that take place, make of modern Europe a sort of Republic, whose members – each independent, but all bound together by a common interest – unite for the maintenance of order and the preservation of liberty. This is what has given rise to the well-known principle of the balance of power, by which is meant an arrangement of affairs so that no State shall be in a position to have absolute mastery and dominate over the others.

The surest means of preserving this balance of power would be to bring it about that no State should be much superior to the others, that all the States, or at least the larger part, should be about equal in strength. This idea has been attributed to Henry IV, but it is one that could not be realized without injustice and violence. And moreover, once this equality were established, how could it be regularly maintained by lawful means? Commerce, industry, the military virtues, would soon put an end to it. The right of inheritance, even in favour of women and their descendants, which has been so absurdly established for succession to the throne, but which after all has been established, would overturn your arrangement.

It is simpler, easier, and more just to have recourse to the method just referred to, of forming alliances in order to make a stand against a very powerful sovereign and prevent him from dominating. This is the plan followed by the sovereigns of Europe at the present day. They look upon the two principal powers, who for that very reason are naturally rivals, as destined to act as a mutual check upon each other, and they unite with the weaker of the two, thereby acting as so much weight thrown into the lighter scale in order to make the balance even. The House of Austria has for a long time been the predominant power; now it is the turn of France. England, whose wealth and powerful navy have given her a very great influence, without, however, causing any State to fear for its liberty, since that power appears to be cured of the spirit of conquest – England, I say, has the honour to hold in her hands the political scales. She is careful to maintain them in equilibrium. It is a policy of great wisdom and justice, and one which will be always commendable, so long as she only makes use of alliances, confederations, and other equally lawful means.

Confederations would be a sure means of preserving the balance of power and thus maintaining the liberty of Nations, if all sovereigns were constantly aware of their true interests, and if they regulated their policy according to the welfare of the State. But powerful sovereigns succeed only too often in winning for themselves partisans and allies who are blindly devoted to their designs. Dazzled by the glitter of a present advantage, seduced by their greed, deceived by unfaithful ministers, how many princes become the instruments of a power which will one day swallow up either themselves or their successors. The safest plan, therefore, is either to weaken one who upsets the balance of power, as soon as a favourable opportunity can be found when we can do so with justice, or, by the use of all upright means, to prevent him from attaining so formidable a degree of power. To this end all Nations should be on their guard above all not to allow him to increase his power by force of arms, and this they are always justified in doing. For if that prince wages an unjust war every Nation has the right to assist the oppressed State; and if he wages a just war, neutral Nations may interpose to bring about a settlement; they may persuade the weak State to offer just satisfaction upon reasonable terms, and may thus prevent it from being subjugated. When one who wages a just war is offered equitable terms, he has all that he can demand. As we shall see later, the justice of his cause never gives him the right to subjugate his enemy, except when this extreme measure becomes necessary to his safety, or when he has no other means of redressing an injury which he has received. Now, that is not the case here, for the Nations that intervene enable him both to insure his safety and to obtain just redress in another manner.

Finally, there is no question but that if that formidable Prince is clearly entertaining designs of oppression and conquest, if he betrays his plans by preparations or other advances, other Nations have the right to check him; and if the fortune of war be favourable to them, they may profit by the favourable opportunity to weaken and reduce his strength, which upsets the balance of power and constitutes a menace to the common liberty of all.

This right on the part of Nations is still more evident as against a sovereign who is always ready to take to arms without cause and without plausible pretext, and who is thus a constant disturber of the public peace.

Book III

CHAPTER XII

THE VOLUNTARY LAW OF NATIONS WITH RESPECT TO THE EFFECTS OF THE REGULAR WAR, INDEPENDENTLY OF THE JUSTICE OF THE CAUSE

The doctrines laid down in the preceding chapter are a logical inference from sound principles, from the eternal rules of justice; they are the provisions of that sacred law which Nature, or the Divine Author of Nature, has imposed upon Nations.[1] He alone whose sword is drawn from necessity and in the cause of justice has the right to make war; he alone has the right to attack his enemy, to take away his life, and to deprive him of his property. Such is the decree of the *necessary Law of Nations*, or of the natural law, as it must be observed in all its strictness by Nations; it is the inviolable law binding upon each of them in conscience. But how shall this law be made to prevail in the quarrels of the Nations and sovereigns who live together in the state of nature? They recognize no superior who shall decide between them and define the rights and obligations of each, who shall say to this one: 'You have a right to take up arms, to attack your enemy and subdue him by force', and to that other: 'Your hostilities are unwarranted, your victories are but murder, your conquests are but the spoil of robbery and pillage'. It belongs to every free and sovereign State to decide in its own conscience what its duties require of it, and what it may or may not do with justice. If others undertake to judge of its conduct, they encroach upon its liberty and infringe upon its most valuable rights. Moreover, since each Nation claims to have justice on its side, it will arrogate

[1] [The previous chapter discusses the sovereign who wages an unjust war.]

to itself all the rights of war and claim that its enemy has none, that his hostilities are but deeds of robbery, acts in violation of the Law of Nations, and deserving of punishment by all Nations. The decision of the rights at issue will not be advanced thereby, and the contest will become more cruel, more disastrous in its effects, and more difficult of termination. Further still, neutral Nations themselves will be drawn into the dispute and implicated in the quarrel. If an unjust war can give rise to no legal rights, no certain possession can be obtained of any property captured in war until a recognized judge, and there is none such between Nations, shall have passed definitely upon the justice of the war; and such property will always be subject to a claim for recovery, as in the case of goods stolen by robbers.

Let us, therefore, leave to the conscience of sovereigns the observance of the natural and necessary law in all its strictness; and indeed it is never lawful for them to depart from it. But as regards the external operation of that law in human society, we must necessarily have recourse to certain rules of more certain and easy application, and this in the interest of the safety and welfare of the great society of the human race. These rules are those of the *voluntary* Law of Nations. The natural law which looks to the greatest good of human society, which protects the liberty of each Nation, and which desires that the affairs of sovereigns be settled and their quarrels come to a speedy issue – the natural law, I say, recommends for the common advantage of Nations the observance of the voluntary Law of Nations, just as it approves of the changes which the civil law makes in the natural law for the purpose of adapting the latter to the conditions of civil society and of making its application easier and more certain. Let us, therefore, apply to the special subject of war the general statements which we made in the Introduction. When a sovereign, or a Nation, is deliberating upon the steps he must take to fulfill his duty, he must never lose sight of the *necessary* law, which is always binding in conscience; but when it is a question of determining what he can demand of other States, he must consider the *voluntary* Law of Nations, and restrict even his just claims within the bounds of a law whose principles are consecrated to the safety and welfare of the universal society of Nations. Let him make the *necessary* law the constant rule of his own conduct; he must allow others to take advantage of the voluntary Law of Nations.

The first rule of that law, with respect to the subject under consideration, is that *regular war, as regards its effects, must be accounted just on both sides.* This principle, as we have just shown, is absolutely necessary if any law or order is to be introduced into a method of redress as violent as that of war, if any bounds are to be set to the disasters it occasions, as if a door is to be left at all times open for the return of peace. Moreover, any other rule would be impracticable as between Nation and Nation, since they recognize no common judge.

Thus the rights founded upon the state of war, the legal nature of its effects, the validity of the acquisitions made in it, do not depend, externally and in the sight of men, upon the justice of the cause, but upon the legality of the means as such, that is to say, upon the presence of the elements constituting a regular war. If the enemy observes all the rules of formal warfare, we are not to be heard in complaint of him as a violator of the Law of Nations; he has the same right as we to assert a just cause; and our entire hope lies in victory or in a friendly settlement.

Second rule: Since two enemies are regarded as having an equally just cause, *whatever is permitted to one because of the state of war is also permitted to the other.* In fact, no Nation, on the ground of having justice on its side, ever complains of the hostilities of its enemy, so long as they remain within the bounds prescribed by the common laws of war. In the preceding chapters we have treated of what may lawfully be done in a just war. It is precisely that, and no more, which the voluntary law equally authorizes both parties in doing. That law makes the same acts lawful on both sides, but it allows neither party any act unlawful in itself, and cannot approve of unbridled licence. Consequently, if Nations overstep those limits, if they carry hostilities beyond what is in general permitted by the internal and necessary law for the support of a just cause, let us be careful not to ascribe these excesses to the voluntary Law of Nations; they are to be attributed solely to a moral degeneracy which has given rise to iniquitous and barbarous customs. Such are those excesses to which soldiers sometimes abandon themselves when a town is taken by assault.

Thirdly, it must never be forgotten that *this voluntary Law of Nations*, established from necessity and for the avoidance of greater evils, *does not confer upon him whose cause is unjust any true rights capable of justifying his conduct and appeasing his conscience, but merely makes his conduct legal in the sight of men, and exempts him from punishment*. This is sufficiently clear from the principles on which the voluntary Law of Nations is based. Consequently, the sovereign who has no just cause in authorization of his hostilities is not less unjust, or less guilty of violating the sacred Law of Nature, merely because that same natural law, in the effort not to increase the evils of human society while seeking to prevent them, requires that he be conceded the same legal rights as more justly belong to his enemy. Thus the civil law allows a debtor to refuse payment in a case of prescription; but the debtor nevertheless violates his moral duty; he takes advantage of a law enacted to prevent a multiplicity of lawsuits, but he acts without any true right.

From the fact that Nations actually concur in observing the rules which we assign to the voluntary Law of Nations, Grotius bases them upon a real consent upon the part of Nations, and refers them to the arbitrary Law of Nations. But apart from the difficulty of proving the existence of such an agreement, it would only be enforceable against those who had formally entered into it. If such an agreement existed, it would come under the conventional Law of Nations, which is a matter of historical proof, not of reasoning, and is based, not upon principles, but upon facts. In this work we are laying down the natural principles of the Law of Nations; we deduce them from nature itself; and what we call the voluntary Law of Nations consists in the rules of conduct, of external law, to which the natural law obliges Nations to consent; so that we rightly presume their consent, without seeking any record of it; for even if they had not given their consent, the Law of Nature supplies it, and gives it for them. Nations are not free in this matter to consent or not; the Nation which would refuse to consent would violate the common rights of all Nations.

The voluntary Law of Nations, thus substantiated, is of very wide application; it is by no means a fantasy, an arbitrary invention destitute of foundation. It is derived from the same source and based upon the same principles as the *natural* or *necessary* law.

Why has nature appointed to men such and such rules of conduct, except because those rules are necessary to the welfare and happiness of the human race? Now, the principles of the necessary Law of Nations are founded directly upon the nature of things, and particularly upon the nature of man and of political society, while the voluntary Law of Nations supposes a further principle, namely, the nature of the great society of Nations and of the intercourse which they have with one another. The necessary law prescribes what is of absolute necessity for Nations and what tends naturally to their advancement and their common happiness; the voluntary law tolerates what it is impossible to forbid without causing greater evils.

JEAN-JACQUES ROUSSEAU

Jean-Jacques Rousseau (1712-78) devoted no single work to the study of international relations but his belief in the importance of the subject to any fully satisfactory account of politics is in evidence throughout his writings.

While working in Venice as the private secretary to the French Ambassador (1743), Rousseau contemplated a comprehensive treatment of politics, to be called the *Institutions Politiques*. This grandiose scheme was later abandoned as being, according to Rousseau himself, in excess of his energy and talents. *The Social Contract*, the most famous of his writings, is itself a fragment designed originally to form part of the larger work and salvaged from the wider enterprise. It is worth noting that the early chapters of *The Social Contract* deal in part with the nature of international relations and take the form of a discussion of war, but that Rousseau had much more to say on the subject is clear from the concluding lines of this book. Here one can gain a more detailed impression of what Rousseau had in mind when he talked about dealing with international relations in the second part of the *Institutions Politiques*.

'After setting out the true principles of political right, and trying to establish the state on the basis of those principles, I should complete my study by considering the foreign relations of the state, including the law of nations, commerce, the rights of war and conquest, international law, leagues, negotiations, treaties and so forth.' (*The Social Contract*. Translated by Maurice Cranston, p. 188. Penguin 1968.)

From Rousseau's writings on international relations presented here it is plain that the subject engaged the best that was in him; the controlled intensity of feeling is matched by keen analytical skill.

The immediate issue raised by the *Abstract of the Abbé de Saint-Pierre's Project for Perpetual Peace* is how much of its content is to be attributed to Rousseau. In 1754 Rousseau took possession of seventeen volumes and six boxes of manuscripts belonging to Saint-Pierre with the idea of preparing a summary or abstract of his works and by making this mass of unreadable material presentable and intelligible to a wider public, help to preserve his ideas. Rousseau had indeed met Saint-Pierre and knew him slightly. The Abbé died in 1743 at the age of eighty-three when Rousseau was thirty-one. In addition to the abstracts, Rousseau planned to add his own views and estimate of Saint-Pierre's ideas in the form of *Judgments*. This scheme as we know progressed no further than the *Project for Perpetual Peace* and the *Polysnodie*, at which stage Rousseau apparently tired of the business. There seems little doubt that whatever the differences between Saint-Pierre and Rousseau – and they could, between a believer in the perfectibility of man through reason and an arch-critic of rationalism, only be considerable – Jean-Jacques held the Abbé in the highest respect. At all events by taking on the work Rousseau found himself confronted with ideas on the most important of subjects at a time when his creative powers were at their stretch.

According to C. E. Vaughan, Rousseau treated Saint-Pierre's *Project for Perpetual Peace*, first published in 1712-13 with 'the freest hand'. 'Except as regards the kernel of the Project', he writes, 'there is much more of Rousseau than of Saint-Pierre in the whole.' (*The Political Writings of Jean-Jacques Rousseau*. C. E. Vaughan. Vol. 1, p. 360.) The *Abstract* was completed between 1756 and 1758, and first published in 1761, though because his publisher got cold feet, in Amsterdam and not in Paris. It was translated into English in the same year. The *Judgment*, however, was only published posthumously in 1782 and this may go some way to explain why his contemporaries immediately identified Rousseau's own views with those of Saint-Pierre. From Ferney Voltaire satirized the *Abstract of the Abbé Saint-Pierre's Project for Perpetual Peace* lumping Rousseau and Saint-Pierre together in his criticism of their 'esprit chimérique'.

The translation of the *Abstract* and *Judgment* is that by C. E. Vaughan.

The important fragment *The State of War* raises several questions. First the original manuscript is hard to decipher. Rousseau clearly reworked these passages several times and on this occasion his handwriting is difficult to read. Secondly there has been a dispute over the correct ordering of the manuscript – three quarto sheets folded in two – which affects the way in which Rousseau's argument is to be taken. And thirdly there is the question of when this fragment was written and where it fits into the body of Rousseau's work. On all these points the views of C. E. Vaughan have been accepted as providing the most convincing interpretation. Vaughan's views have been largely accepted in the Pléiade edition of Rousseau's complete works where the only substantial difference concerns the dating of the fragment. Vaughan places it somewhere between 1753 and 1755, whereas Sven Stelling-Michaud in the Pléiade suggests 1757 and 1758.

Vaughan argues that *The State of War*, a title Rousseau did not use but which is retained for convenience, is best considered as initially designed to form part of the *Institutions Politiques*. The year before

Rousseau abandoned this work he mentions another title, the *Principes de droit de la guerre*, and this has led some to believe in a separate work of which *The State of War* is a part. This further work is mentioned only once by Rousseau and came to nothing. Vaughan suggests that this too may have been a plan to save something from the *Institutions Politiques*. In this roundabout way one returns to the contention that the fragment, *The State of War* is to be taken as written in connection with Rousseau's large-scale work on politics.

The State of War was first published in 1896. The translation is by Murray Forsyth.

The *Fragments on War* provide further clues to Rousseau's concept of war. They are likely to be earlier or alternative versions to the early part of the *Social Contract* where Rousseau discusses the nature of war (Book I, Chapter IV). Taken with *The State of War*, these fragments, though slight, emphasize Rousseau's concentrated attempts to elaborate his fundamental ideas on international relations. The translation is by Maurice Keens-Soper.

The controlled passion of Rousseau's interest in international relations is apparent in the firmness and eloquence of his style. In his writings on international relations there is clarity and incisiveness of a very high order. Rousseau was, however, pessimistic about the subject. Men might reform themselves, as well as states their constitutions, but strife between states derives principally from the setting of their mutual relations.

Men are organized within states only to find that they have inescapably created a permanent state of mutual antagonism between states. In a world of states each is condemned to insecurity, 'is forced to compare itself in order to know itself; it depends on its whole environment'. Rousseau's achievement is to have riveted attention on the arbitrariness and instability of international society and not just on the wilfulness of individual men and the imperfections of political regimes. His other achievement is to resist the easy conclusion that if the co-existence of states entails conflict then one must progress beyond the state to some form of supra-national management of international relations. Rousseau grasps the inherent complications of such an enterprise; how at any particular moment a scheme for lasting peace would codify the pre-existing balance of power and interest, and how because of diversity and inequality, the timing is always right for the satisfied but wrong for the discontented.

The price of perpetual peace would be war and revolution, in which case, Rousseau asks, are schemes of perpetual peace more to be desired or feared? In a condition of mutual isolation – Rousseau's original state of nature – states would necessarily live in peace because they would have no occasion for war. There is, however, no going back. Hence his pessimism; men are condemned to politics and given the nature of international society they are also exposed to war.

The *Abstract* and *Judgment* are from C. E. Vaughan, *A Lasting Peace Through the Federation of Europe*, 1917. The *State of War* and the *Fragments on War* are from Vol. 1, pp. 292-307 and pp. 308-314 of C. E. Vaughan, *The Political Writings of Jean-Jacques Rousseau*, 1915.

Suggested Reading

Stanley Hoffman, *The State of War*, 1965.
C. E. Vaughan, *The Political Writings of Jean-Jacques Rousseau*, Vol. 1, 1915.

Abstract of the Abbé de Saint-Pierre's Project for Perpetual Peace

Never did the mind of man conceive a scheme nobler, more beautiful, or more useful than that of a lasting peace between all the peoples of Europe. Never did a writer better deserve a respectful hearing than he who suggests means for putting that scheme into practice. What man, if he has a spark of goodness, but must feel his heart glow within him at so fair a prospect? Who would not prefer the illusions of a generous spirit, which overleaps all obstacles, to that dry, repulsive reason whose indifference to the welfare of mankind is ever the chief obstacle to all schemes for its attainment?

I doubt not that many readers will forearm themselves with scepticism, as the best defence against the pleasure of yielding to conviction. I pity the melancholy mood which makes them take obstinacy for wisdom. On the other hand, I trust that every generous spirit will share the thrill of emotion with which I take up the pen on a subject which concerns mankind so closely. I see in my mind's eye all men joined in the bonds of love. I call before my thoughts a gentle and peaceful brotherhood, all living in unbroken harmony, all guided by the same principles, all finding their happiness in the happinesss of all. And, as I dwell upon this touching picture, the idea of an imaginary happiness will cheat me for a few moments into the enjoyment of a real one.

In these opening words, I could not refrain from giving way to the feelings which filled my heart. Now let us do our best to reason coolly. Resolved as I am to assert nothing which I cannot prove, I have the right to ask the reader in his turn to deny nothing which he is unable to refute. It is not so much the reasoners I am afraid of as those who, without yielding to my proofs, steadily refuse to bring any arguments against them.

No man can have thought long upon the means of bringing any

Government to perfection without realizing a host of difficulties
and obstacles which flow less from its inherent nature than from
its relation to its neighbours. The result of this is that the care
which ought to be given to its internal welfare has to be largely
spent upon its outward security; and we are compelled to think
more of providing for its defence against others than of making
it as good as may be in itself. If the social order were really,
as is pretended, the work not of passion but of reason, should we
have been so slow to see that, in the shaping of it, either too much
or too little, has been done for our happiness? that, each one of us
being in the civil state as regards our fellow citizens, but in the
state of nature as regards the rest of the world, we have taken all
kinds of precautions against private wars only to kindle national
wars a thousand times more terrible? and that, in joining a particular group of men, we have really declared ourselves the enemies
of the whole race?

If there is any way of reconciling these dangerous contradictions,
it is to be found only in such a form of federal Government as
shall unite nations by bonds similar to those which already unite
their individual members, and place the one no less than the
other under the authority of the Law. Even apart from this, such
a form of Government seems to carry the day over all others,
because it combines the advantages of the small and the large
State, because it is powerful enough to hold its neighbours in
awe, because it upholds the supremacy of the Law, because it is the
only force capable of holding the subject, the ruler, the foreigner
equally in check.

Such a form of Government is to some extent a novelty, and its
principles have been fully understood only by the moderns. But
it was not unknown among the ancients. The Greeks had their
Amphictyons and the Etruscans their Lucumonies; the Latins
had their feriæ and the Gauls their city-leagues; the Achæan
League gave lustre to the death-struggles of Greece. But not one
of these Federations was built up with half the wisdom which has
gone to the making of the Germanic Body, of the Helvetic League,
or of the States General. And if these Bodies are still so scarce
and so far from the perfection which we feel they might attain,
that is because the realization of the good invariably falls short of
the ideal; because in politics as in morals, the more we enlarge

our knowledge, the more we are forced to recognize the extent of our misery.

In addition to these formal Confederations, it is possible to frame others, less visible but none the less real, which are silently cemented by community of interests, by conformity of habits and customs, by the acceptance of common principles, by other ties which establish mutual relations between nations politically divided. Thus the Powers of Europe constitute a kind of whole, united by identity of religion, of moral standard, of international law: by letters, by commerce, and finally by a species of balance which is the inevitable result of all these ties and, however little any man may strive consciously to maintain it, is not to be destroyed so easily as many men imagine.

This concert of Europe has not always existed, and the special causes which produced it are still working to preserve it. The truth is that, before the conquests of the Romans, the nations of this continent, all sunk in barbarism and each utterly unknown to the others, had nothing in common beyond the character which belonged to them as men: a character which, degraded by the practice of slavery, differed little enough in their eyes from that which constitutes the brute. Accordingly the Greeks, vain and disputatious, divided mankind, it may almost be said, into two distinct races: the one – their own, of course – made to rule; the other – the entire rest of the world – created solely to be slaves. From this principle it followed that a Gaul or a Spaniard was no more to a Greek than a Kaffir or Red Indian; and the barbarians themselves were as deeply divided from each other as the Greeks from all of them.

But when these men, born to rule, had been conquered by their slaves the Romans, when half of the known universe had passed beneath the same yoke, a common bond of laws and government was established, and all found themselves members of the same empire. This bond was still further tightened by the recognized principle, either supremely wise or supremely foolish, imparting to the conquered all the rights of the conqueror; above all, by the famous decree of Claudius, which placed all the subjects of Rome on the roll of her citizens.

Thus all members of the Empire were united in one body politic. They were further united by laws and civil institutions

133

which reinforced the political bond by defining equitably, clearly and precisely, so far as this was possible in so vast an empire, the mutual rights and duties of the ruler and the subject, of one citizen as against another. The Code of Theodosius and the later legislation of Justinian constituted a new bond of justice and reason, which came in to replace the sovereign power at the very moment when it showed unmistakable signs of slackening. This did more than anything else to stave off the break-up of the Empire and to maintain its authority even over the barbarians who ravaged it.

A third and yet stronger bond was furnished by religion: and it cannot be denied that Europe, even now, is indebted more to Christianity than to any other influence for the union, however imperfect, which survives among her members. So true is this that the one nation which has refused to accept Christianity has always remained an alien among the rest. Christianity, so despised in its infancy, ended by serving as a sanctuary to its slanderers. And the Roman Empire, which had persecuted it for centuries with fruitless cruelty, drew from it a power which she could no longer find in her own strength. The missionaries did more for her than any victory; she despatched Bishops to redeem the mistake of her generals and triumphed by the aid of the priests when her soldiers were defeated. It is thus that the Franks, the Goths, the Burgundians, the Lombards, the Avars and many others ended by recognizing the authority of the Empire which they had mastered, by admitting at least in appearance, not only the law of the Gospel, but also that of the Prince at whose command it had been preached to them.

Such was the respect which this august body inspired even in its death-throes that, to the very end, its conquerors felt themselves honoured by the acceptance of its titles. The very generals who had humbled the Empire became its ministers and officials; the proudest Kings welcomed, nay even canvassed for, the patriciate, the prefecture, the consulate; and, like the lion who fawns upon the man he could easily devour, these terrible conquerors did homage to the imperial throne which they might at any moment have cast down.

Thus the priesthood and the Empire wove a bond between various nations which, without any real community of interests, of rights, or of mutual dependence, found a tie in common principles and beliefs, the influence of which still survives even after its foundation is withdrawn. The venerable phantom of the Roman Empire has never ceased to unite the nations which once formed part of it; and as, after the fall of the Empire, Rome still asserted her authority under another form,[1] Europe, the home of the temporal and spiritual Powers, still retains a sense of fellowship far closer than is to be found elsewhere. The nations of the other continents are too scattered for mutual intercourse; and they lack any other point of union such as Europe has enjoyed.

There are other, and more special causes for this difference. Europe is more evenly populated, more uniformly fertile; it is easier to pass from one part of her to another. The interests of her Princes are united by ties of blood, by commerce, arts and colonies. Communication is made easy by countless rivers winding from one country to another. An inbred love of change impels her inhabitants to constant travel, which frequently leads them to foreign lands. The invention of printing and the general love of letters has given them a basis of common knowledge and common intellectual pursuits. Finally, the number and smallness of her States, the cravings of luxury and the large diversity of climates which Europe offers for their satisfaction, make them all necessary to each other. All these causes combine to make of Europe not, like Asia and Africa, a purely imaginary assemblage of peoples with nothing in common save the name, but a real community with a religion and a moral code, with customs and even laws of its own, which none of the component nations can renounce without causing a shock to the whole frame.

Now look at the other side of the picture. Observe the perpetual quarrels, the robberies, the usurpations, the revolts, the wars, the murders, which bring daily desolation to this venerable home of philosophy, this brilliant sanctuary of art and science. Consider our fair speeches and our abominable acts, the boundless humanity

[1] Respect for the Roman Empire has so completely survived her power that many jurists have questioned whether the Emperor of Germany is not the natural sovereign of the world; and Bartholus carried this doctrine so far as to treat anyone who dared to deny it as a heretic. The writings of the canonists are full of the corresponding doctrine of the temporal supremacy of the Roman Church. (Rousseau's note.)

of our maxims and the boundless cruelty of our deeds; our religion so merciful and our intolerance so ferocious; our policy so mild in our textbooks and so harsh in our acts; our rulers so beneficent and our people so wretched; our Governments so temperate and our wars so savage: and then tell me how to reconcile these glaring contradictions: tell me if this alleged brotherhood of the nations of Europe is anything more than a bitter irony to denote their mutual hatred.

But, in truth, what else was to be expected? Every community without laws and without rulers, every union formed and maintained by nothing better than chance, must inevitably fall into quarrels and dissensions at the first change that comes about. The historic union of the nations of Europe has entangled their rights and interests in a thousand complications: they touch each other at so many points that not one of them can move without giving a jar to all the rest; their variances are all the more deadly, as their ties are more closely woven; their frequent quarrels are almost as savage as civil wars.

Let us admit then that the Powers of Europe stand to each other strictly in a state of war, and that all the separate treaties between them are in the nature rather of a temporary truce than a real peace: whether because such treaties are seldom guaranteed by any except the contracting parties; or because the respective rights of those parties are never thoroughly determined and are therefore bound – they, or the claims which pass for rights in the eyes of Powers who recognize no earthly superior – to give rise to fresh wars as soon as a change of circumstances shall have given fresh strength to the claimants.

More than this: the public Law of Europe has never been passed or sanctioned by common agreement: it is not based upon any general principles; it varies incessantly from time to time and from place to place: it is therefore a mass of contradictory rules which nothing but the right of the stronger can reduce to order: so that, in the absence of any sure clue to guide her, reason is bound, in every case of doubt, to obey the promptings of self-interest which, in itself, would make war inevitable, even if all parties desired to be just. With the best intentions in the world, all that can be done is to appeal to arms, or put the question to rest for the moment by a treaty. But the old quarrel soon comes to life again, complicated by others which have arisen in the interval; all is confusion and bewilderment; the truth is obscured so hopelessly that usurpation passes for right and weakness for wrong. In this general welter, all bearings have been so utterly lost that, if we could get back to the solid ground of primitive right, few would be the Sovereigns in Europe who would not have to surrender all that they possess.

Another source of war, less obvious but not less real, is that things often change their spirit without any corresponding change of form; that States, hereditary in fact, remain elective in appearance; that we find Parliaments or States-General in Monarchies and hereditary rulers in Republics; that a Power, in fact dependent on another, often retains the semblance of autonomy; that all the provinces ruled by the same sovereign are not always governed by the same laws; that the laws of succession differ in different dominions of the same sovereign; finally, that the tendency of every Government to degenerate is a process which no human power can possibly arrest. Such are the causes, general and special, which unite us only to work our ruin. Such are the reasons which condemn us to write our high-sounding theories of fellowship with hands ever dyed afresh in blood.

The causes of the disease, once known, suffice to indicate the remedy, if indeed there is one to be found. Everyone can see that what unites any form of society is community of interests, and what disintegrates is their conflict; that either tendency may be changed or modified by a thousand accidents; and therefore that, as soon as a society is founded, some coercive power must be provided to co-ordinate the actions of its members and give to their common interests and mutual obligations that firmness and consistency which they could never acquire of themselves.

It would, indeed, be a great mistake to suppose that the reign of violence, described above, could ever be remedied by the mere force of circumstances, or without the aid of human wisdom. The present balance of Europe is just firm enough to remain in perpetual oscillation without losing itself altogether and, if our troubles cannot increase, still less can we put an end to them, seeing that any sweeping revolution is henceforth an impossibility.

In proof of this conclusion, let us begin by glancing at the present condition of Europe. The lie of the mountains, seas and rivers, which serve as frontiers for the various nations who people it, seems to have fixed for ever their number and their size. We may fairly say that the political order of the continent is, in some sense, the work of nature.

In truth, we must not suppose that this much vaunted balance is the work of any man, or that any man has deliberately done anything to maintain it. It is there; and men who do not feel themselves strong enough to break it conceal the selfishness of their designs under the pretext of preserving it. But, whether we are aware of it or no, the balance continues to support itself without the aid of any special intervention; if it were to break for a moment on one side, it would soon restore itself on another; so that, if the Princes who are accused of aiming at universal monarchy were in reality guilty of any such project, they gave more proof of ambition than of genius. How could any man look such a project in the face without instantly perceiving its absurdity, without realizing that there is not a single potentate in Europe so much stronger than the others as ever to have a chance of making himself their master? No conqueror has ever changed the face of the world unless, appearing suddenly with an army of unexpected strength, or with foreign troops hardened to war in other service, he fell upon nations who were undisciplined. But where is a European Prince to find an army of unexpected strength sufficient to crush all the others, when the most powerful of them has only a fraction of the strength belonging to the whole body and all the rest are watching so carefully to prevent him? Will he have a larger army than all of them put together? It is impossible; or he will only ruin himself the sooner; or his troops will be less good, just because they are more numerous. Will his troops be better trained? They will be proportionally fewer; not to mention that discipline is now everywhere the same, or will have become so before long. Will he have more money? Its sources are open to all, and no great conquest was ever made by money. Will he fall upon his enemies suddenly? Famine, or fortresses, will bar his way at every step. Will he strive to win his way inch by inch? Then he will give his enemies time to unite their forces to resist him; time, money and men will all be bound to fail him. Will he try to divide the other Powers and conquer them one by one? The traditional maxims of Europe make such a policy impossible; the most stupid of Princes would never fall into such a trap as that. In a word, as all the sources of power are equally open to them all, the resistance is in the long run as strong as the attack; and time soon repairs the sudden accidents of fortune, if not for each Prince individually, at least for the general balance of the whole.

Now let us take the supposition that two or three potentates league themselves together to conquer all the rest. Those three potentates, take them where you please, will not together have behind them as much as half of Europe. The other half will, quite certainly, make common cause against them. They will therefore have to conquer an enemy stronger than themselves. I may add that their interests are too contradictory and their mutual jealousies too great to allow of such a project ever being formed. I may add further that, even if it were formed, even if it were put in act, even if it had some measure of success, that very success would sow the seeds of discord among our victorious allies. It is beyond the bounds of possibility that the prizes of victory should be so equally divided, that each will be equally satisfied with his share. The least fortunate will soon set himself to resist the further progress of his rivals, who in their turn, for the same reason, will speedily fall out with one another. I doubt whether, since the beginning of the world, there has been a single case in which three, or even two, Powers have joined forces for the conquest of others, without quarrelling over their contingents, or over the division of the spoil, and without, in consequence of this disagreement, promptly giving new strength to their common enemy. From all this it appears improbable that, under any supposition, either a King, or a league of Kings, is in a position to bring about any serious or permanent change in the established order of Europe.

This does not mean that the Alps, the Rhine, the sea and the Pyrenees are in themselves a barrier which no ambition can surmount; but that these barriers are supported by others which either block the path of the enemy, or serve to restore the old frontiers directly the first onslaught has spent its force. The real strength of the existing order is, in truth, to be found partly in the play of conflicting policies which, in nine cases out of ten, keep each other mutually in check. But there is another bulwark more formidable yet. This is the Germanic Body, which lies almost in the centre of Europe and holds all the other parts in their place, serving still more perhaps for the protection of its neighbours than for that of its own members: a Body formidable to all by its size and by the number and valour of its component peoples; but of service to all by its constitution which, depriving it both of the means and the will to conquer, makes it the rock on which all schemes of conquest are doomed infallibly to break. In spite of all its defects, it is certain that, so long as that constitution endures, the balance of Europe will never be broken; that no potentate need fear to be cast from his throne by any of his rivals; and that the Treaty of Westphalia will perhaps for ever remain the foundation of our international system. Accordingly, the system of public Right, which the Germans study so diligently, is even more important than they suppose. It is the public Right not only of Germany, but even, in many ways, of Europe as a whole.

But the established order, if indestructible, is for that very reason the more liable to constant storms. Between the Powers of Europe there is a constant action and reaction which, without overthrowing them altogether, keeps them in continual agitation. Ineffectual as they are, these shocks perpetually renew themselves, like the waves which for ever trouble the surface of the sea without ever altering its level. The nations are incessantly ravaged, without any appreciable advantage to the sovereigns.

It would be easy for me to draw the same lesson from a study of the special interests of all the Courts of Europe; to show that those interests are so cunningly interwoven as to hold their respective forces mutually in check. But current theories of commerce and money have bred a political bigotry which works such rapid changes in the apparent interests of princes that it is impossible to arrive at any firm conclusion as to their real interests, seeing that everything now depends upon the economic systems, for the most part thoroughly crazy, which chance to flit through a minister's brain. For all that, commerce tends more and more to establish a balance between State and State; and by depriving certain Powers of the exclusive advantages they once drew from it, deprives them at the same time of one of the chief weapons they once employed for imposing their will upon the rest.

If I have dwelt upon the equal distribution of forces which springs from the present constitution of Europe, it was in order to draw from it a conclusion of the highest importance to the project for establishing a general league among her peoples. For, if we are to form a solid and lasting Confederation, we must have put all the members of it in a state of such mutual dependence that no one of them is singly in a position to overbear all the others, and that separate leagues, capable of thwarting the general League, shall meet with obstacles formidable enough to hinder their formation. Failing this, the Confederation will be nothing but an empty name; and under an appearance of subjection, every member of it will in reality be independent. But, if those obstacles are such as I have described at the present moment – a moment when all the Powers are entirely free to form separate leagues and offensive alliances – judge what they would become if they were a general League, fully armed and ready at any moment to forestall those who should conceive the design of destroying or resisting it. That in itself is enough to show that such a Federation, so far from ending in mere vain discussions to be set at defiance with impunity, would on the contrary give birth to an effective Power, capable of forcing any ambitious ruler to observe the terms of the general treaty which he has joined with others to set up.

From the above survey three certain conclusions may be drawn: the first that, Turkey excepted, there already exists among the nations of Europe a bond, imperfect indeed but still closer than the loose and general ties which exist between man and man in the state of nature; the second, that the imperfections of this association make the state of those who belong to it worse than it would be if they formed no community at all; the third, that these rudimentary ties, which make such an association injurious, make it at the same time readily capable of improvement, that all its members might easily find their happiness in what actually makes their misery, that from the state of war which now reigns among them they might perfectly well draw an abiding peace.

Let us now consider the means by which this great work, begun by chance, may be completed by wisdom. Let us ask how the free and voluntary association which now unites the States of Europe may be converted, by taking to itself the strength and firmness of a genuine Body politic, into an authentic Confederation. There is no doubt that such a creation, by giving to the existing bond the completeness which it now lacks, will increase all its advantages and compel all the parts to unite for the benefit of the whole body. But in order that this can be brought about this Confederation must be sufficiently general that it includes all important powers; it must have a judicial body equipped to establish laws and ordinances binding upon all its members; sufficient power to oblige any state either to perform or abstain from actions commonly agreed upon. Finally it must be solid and durable enough to prevent members from withdrawing the moment they perceive their own interests opposed to the general interest. These factors will ensure that the institution is wise, useful and indestructible. It is now a question of developing these ideas to see what consequences follow, what measures are called for in order to establish it and what reasonable expectations one may have that it can be put into practice.

From time to time there takes place among us kinds of general Diets under the name of Congresses to which men come from all the states of Europe only to return to them; where men assemble in order to say nothing of importance; where public issues are treated as private matters; where there is general deliberation over whether the table is to be round or square, the room is to have this or that number of doors, a certain negotiator his face or his back towards the window, or whether another is to advance a couple of inches this way or that during his reception. These and a thousand similar topics of like importance have been uselessly argued about over the last three hundred years and are worthy, to be sure, of detaining politicians of our own century.

It could come about that at one of these assemblies the members may be endowed with some common sense; it is not entirely impossible that they sincerely want the public good; and that, for reasons which will be worked-out hereafter, one can further conceive, that having overcome many difficulties, they will be instructed by their respective sovereigns to sign the general Confederation that I take in its essentials to be contained in the following five Articles.

By the first, the sovereigns will establish between themselves a perpetual and irrevocable alliance, and designate negotiators to convene in a specific place, a Diet or a permanent Congress in which all the outstanding issues arising between the contracting parties are to be regulated and brought to an end by means of arbitration or decision.

By the second shall be specified the number of the Sovereigns whose plenipotentiaries shall have a vote in the Diet; those who shall be invited to accede to the Treaty; the order, date and method by which the presidency shall pass, at equal intervals, from one to another; finally the quota of their respective contributions and the method of raising them for the defrayal of the common expenses.

By the third, the Confederation shall guarantee to each of its members the possession and government of all the dominions which he holds at the moment of the Treaty, as well as the manner of succession to them, elective or hereditary, as established by the fundamental laws of each Province. Further, with a view to suppressing at a single stroke and at the source those incessant disputes which arise between them, it shall be agreed to take as the basis of the respective rights of the contracting Parties the possession of the moment, as settled in each case by the last treaty concluded, with a general renunciation on all sides of every anterior claim: exception being made for all disputed successions and other claims to fall due in the future, all which shall be determined by arbitration of the Diet, to the absolute exclusion of all attempts to settle the matter by force or to take arms against each other under any pretext whatsoever.

By the fourth shall be specified the conditions under which any Confederate who may break this Treaty shall be put to the ban of Europe and proscribed as a public enemy: namely, if he shall have refused to execute the decisions of the Grand Alliance, if he shall have made preparations for war, if he shall have made a treaty hostile to the ends of the Confederation; if he shall have taken up arms to resist it or to attack any one of the Confederates.

By the same article, it shall be argued that all the Confederates shall arm and take the offensive, conjointly and at the common expense, against any State put to the ban of Europe, and that they shall not desist until the moment when he shall have laid down his arms, carried out the decisions and orders of the Diet, made amends for his offence, paid all the costs and atoned even for such warlike preparations as he may have made in defiance of the Treaty.

Finally, by the fifth Article, the plenipotentiaries of the Confederation of Europe shall receive standing powers to frame – provisionally by a bare majority, definitively (after an interval of five years) by a majority of three-quarters – those measures which, on the instruction of their Courts, they shall consider expedient with a view to the greatest possible advantage of the Common-wealth of Europe and of its members, all and single. In none of the above five Articles, however, shall any change ever be made except with the unanimous consent of the Confederates.

These five Articles, summarized and reduced to the most general form, are, I am aware, exposed to countless petty objections, several of which would call for lengthy explanations. But petty objections are easily removed in case of need; and, in an enterprise of this importance, they are beside the point. When the policy of the Congress comes to be considered, a thousand obstacles will present themselves and ten thousand ways of removing them. It is *our* business to ask whether in the nature of the case, the enterprise is possible or no. We should lose ourselves in volumes of trifles, if we had to foresee all and find an answer to all. Confining ourselves, as we do, to incontestable principles, we have no call to satisfy every reader, not to solve every objection, nor to say how every detail will be settled. It is enough to show that a settlement is possible.

In judging of this scheme, then, what are the questions that have to be considered? Two only; for I will not insult the reader by proving to him the general proposition that the state of peace is a better thing than the state of war.

The first question is whether the Confederation suggested would be certain to answer its purpose and give a solid and abiding peace to Europe. The second, whether it is in the interest of the various sovereigns to establish such a Confederation and to pay the price I have mentioned to obtain a lasting peace.

When we have thus proved our scheme to be for the advantage both of Europe as a whole and of all the States composing her, what obstacle is left, we ask, that can possibly prevent the execution of a design which, after all, depends solely upon the will of those concerned?

In discussion the first Article, for instance, let us apply what has been said above of the general order now established in Europe and of the common resolve which confines each Power practically within its traditional limits and does not allow it wholly to crush any of the others. In order to make my argument clear, I give here a list of the nineteen Powers here assumed to constitute the Commonwealth of Europe, to each of which I give an equal voice, making altogether nineteen votes, in the deliberations of the Diet: the Emperor of the Romans, the Emperor of Russia, the King of France, the King of Spain, the King of England, the States General, the King of Denmark, Sweden, Poland, the King of Portugal, the Sovereign of Rome, the King of Prussia, the Elector of Bavaria and his associates, the Elector Palatine and his associates, the Swiss and their associates, the ecclesiastical Electors and their associates, the Republic of Venice and her associates, the King of Naples, the King of Sardinia.

Several minor sovereigns – for instance, the Republic of Genoa, the dukes of Parma and Modena, and others – are omitted from the list. They will be associated with one or other of the less powerful States, with whom they will share a vote, after the fashion of the joint vote (*votum curiatum*) of the Counts of the Empire. It is useless to make the list more precise because, at any moment before the scheme is put in force, things may happen which, without affecting the principle of the measure, may call for alterations of detail.

A glance at the list will be enough to prove conclusively that it is impossible either for any single Power to resist the united action of all the others, or for any partial league to be formed capable of defying the Confederation as a whole.

How, indeed, could such a league be formed? Between the more powerful of the Confederates? We have already proved that such a league could never last; and with the list before us, it is easy enough to see that it could never be reconciled with the traditional policy of any of the great Powers, or with the interests inherent in their respective positions. Between a large State and a number of small ones? Then the other large States, with the Federation behind them, will crush such a league in no time; and it is clear that the Grand Alliance, being perpetually armed and concerted for action, will find no difficulty in forestalling and crushing in advance any partial and seditious alliance, likely to trouble the peace and the public order of Europe. Look at the cohesion of the Germanic Body: and that, in spite of its defective discipline and the glaring inequality of its members. Is there a single Prince, not even excepting the most powerful, who would dare to expose himself to the ban of the Empire by openly defying its laws, unless indeed he had good reason to suppose that the Empire would never have the courage to take action against the culprit in good earnest?

That is why I regard it as proved that the Diet of Europe, once established, will have no rebellion to fear and that no abuses which may creep in are ever likely to defeat the aims with which it was founded. It remains to ask whether those aims are really secured by the proposed institution.

With a view to answering this question, let us consider the motives by which Princes are commonly led to take up arms. These motives are: either to make conquests, or to protect themselves from aggression, or to weaken a too powerful neighbour, or to maintain their rights against attack, or to settle a difference which has defied friendly negotiation, or lastly, to fulfil some treaty obligation. There is no cause or pretext of war which cannot be brought under one or other of these six heads; and it is manifest that not one of the six is left standing under the new order which I propose.

As for the first, the thought of conquest will have to be given up from the absolute impossibility of making them. The aggressor is sure to find his way barred by forces stronger than his own; he is powerless to gain anything, and he risks the loss of all he has. At present, an ambitious Prince, who wishes to extend his dominions in Europe, relies upon two weapons; he begins by securing strong allies, and then seeks to catch his enemy unawares. But, under the new conditions, no special alliance could stand for a moment before the General Alliance which is stronger and subsists permanently; and as there is no longer any pretext for arming, no Prince can do so without being at once detected, stopped and punished by the Federation always under arms.

Again, the very thing which destroys all hope of conquest relieves him at the same time from all fear of being attacked. And, under the guarantee of all Europe, not only are his territories as strongly assured to him as the possessions of any citizen in a well-ordered community, but they are even more so than they were when he was their sole and only defender; in exactly the same proportion as the whole of Europe is stronger than any one of her Princes taken singly.

Thirdly, having no more reason to fear his neighbour, neither has he any more reason for desiring to weaken him; and having no hope of success in such an enterprise, he is under no temptation to attempt it.

As for the maintenance of his rights, I begin by remarking that a whole host of pettifogging claims and obscure pretensions will be swept away at one stroke by the third Article of Federation, which settles for ever all the conflicting rights of the allied Princes, on the basis of what they actually hold. By the same Article, we have a clear principle for settling all claims and pretensions which may be raised in the future: each will be decided in the Diet, as it arises. It may be added that, if my rights are attacked, I am bound to defend them by the weapon used against me. They cannot be attacked by force of arms without bringing the ban of the Diet upon the assailant. It is not by arms then that I shall have to defend them. The same may be said of injuries, wrongs and claims for damage – in short, of all the unforeseen differences which may arise between two Sovereigns. The same Power which is bound to maintain their rights is bound also to redress their grievances.

As for the last head, the question settles itself. It is clear at a glance that, having no longer any assailant to fear, I have no longer any use for treaties of defence; and that, as no treaty can be so strong or so trustworthy as that guaranteed by the Grand Confederation, any other treaty would be useless, illegitimate and consequently null and void.

For all these reasons it is impossible that the Confederation, once established, can leave any seed of war between its members; impossible that our object, an abiding peace, should not be absolutely attained by the proposed system, if it were once set on foot.

It now remains to settle the other question: that relating to the interests of the several parties concerned. For everyone knows that the general interest is powerless to silence that of the individual. To prove that peace, as a general principle, is a better thing than war is to say nothing to the man who has private reasons for preferring war to peace; to show him the means for securing a lasting peace is only to encourage him to work against them.

In truth, we shall be told: 'You are taking from Sovereigns the right of doing themselves justice; that is to say, the precious right of being unjust when they please. You are taking from them the

power of making themselves great at the expense of their neighbours. You are forcing them to renounce those antiquated claims
whose value depends on their obscurity and which grow with
every fresh growth in power; that parade of might and terror with
which they love to awe the world; that pride of conquest which
is the chief source of their glory. In one word, you are forcing
them to be equitable and peaceful. What amends do you propose
to make them for all these cruel privations?'

I do not venture to answer, with the Abbé de Saint-Pierre, that
the true glory of Princes lies in serving the good of the community
and the happiness of their subjects, that their highest interest is
to win a good name, and that such a name is awarded by the wise
in exact proportion to the good which the ruler had done in the
world; that the scheme of founding a lasting peace is the most
lofty ever conceived and the most certain, if executed, to cover its
author with undying glory; that such a scheme would not only do a
greater service than any other to the people but also confer higher
honour upon the Sovereign; that this is the only ideal not stained
with blood, rapine, curses and tears; in a word, that the surest
way for a Sovereign to raise himself above the common herd of
kings is to labour for the good of the community. Let such language,
which has covered the author and his projects with ridicule in all
the council-chambers of Europe, be left to irresponsible declaimers.
But let us never join in the cry against the arguments it embodies;
and, whatever may be the truth as to the virtues of princes, let us
confine ourselves to their interests.

All the Powers of Europe have rights, or claims, as against each
other. These rights are, from the nature of the case, incapable of
ever being finally adjusted, because there is no common and
unvarying standard for judging of their merits and because they
are often based upon facts which are either disputed or of doubtful
interpretation. Nor are the quarrels which spring from them any
more capable of being settled beyond appeal, whether in default of
any recognized umpire, or because, when the chance offers, every
Prince goes back shamelessly upon the cessions which have been
forcibly torn from him by a stronger Power through treaties, or
after an unsuccessful war. It is therefore a mistake to think only of
the claims we have on others, and to forget those they have on us,
when in reality there is no more justice on one side than on the

other and both are equally capable of acquiring the means for enforcing their demands. Directly fortune is taken for arbiter, actual possession acquires a value which no wise man will stake against a possible gain in the future, even where chances are equal on both sides; and the rich man who, in the hope of doubling his fortune, ventures to risk it all upon one throw is blamed by the whole world. We have shown, however, that in schemes of self-aggrandizement the chances are never equal and that, even in the present order of things, the aggressor is always bound to find his enemy stronger than himself. The inevitable conclusion is that, the more powerful having no motive for staking his possessions and the weaker no hope of gaining on the throw, both will find their advantage in renouncing what they would like to win, in order to secure what they possess.

Think of the waste of men, of money, of strength in every form; think of the exhaustion in which any State is plunged by the most successful war; compare these ravages with the profit which results; and we shall find that we commonly lose where we suppose ourselves to gain; that the conqueror, always enfeebled by the war, can only console himself with the thought that the conquered is still more enfeebled than himself. And even this advantage is more in appearance than reality; for the strength which has been gained upon our opponent has been lost against the neutrals, who without changing themselves, are nevertheless stronger relatively to us by all the strength that we have lost.

If all Kings have not yet thrown off the folly of conquests, it would seem that the wiser of them at any rate are beginning to realize that they sometimes cost more than they are worth. Without going into a thousand distinctions which would only distract us from our purpose, we may say broadly that a Prince who, in extending his frontiers, loses as many of his old subjects as he gains new ones in the process only weakens himself by his aggrandizement; because, with a larger territory to defend, he has no more soldiers to defend it. Everyone knows, however, that, as war is waged nowadays, the smallest part of the resultant loss of life is due to losses in the field. Certainly, that is the loss which everyone sees and feels. But all the time there is taking place through the whole kingdom a loss far more serious and more irreparable than that of those who die: a loss due to those who are not born, to the increase of taxes, to the interruption of trade, to the desertion of the fields, to the neglect of their cultivation. This evil, which no one sees at first, makes itself felt cruelly in the end. And then the King is astonished to find himself so weak, as the result of making himself so strong.

There is another thing which makes conquests even less profitable than they used to be. It is that Kings have at last learned the secret of doubling or trebling their power not only without enlarging their territory but even, it may be, by contracting it, after the wise example of Hadrian. The secret is that the strength of Kings lies only in that of their subjects; and it follows from what I have just said that, given two States supporting an equal number of inhabitants, that which covers the smaller extent of territory is in reality the more powerful. It is then by good laws, by a wise discipline, by large views on economic policy that a sagacious Sovereign is sure of increasing his power without incurring any hazard. It is in carrying out works more useful than his neighbours' that he makes conquests – the early true conquests – at their expense; and every subject born to him in excess of theirs is another enemy killed.

It may be objected that I prove too much and that, if the matter were as I put it, everyone being manifestly interested in avoiding war and the public interest combining with that of individuals for the preservation of peace, that peace ought to come of itself and of itself last for ever without any need of Federation. Given the present state of things, however, that would be to reason very ill. It is quite true that it would be much better for all men to remain always at peace. But so long as there is no security for this, everyone, having no guarantee that he can avoid war, is anxious to begin it at the moment which suits his own interest and so forestall a neighbour, who would not fail to forestall the attack in his turn at any moment favourable to himself, so that many wars, even offensive wars, are rather in the nature of unjust precautions for the protection of the assailant's own possessions than a device for seizing those of others. However salutary it may be in theory to obey the dictates of public spirit, it is certain that, politically and even morally, those dictates are liable to prove fatal to the man who persists in observing them with all the world when no one thinks of observing them towards him.

I have nothing to say on the question of military parade because, when supported by no solid foundation either of hope or fear, such parade is mere child's play, and Kings have no business to keep dolls. I am equally silent as to the glory of conquest because, if there really were men who would break their hearts at the thought of having no one to massacre, our duty would be not to reason with such monsters but to deprive them of all means for putting their murderous frenzy into act. All solid grounds of war being swept away by the third Article, no King can have any motive for kindling its horrors against a rival which would not furnish that rival with equally strong grounds for kindling them against him. And it is a great gain to be delivered from a danger in which each finds himself alone against the world.

As for the dependence of all upon the Tribunal of Europe, it is abundantly clear by the same Article that the rights of sovereignty, so far from being weakened, will, on the contrary, be strengthened and confirmed. For that Article guarantees to each Sovereign not only that his dominions shall be protected against foreign invasion, but also that his authority shall be upheld against the rebellion of his subjects. The Prince accordingly will be none the less absolute, and his crown will be more fully assured. By submitting to the decision of the Diet in all disputes with his equals, and by surrendering the perilous right of seizing other men's possessions, he is, in fact, doing nothing more than securing his real rights and renouncing those which are purely fictitious. Besides, there is all the difference in the world between dependence upon a rival and dependence upon a Body of which he is himself a member and of which each member in turn becomes the head. In the latter case, the pledges that are given him are really the security for his freedom: it would be forfeited, if lodged with a superior; it is confirmed, when lodged with equals. In support of this, I appeal to the example of the Germanic Body. It is quite true that the constitution of this is such as to trench in many ways upon the sovereignty of its members. It is quite true that their position is consequently less favourable than it would be in the Confederation of Europe. But, in spite of those drawbacks, there is not one of them, however jealous he may be of his dignity, who would choose, even if he had the power, to win absolute independence at the cost of severance from the Empire.

Observe further that the head of the Germanic Body, being permanent, is bound to usurp ceaselessly upon the rights of the other members. In the Diet of Europe, where the presidency passes from one to another without any regard to disparities of power, no such danger is to be feared.

There is yet another consideration which is likely to weigh even more with men so greedy of money as Princes always are. Not only will an unbroken peace give them, as well as their subjects, every means of amassing abundant riches; they will also be spared vast expenses by the reduction of their military budget, of those innumerable fortresses, of those enormous armies, which swallow up their revenue and become daily more and more of a burden to their subjects and themselves. I know that it will not suit all Sovereigns to suppress their army bodily and leave themselves with no force in hand to crush an unexpected revolt or repel a sudden invasion. I know also that they will have their contingent to furnish to the Confederation with a view both to guarding the frontiers of Europe and to maintaining the federal arm whose duty it will be, in case of need, to carry out the decrees of the Diet. But, when all these charges are met and, at the same time, the extraordinary expenses of war suppressed for ever, there will still be a saving of more than half the ordinary military budget; and that saving can be divided between the relief of the subject and the coffers of the Prince. The result will be that the people will have to pay much less; that the Prince, being much better off, will be in a position to encourage commerce, agriculture and the arts and to create useful foundations which will still further increase his subjects' riches, and his own; and, over and above all this, that the State will enjoy a security far greater than it now draws from all its armies and from all that warlike parade which drains its strength in the very bosom of peace.

It will be said perhaps that the frontier countries of Europe will then be relatively worse off, they will still have to face the chance of war either with the Turk, or the African Corsairs, or the Tartars.

The answer to this is (1) that those countries are under the same necessity at present, from which it follows that they will not be put to any positive disadvantage, but will only have an advantage the less; and this, in fact, is an inevitable consequence of their geographical position; (2) that, being freed from all anxiety on the side of Europe, they will be much more capable of resisting attacks from other quarters; (3) that the suppression of all fortresses in the inner parts of Europe and of all expenses needed for their maintenance would enable the Federation to build a large number on the eastern frontiers without bringing any fresh charge upon its members; (4) that these fortresses, built, maintained and garrisoned at the common charge, will mean so many fresh guarantees, and so much expense saved to the frontier Powers for whose benefit they are built; (5) that the troops of the Federation, posted on the frontiers of Europe, will stand permanently ready to drive back the invader; (6) and finally, that a Body so formidable as the Commonwealth of Europe will make the foreigner think twice before attacking any of its members: just as the Germanic Body, though infinitely less powerful, is still strong enough to command the respect of its neighbours and offer valuable protection to all the Princes who compose it.

It may be further objected that, when the nations of Europe have ceased to war among themselves, the art of war will be gradually forgotten, that her armies will lose their courage and discipline, that there will be no more soldiers or generals, and that Europe will lie at the mercy of the first comer.

My answer is that one of two things will happen. Either the neighbours of Europe will attack her and wage war against her; or they will be afraid of the Confederation and leave her in peace.

In the former case, there will be plenty of opportunities for training military genius and talent, for practising and hardening our troops. The armies of the Confederation will, in this way, be the school of Europe. Men will go to the frontiers to learn war, while in the heart of Europe there will reign the blessings of peace. The advantages of war and peace will be combined. Does anyone believe that no nation can become warlike without perpetual civil war? And are the French the less brave because Anjou and Touraine are not constantly fighting with each other?

In the latter case, it is true that there can be no more hardening for war. But neither will there be any more need for it. Of what use would it be to train for war, when you have no intention of ever making it? And which is the better course – to cultivate a pernicious art, or to destroy the need of it for ever? If the secret of perpetual health were discovered, would there be any sense in rejecting it, on the ground that doctors must not be deprived of the chance of gaining experience? And in making this parallel we have still to ask which of the two arts is the more beneficent in itself and the more deserving of encouragement.

Let no one threaten us with a sudden invasion. It is perfectly obvious that Europe has no invader to fear, and that the 'first comer' will never come. The day of those barbarian eruptions, which seemed to fall from the clouds, is gone for ever. Now that the whole surface of the earth lies bare to our scrutiny, no danger can reach us which we have not foreseen for years. There is no Power in the world now capable of threatening all Europe; and if one ever appears, Europe will either have time to make ready or, at the worst, will be much more capable of resisting him when she is united in one corporate body than she is now, when she would have to put a sudden end to all her quarrels and league herself in haste against the common invader.

We have thus seen that all the alleged evils of Confederation, when duly weighed, come to nothing. I now ask whether anyone in the world would dare to say as much of those which flow from the recognized method of settling disputes between one prince and another – the appeal to the sword; a method inseparable from the state of anarchy and war, which necessarily springs from the absolute independence conceded to all Sovereigns under the imperfect conditions now prevailing in Europe. In order to put the reader in a better position to estimate these evils, I will give a short summary of them and leave him to judge of their significance.

(1) The existence of no solid right, except that of the stronger. (2) The perpetual and inevitable shifting of the balance from nation to nation, which makes it impossible for any one of them to keep in its grasp the power it holds at any moment. (3) The absence of complete security for any nation, so long as its neighbours are not subdued or annihilated. (4) The impossibility of annihilating them, in view of the fact that, directly one is conquered, another springs up in its place. (5) The necessity of endless precautions and expenses to keep guard against possible enemies. (6) Weakness, and consequent exposure to attack, during minorities or revolts; for, when the State is divided, who can support one faction against the other? (7) The absence of any guarantee for international agreements. (8) The impossibility of obtaining

justice from others without enormous cost and loss, which even so do not always obtain it, while the object in dispute is seldom worth the price. (9) The invariable risk of the Prince's possessions, and sometimes of his life, in the quest of his rights. (10) The necessity of taking part against his will in the quarrels of his neighbours and of engaging in war at the moment when he would least have chosen it. (11) The stoppage of trade and revenue at the moment when they are most indispensable. (12) The perpetual danger threatened by a powerful neighbour, if the Prince is weak, and by an armed alliance, if he is strong. (13) Finally, the uselessness of prudence, when everything is left to chance; the perpetual impoverishment of nations; the enfeeblement of the State alike in victory and defeat; and the total inability of the Prince ever to establish good government, ever to count upon his own possessions, ever to secure happiness either for himself or for his subjects.

In the same way, let us sum up the advantages which the arbitration of Europe would confer upon the Princes who agree to it.

1. Absolute certainty that all their disputes, present and future, will always be settled without war: a certainty incomparably more useful to Princes than total immunity from lawsuits to the individual.

2. The abolition, either total or nearly so, of matters of dispute, thanks to the extinction of all existing claims – a boon which, in itself, will make up for all the Prince renounces and secure what he possesses.

3. An absolute and indefeasible guarantee not only for the persons of the Prince and his family, but also for his dominions and the law of succession recognized by the custom of each province: and this, not only against the ambition of unjust and grasping claimants, but also against the rebellion of his subjects.

4. Absolute security for the execution of all engagements between Princes, under the guarantee of the Commonwealth of Europe.

5. Perfect freedom of trade for all time whether between State and State, or between any of them and the more distant regions of the earth.

6. The total suppression for all time of the extraordinary military expenses incurred by land and sea in time of war, and a

considerable reduction of the corresponding expenses in time of peace.

7. A notable increase of population and agriculture, of the public wealth and the revenues of the Prince.

8. An open door for all useful foundations, calculated to increase the power and glory of the Sovereign, the public wealth and the happiness of the subject.

As I have already said, I leave it to the reader to weigh all those points and to make his own comparison between the state of peace which results from Confederation and the state of war which follows from the present anarchy of Europe.

If our reasoning has been sound in the exposition of this Project, it has been proved; firstly, that the establishment of a lasting peace depends solely upon the consent of the Sovereigns concerned and offers no obstacle except what may be expected from their opposition; secondly, that the establishment of such a peace would be profitable to them in all manner of ways, and that, even from their point of view, there is no comparison between its drawbacks and advantages; thirdly, that it is reasonable to expect their decision in this matter will coincide with their plain interest; and lastly, that such a peace, once established on the proposed basis, will be solid and lasting and will completely fulfil the purpose with which it was concluded.

This is not, of course, to say that the Sovereigns will adopt this project – who can answer for the reason of another? – but only that they would adopt it, if they took counsel of their true interest. It must be observed that we have not assumed men such as they ought to be, good, generous, disinterested and devoted to the public good from motives of pure humanity; but such as they are, unjust, grasping and setting their own interest above all things. All that I do assume in them is understanding enough to see their own interest, and courage enough to act for their own happiness. If, in spite of all this, the project remains unrealized, that is not because it is utopian; it is because men are crazy, and because to be sane in a world of madmen is in itself a kind of madness.

Judgment on Saint-Pierre's Project for Perpetual Peace

The scheme of a lasting peace was of all others the most worthy to fascinate a man of high principle. Of all those which engaged the Abbé de Saint-Pierre, it was therefore that over which he brooded the longest and followed up with the greatest obstinacy. It is indeed hard to give any other name to the missionary zeal which never failed him in this enterprise: and that, in spite of the manifest impossibility of success, the ridicule which he brought upon himself day by day and the rebuffs which he had continually to endure. It would seem that his well-balanced spirit, intent solely on the public good, led him to measure his devotion to a cause purely by its utility, never letting himself be daunted by difficulties, never thinking of his own personal interest.

If ever moral truth were demonstrated, I should say it is the utility, national no less than international, of this project. The advantages which its realization would bring to each Prince, to each Nation, to the whole of Europe, are immense, manifest, incontestable; and nothing could be more solid or more precise than the arguments which the author employs to prove them. Realize his Commonwealth of Europe for a single day, and you may be sure it will last for ever; so fully would experience convince men that their own gain is to be found in the good of all. For all that, the very Princes who would defend it with all their might, if it once existed, would resist with all their might any proposal for its creation; they will as infallibly throw obstacles in the way of its establishment as they would in the way of its abolition. Accordingly Saint-Pierre's book on *A Lasting Peace* seems to be ineffectual for founding it and unnecessary for maintaining it. 'It is then an empty dream', will be the verdict of the impatient reader. No: it is a work of solid judgment, and it is of great importance for us to possess it.

Let us begin by examining the criticisms of those who judge of reasons not by reason, but by the event, and who have no objection to bring against the scheme except that it has never been put in practice. Well, such men will doubtless say, if its advantages are so certain, why is it that the Sovereigns of Europe have never adopted it? Why do they ignore their own interest, if that interest is demonstrated so clearly? Do we see them reject any other means of increasing their revenue and their power? And, if this means were as efficacious as you pretend, is it conceivable that they should be less eager to try it than any of the schemes they have pursued for all these centuries? that they should prefer a thousand delusive expedients to so evident an advantage?

Yes, without doubt, that is conceivable; unless it be assumed that their wisdom is equal to their ambition, and that the more keenly they desire their own interest, the more clearly do they see it. The truth is that the severest penalty of excessive self-love is that it always defeats itself, that the keener the passion the more certain it is to be cheated of its goal. Let us distinguish then, in politics as in morals, between real and apparent interest. The former will be secured by an abiding peace; that is demonstrated in the *Project*. The latter is to be found in the state of absolute independence which frees Sovereigns from the reign of Law only to put them under that of chance. They are, in fact, like a madcap pilot who, to show off his idle skill and his power over his sailors, would rather toss to and fro among the rocks in a storm than moor his vessel in safety.

The whole life of Kings, or of those on whom they shuffle off their duties, is devoted solely to two objects: to extend their rule beyond their frontiers and to make it more absolute within them. Any other purpose they may have is either subversient to one of these aims, or merely a pretext for attaining them. Such pretexts are 'the good of the community', 'the happiness of their subjects', or 'the glory of the Nation': phrases for ever banished from the council chamber, and employed so clumsily in proclamations that they are always taken as warnings of coming misery and that the people groans with apprehension when its masters speak to it of their 'fatherly solicitude'.

From these two fundamental maxims we can easily judge of the spirit in which Princes are likely to receive a proposal which runs directly counter to the one and is hardly more favourable to the other. Anyone can see that the establishment of the Diet of Europe will fix the constitution of each State as inexorably as its frontiers; that it is impossible to guarantee the Prince against the rebellion of his subjects without at the same time securing the subjects against the tyranny of the Prince; and that, without this, the Federation could not possibly endure. And I ask whether there is in the whole world a single Sovereign who, finding himself thus bridled for ever in his most cherished designs, would endure without indignation the very thought of seeing himself forced to be just not only with the foreigner, but even with his own subjects?

Again, anyone can understand that war and conquest without and the encroachments of despotism within give each other mutual support; that money and men are habitually taken at pleasure from a people of slaves, to bring others beneath the same yoke; and that conversely war furnishes a pretext for exactions of money and another, no less plausible, for keeping large armies constantly on foot, to hold the people in awe. In a word, anyone can see that aggressive Princes wage war at least as much on their subjects as on their enemies, and that the conquering nation is left no better off than the conquered. 'I have beaten the Romans,' so Hannibal used to write to Carthage, 'send me more troops. I have exacted an indemnity from Italy, send me more money.' That is the real meaning of the *Te Deums*, the bonfires and rejoicings with which the people hail the triumphs of their masters.

As for disputes between Prince and Prince, is it reasonable to hope that we can force before a higher tribunal men who boast that they hold their power only by the sword, and who bring in the name of God solely because He 'is in heaven'? Will Sovereigns ever submit their quarrels to legal arbitration, when all the rigour of the laws has never succeeded in forcing private individuals to admit the principle in theirs? A private gentleman with a grievance is too proud to carry his case before the Court of the Marshals of France; and you expect a King to carry his claims before the Diet of Europe? Not to mention that the former offends against the laws, so risking his life twice over, while the latter seldom risks anything but the life of his subjects; and that, in taking up arms, he avails himself of a right recognized by all the world – a right for the use of which he claims to be accountable to God alone.

A Prince who stakes his cause on the hazards of war knows well enough that he is running risks. But he is less struck with the risks than with the gains on which he reckons, because he is much less afraid of fortune than he is confident in his own wisdom. If he is strong, he counts upon his armies; if weak, upon his allies. Sometimes he finds it useful to purge ill humours, to weaken restive subjects, even to sustain reverses; and the wily statesman knows how to draw profit even from his own defeats. I trust it will be remembered that it is not I who reason in this fashion, but the court sophist, who would rather have a large territory with few subjects, poor and submissive, than that unshaken rule over the hearts of a happy and prosperous people, which is the reward of a Prince who observes justice and obeys the laws.

It is on the same principle that he meets in his own mind the argument drawn from the interruption of commerce, from the loss of life, from the financial confusion and the real loss which result from an unprofitable conquest. It is a great miscalculation always to estimate the losses and gains of Princes in terms of money; the degree of power they aim at is not to be reckoned by the millions in their coffers. The Prince always makes his schemes rotate; he seeks to command in order to enrich himself, and to enrich himself in order to command. He is ready by turns to sacrifice the one aim to the other, with a view to obtaining whichever of the two is most wanting at the moment. But it is only in the hope of winning them both in the long run that he pursues each of them apart. If he is to be master of both men and things, he must have empire and money at the same time.

Let us add finally that, though the advantages resulting to commerce from a general and lasting peace are in themselves certain and indisputable, still, being common to all States, they will be appreciated by none. For such advantages make themselves felt only by contrast, and he who wishes to increase his relative power is bound to seek only such gains as are exclusive.

So it is that, ceaselessly deluded by appearances, Princes would have nothing to do with peace on these terms, even if they calculated their interests for themselves. How will it be, when the calculation is made for them by their ministers, whose interests are always opposed to those of the people and almost always to the Princes'? Ministers are in perpetual need of war, as a means of making themselves indispensable to their master, of throwing him into difficulties from which he cannot escape without their aid, of ruining the State, if things come to the worst as the price of keeping their own office. They are in need of it, as a means of oppressing the people on the plea of national necessity, of finding places for their creatures, of rigging the market and setting up a thousand odious monopolies. They are in need of it, as a means of gratifying their passions and driving their rivals out of favour. They are in need of it, as a means of controlling the Prince and withdrawing him from court whenever a dangerous plot is formed against their power. With a lasting peace, all these resources would be gone. And the world still persists in asking why, if such a scheme is practicable, these men have not adopted it. Is it not obvious that there is nothing impracticable about it, except its adoption by these men? What then will they do to oppose it? What they have always done: they will turn it into ridicule.

Again, even given the goodwill that we shall never find either in Princes or their ministers, we are not to assume, with the Abbé de Saint-Pierre, that it would be easy to find the right moment for putting the project into act. For this, it would be essential that all the private interests concerned, taken together, should not be stronger than the general interest, and that everyone should believe himself to see in the good of all the highest good to which he can aspire for himself. But this requires a concurrence of wisdom in so many heads, a fortuitous concourse of so many interests, such as chance can hardly be expected ever to bring about. But, in default of such spontaneous agreement, the one thing left is force; and then the question is no longer to persuade but to compel, not to write books but to raise armies.

Accordingly, though the scheme in itself was wise enough, the means proposed for its execution betray the simplicity of the author. He fairly supposed that nothing was needed but to convoke a Congress and lay the Articles before it; that they would be signed directly and all be over on the spot. It must be admitted that, in all his projects, this good man saw clearly enough how things would work, when once set going, but that he judged like a child of the means for setting them in motion.

To prove that the project of the Christian Commonwealth is not utopian, I need do no more than name its original author.

For no one will say that Henry IV was a madman, or Sully a dreamer. The Abbé de Saint-Pierre took refuge behind these great names, to revive their policy. But what a difference in the time, the circumstances, the scheme itself, the manner of bringing it forward and, above all, in its author!

To judge of this, let us glance at the state of Europe as it was at the moment which Henry chose for the execution of his project.

The power of Charles V, who reigned over one half of the world and struck awe into the other, had led him to aspire to universal empire, with great chances of success and great talents for making use of them. His son, more rich and less powerful, never ceased to nurse a design which he was incapable of carrying out, and throughout his reign kept Europe in a state of perpetual alarm. In truth, the House of Austria had acquired such an ascendancy over the other Powers that no Prince was safe upon his throne, unless he stood well with the Hapsburgs. Philip III, with even fewer talents, inherited all his father's pretensions. Europe was still held in awe by the power of Spain, which continued to dominate the others rather by a long habit of commanding than from any power to make herself obeyed. In truth, the revolt of the Low Countries, the struggle against England, the long drain of the civil wars in France had exhausted the strength of Spain and the riches of the Indies. The House of Austria, now divided into two branches, has ceased to act with the same unity; and the Emperor, although he strained every nerve to maintain or recover the authority of Charles V, only succeeded in affronting the lesser Princes and provoking conspiracies which speedily broke out and came near to costing him his throne. Such were the slow stages which prepared the fall of the House of Austria and the new birth of the liberties of Europe. No one, however, had the courage to be first to risk throwing off the yoke and exposing himself alone to the dangers of war; the example of Henry himself, who had come so ill out of the enterprise, damped the courage of all the rest. Moreover, if we except the Duke of Savoy, who was too weak and too much under the curb to move a step, there was not among all the Sovereigns of the time a single one of ability enough to form and carry through such an enterprise; each one of them waited on time and circumstances for the moment to break his chains. Such, in rough outline, was the state of things at the time when Henry formed the plan of the Christian Commonwealth and prepared to put it in act. The project was vast indeed and, in itself, quite beyond praise. I have no wish to dim its glory. But, prompted as it was by the secret hope of humbling a formidable enemy, it took from this urgent motive an impulse which could hardly have come from humanity alone.

Let us now see what were the means employed by this great man to pave the way for so lofty an undertaking. In the front rank of these I should be disposed to put that he had clearly recognized all the difficulties of the task; so that, having formed the project in his youth, he brooded over it all his life and reserved its accomplishment for his old age. This proves in the first place that ardent and sustained passion by which alone great obstacles can be overcome; and secondly, that patient and considerate wisdom which smoothes the way in advance by forethought and calculation. For there is a great difference between an enforced undertaking, in which prudence itself counsels to leave something to chance, and one which is to be justified only by success; seeing that, being under no compulsion to engage in it, we ought never to have attempted it unless that success were beyond doubt. Again, the deep secrecy which he maintained all his life, until the very moment of action, was as essential as it was difficult in so vast an enterprise, where the concurrence of so many men was a necessity and which so many men were interested in thwarting. It would seem that, though he had drawn the greater part of Europe to his side and was in league with her chief potentates, there was only one man to whom he had confided the full extent of his design; and, by a boon granted by heaven only to the best of Kings, that one man was an honest minister. But, though nothing was allowed to transpire of these high aims, everything was silently moving towards their execution. Twice over did Sully make the journey to London: James I was a party to the plan, and the King of Sweden had fallen in with it. A league was made with the Protestants of Germany; even the Princes of Italy had been secured. All were ready to join in the great purpose, though none could say what it was; just as workmen are employed in making the separate parts of a new machine, of whose shape and use they know nothing. What was it then that set all these springs in motion? Was it the craving for a lasting peace, which was foreseen by no one and with which few would have troubled their heads? Was it the public interest, which is never the interest of anyone? The Abbé de Saint-Pierre might have supposed so. But the truth is that each of them was working for his own private interest which Henry had been clever enough to display to all of them in the most attractive light. The King of England was glad to deliver himself from the perpetual conspiracies of his Catholic subjects, all of them fomented by Spain. He found a further advantage in the liberation of the United Provinces, in whose support he was spending large sums, while every moment he was placed on the brink of a war which he dreaded, or in which he preferred to join once for all with the whole of Europe and then be quit of it for ever. The King of Sweden was anxious to make sure of Pomerania and so win a footing in Germany. The Elector Palatine, at that time a Protestant and head of the Lutheran Confession, had designs on Bohemia and shared all the plans of the King of England. The Princes of Germany aimed at checking the encroachments of the House of Austria. The Duke of Savoy was to receive Milan and the crown of Lombardy which he passionately coveted. The Pope himself, weary of the Spanish tyranny, was in the league, bribed by the promise of the Kingdom of Naples. The Dutch, better paid than all the rest, gained the assurance of their freedom. In a word, quite apart from the common interest of humbling a haughty Power which was striving to tyrannize over all of them, each State had a private interest all the more keenly felt because it was not countered by the fear of exchanging one tyrant for another. It was agreed that the conquests should be distributed among all the Allies to the exclusion of France and England, who were bound to keep nothing for themselves. This was enough to quiet the most suspicious as to the ambitions of Henry. But that wise prince was well aware that in keeping nothing for himself by this treaty, he gained more than all the rest. Without adding a yard to his own patrimony, it was enough to partition that of the only man who excelled him in power, and he became the most powerful himself. And it is perfectly clear that, in taking all the precautions which would assure the success of his enterprise, he in no wise neglected those which were sure to give him the first place in the Body he was creating.

More than that: he did not confine himself to forming formidable leagues beyond his frontiers, to making alliances with his own neighbours and the neighbours of his enemy. While engaging all these nations in the abasement of the first Power in Europe, he did not forget to put himself in the way of securing the coveted position for himself. He spent fifteen years of peace in preparations worthy of the enterprise he had in mind. He filled his coffers with money, his arsenals with artillery, arms and munitions. He amassed resources of all kinds against unforeseen demands. But he did more than all, we may be very sure, by governing his people wisely, by silently removing all seeds of division, by putting his finances in such order as to meet all possible needs without any vexation of his subjects. So it was that, at peace within and formidable abroad, he saw himself in a position to arm and maintain sixty thousand men and twenty vessels of war, to quit his kingdom without leaving behind him the smallest germ of disorder and to carry on war for six years without touching his ordinary revenue or laying on a penny of new taxes.

To all these preparations must be added the assurance that the enterprise would be carried out, both by his minister and himself, with the same energy and prudence that had conceived and framed it. And, finally, the knowledge that all the military operations would be directed by a captain of his skill, while the enemy had none left to put against him. From all this it may be judged if any element which could promise success was wanting to his prospects. Without having fathomed his designs, all Europe was watching his preparations with a kind of awe. The great revolution was about to be launched on a slight pretext. A war, destined to be the end of all wars, was about to usher in eternal peace, when a deed, the horror of which is only increased by its mystery, came to quench for ever the last hope of the world. The blow which cut short the days of this good King, also plunged Europe back into ceaseless wars, of which she can now never hope to see the end.

Such were the means prepared by Henry IV for founding the Federation which the Abbé de Saint-Pierre proposed to set up by a book.

Let us not say, then, if his system has not been adopted, that is because it was not good. Let us rather say that it was too good to be adopted. Evils and abuses, by which so many men profit, come in of themselves. Things of public utility on the other hand, are seldom brought in but by force, for the simple reason that private interests are almost always ranged against them. Beyond doubt, a lasting peace is, under present circumstances, a project ridiculous enough. But give us back Henry IV and Sully, and it will become once more a reasonable proposal. Or rather, while we admire so fair a project, let us console ourselves for its failure by the thought that it could only have been carried out by violent means from which humanity must needs shrink.

No Confederation could ever be established except by a revolution. That being so, which of us would dare to say whether the League of Europe is a thing more to be desired or feared? It would perhaps do more harm in a moment that it would guard against for ages.

The State of War[1]

. . . But even if it were true that this boundless and uncontrollable greed had developed in all men to the extent which our sophist imagines, it still would not produce that state of universal war between everyone which Hobbes dares to depict in all its repulsiveness. The frantic desire to possess everything is incompatible with the desire to destroy all one's fellow men; and the conqueror who had the misfortune to remain alone in the world, having killed everyone else, would not thereby enjoy anything for the very reason that he would possess all. What are riches themselves good for if not to be imparted to others? What would be the use of possessing the whole universe, if he was its sole inhabitant? What! Would his stomach devour all the fruits of the earth? Who would gather the produce of the world's climates for him? Who would witness his empire in the vast solitudes where he did not live? What would he do with his treasures? Who would eat his food? For whose eyes would he display his power? I see. Instead of massacring everyone, he would put them all in irons, so that at least he would have slaves. This immediately changes the whole nature of the question; since it is no longer a question of destroying, the state of war is abolished. The reader may here suspend judgment. I shall not omit to discuss this point.

Man is naturally peaceful and timid; at the least danger, his first action is to flee; he only fights through the force of habit and experience. Honour, interest, prejudices, vengeance, all those passions which make him brave danger and death, are remote from him in the state of nature. It is only when he has entered into society with other men that he decides to attack another, and he only becomes a soldier after he has become a citizen. There are no strong natural dispositions to make war on all one's

[1] The original title, 'That the State of War arises from the Social State', was cancelled by Rousseau. The present title is used for convenience.

fellow men. But I am lingering too long over a system both revolting and absurd, which has already been refuted a hundred times.

There is then no general war between men; and the human species has not been created solely in order to engage in mutual destruction. It remains to consider war of an accidental and exceptional nature which can arise between two or more individuals.

If natural law were inscribed solely in human reason, it would scarcely be capable of guiding the bulk of our actions. But it is also indelibly engraved in the human heart; and it is there that it speaks to man more powerfully than all the precepts of philosophers; it is there that it tells him that he is not permitted to sacrifice the life of his fellow man except in order to preserve his own, and it is there that it gives him a horror of killing in cold blood, even when he is obliged to do so.

I can conceive that in the unarbitrated quarrels which can arise in the state of nature, a man whose anger has been roused can sometimes kill another, either by open force or by surprise. But if a real war were to take place, imagine the strange position which this same man would have to be in if he could only preserve his life at the expense of that of another, and if an established relationship between them required that one died so that the other could live. War is a permanent state which presupposes constant relations; and these relations are a rare occurrence between men, for between individuals there is a continual flux which constantly changes relationships and interests. Thus a matter of dispute rises and disappears almost at the same moment; a quarrel begins and ends within a day; and one can have fights and murders, but never, or very rarely, long enmities and wars.

In the civil state, where the life of all the citizens is in the power of the Sovereign and where no one has the right to dispose either of his own life or that of another person, the state of war can no longer take place between private individuals; as for duels, challenges, agreements or appeals to single combat, apart from the fact that they represent an illegal and barbarous abuse of a military settlement, they do not give rise to a true state of war, but only to a specific event, limited in time and space, which requires a new challenge if a second combat is to take place. An exception must be made for those private wars which were suspended by daily truces, called the peace of God, and which were sanctioned by the Institutions of St Louis. But this example is unique in history.

It may still be asked whether Kings, who are in fact independent of all human power, can establish personal and private wars between themselves, separate from those of the State. This is surely a trifling question; for as one knows it is not the custom of Princes to spare others in order to expose themselves personally. Moreover, this question depends on another which it is not incumbent upon me to decide; that is whether the Prince is himself subject to the State's laws or not; for if he is subject to them, his person is bound and his life belongs to the state, like that of the lowest citizen. But if the Prince is above the laws, he lives in the pure state of nature and is accountable neither to his subjects nor to anyone for any of his actions.

The social state

We now enter a new order of things. We are about to see men, united in artificial harmony, band together to cut each other's throats, and to see all the horrors of war arise from the very efforts which have been taken to prevent them. But first it is crucial to formulate a more exact idea of the essence of the body politic than has been done so far. The reader must realize that it is here less a question of history and facts than of right and justice, and that I wish to examine things according to their nature rather than according to our prejudices.

As soon as the first society is formed the formation of all the others necessarily follows. One has either to join it or to unite to resist it; to imitate it or let oneself be swallowed up by it. Thus the whole face of the earth is changed; everywhere nature has disappeared; everywhere human artifice takes its place; independence and natural liberty give way to laws and slavery; free beings no longer exist; the philosopher searches for man and no longer finds him. But it is fruitless to expect the annihilation of nature; it springs to life again and reveals itself where one least expects it. The independence which is removed from men takes refuge in societies; and these great bodies, left to their own impulses, produce collisions which grow more terrible the more their weight takes a precedence over that of individuals.

But how, it will be asked, is it possible that these bodies, each of which has so solid a foundation, should ever come to run up against one another? Ought not their very formation to keep perpetual peace between them? Are they obliged, like men, to look outside themselves for the satisfaction of their needs? Do they not possess in themselves all that is necessary for their preservation? Are competition and trade a source of inevitable discord? And have not people existed in all lands before commerce started, an irrefutable proof that they are able to survive without it?

(End of the chapter: there is no war between man;
it only exists between states)

I could content myself with replying to this question with facts, and I would fear no rejoinder. However, I have not forgotten that I am reasoning here about the nature of things and not about events, which can have a thousand particular causes, independent of the common principle. Let us consider closely the formation of political bodies, and we will find that, although each of them has, if need be, enough for its own preservation, their mutual relations are none the less far more intimate that those of individuals. For basically man has no necessary connection with his fellow men; he can maintain his full strength without their help; his need is not so much for men's care as for the earth's produce; and the earth produces more than enough to feed its inhabitants. Also the strength and size of man has a limit set by nature which he cannot go beyond. Whichever way he looks at himself, he finds all his faculties are limited. His life is short, his years are numbered. His stomach does not grow with his riches; his passions increase in vain, his pleasures are bounded; his heart is confined, like all the rest; his capacity for enjoyment is always the same. He can rise up in his imagination, he always remains small.

The State on the other hand, being an artificial body, has no fixed measure; its proper size is undefined; it can always grow bigger; it feels weak so long as there are others stronger than itself. Its safety and preservation demand that it makes itself stronger than its neighbours. It cannot increase, foster, or exercise its strength except at their expense; and even if it has no need to seek for provisions beyond its borders, it searches ceaselessly for new members to give itself a more unshakeable position. For the inequality of men has its limits set by nature, but the inequality of societies can grow incessantly, until one of them absorbs all the others.

Thus the size of the body politic being purely relative, it is forced to compare itself in order to know itself; it depends on its whole environment and has to take an interest in all that happens. In vain it wishes to stay within its own bounds, neither gaining nor losing; it becomes big or small, strong or weak according to the extent that its neighbour expands or contracts, grows stronger or weaker. Finally its very consolidation, by making its relations more constant, gives greater sureness to all its actions and makes all its quarrels more dangerous.

It looks as if one has set out to turn every true idea of things upside down. Everything inclines natural man to peace; the sole needs he knows are eating and sleeping, and only hunger drags him from idleness. He is made into a savage continually ready to torment his fellow men because of passions of which he knows nothing. On the contrary, these passions, aroused in the bosom of society by everything that can inflame them, are considered not to exist there at all. A thousand writers have dared to say that the body politic is passionless, and that there is no other *raison d'État* than reason itself. As if no one saw that, on the contrary, the essence of society consists in the activity of its members, and that a state without movement would be nothing but a corpse. As if all the world's histories do not show us that the best constituted societies are also the most active and that the continual action and reaction of all their members, whether within or without, bear witness to the vigour of the whole body.

The difference between human artifice and the work of nature is made evident in its effects. The citizens may well call themselves members of the State, but they are incapable of uniting themselves to it like the real members of a body; it is impossible to prevent each one of them from having a separate and individual existence through which he can be self-sufficing; the nerves are less sensitive, the muscles have less strength, all the bonds are looser, the slightest accident can break everything asunder.

If one considers how inferior the public power is to the sum of particular powers within the totality of the body politic, and how much, so to speak, friction there is in the working of the whole

machine, one will discover that the feeblest man has proportionately more power to preserve himself than the strongest state has
to preserve itself.

For the State to survive then, it is necessary for the intensity
of its passions to compensate for that of its movements and for
its will to quicken as its power slackens. This is the law of preservation that nature herself establishes between the species, and
which maintains them all, despite their inequality. It is also, one
may note in passing, the reason why small states have proportionately more vigour than big ones. Public feeling does not grow with
territory; the more the latter extends, the more the will relaxes
and movements grow weaker, until finally the huge body, over-
loaded with its own weight, caves in, and falls into listlessness
and decay.

These examples suffice to give an idea of the various methods
whereby a state can be weakened, and of those which war seems
to sanction in order to harm its enemy. As for treaties in which
some of these means are incorporated, what basically is a peace
of this sort except a war continued with all the more cruelty in
that the enemy no longer has the right to defend himself? I will
speak of this elsewhere.

Add to this the visible signs of ill will, which indicate the
intention to do harm; such as refusing to accord a Power the
status due to it, or ignoring its rights, rejecting its claims, refusing
its subjects freedom to trade, rousing enemies against it, or finally
breaking international law towards it, under some pretext or
other. These various ways of offending a body politic are neither
equally practicable nor equally useful to the state that uses them,
and those which result simultaneously in our own advantage and
the enemy's disadvantage are naturally preferred. Land, money,
men, all the booty that one can carry off thus become the principal
object of reciprocal hostilities. As this base greed imperceptibly
changes people's ideas about things, war finally degenerates into
brigandage, and little by little enemies and warriors become
tyrants and thieves.

From fear of thoughtlessly adopting this change of ideas ourselves, let us fix our own thoughts by a definition, and try to
make it so simple that it cannot be abused.

I call then war between Power and Power the effect of a constant, overt, mutual disposition to destroy the enemy State, or at least to weaken it by all the means one can. When this disposition is transformed into action it is war properly called; in so far as it remains untransformed it is only the state of war.

I foresee an objection: since according to me the state of war is natural between Powers, why does the disposition in which it results have to be overt? To this I reply that I have been speaking up to now of the natural state and that I am here speaking of the legitimate state, and that I shall show below how, in order to make it legitimate, war must be declared.

Fundamental Distinctions

I beg readers not to forget that I am not searching for what makes war advantageous to him who wages it, but for what makes it legitimate. It almost always costs something to be just. Is one therefore exempted from being so?

If there has never been, and if it is impossible to have, a true war between individuals, between whom then does it take place, and who can really call themselves enemies? I reply that they are public persons. And what is a public person? I reply that it is the moral being which one calls sovereign, which has been brought into existence by the social pact, and whose will always carries the name of law. Let us apply here the distinctions made earlier; one can say that, in considering the effects of war, the Sovereign inflicts the injury and the State receives it.

If war only takes place between moral beings, it is not intended to be between men, and one can conduct a war without depriving anyone of their life. But this requires an explanation.

If one looks at things solely and strictly in the light of the social pact, land, money, men, and everything contained within the boundary of the State, belongs unreservedly to it. But as the rights of society, founded on those of nature, cannot abolish the latter, all these objects must be considered in a double context: that is, the earth must be seen both as public land and as the patrimony of individuals; goods belong in one sense to the Sovereign, and in another to their owners; people are both citizens and men. Basically the body politic, in so far as it is only a moral being, is merely a thing of reason. Remove the public convention and immediately the State is destroyed, without the least change in all that composes it; for all man's conventions are unable to change anything in the nature of things. What then does it mean to wage war on a Sovereign? It means an attack on the public convention and all that results from it; for the essence of the State consists solely in that. If the social pact could be sundered with one blow, immediately there would be no more war; and by this one blow the State would be killed, without the death of one man. Aristotle states that in order to authorize the cruel treatment which the Helots were made to suffer in Sparta, the Ephors, when they took charge, solemnly declared war on them. This declaration was as superfluous as it was barbarous. A state of war existed of necessity between them from the very fact that the ones were masters and the others slaves. There can be no doubt that the Helots had the right to kill the Lacedaemonians since the latter killed them.

I open books on law and ethics, and listen to the scholars and legal experts. Permeated with their persuasive talk, I lament the miseries of nature, admire the peace and justice established by the civil order, bless the wisdom of public institutions, and console myself for being a man by looking upon myself as a citizen. Well versed in my duties and happiness, I shut my book, leave the classroom, and look around me. I see unfortunate Nations groaning under yokes of iron, the human race crushed by a handful of oppressors, a starving crowd overwhelmed with pain and hunger, whose blood and tears the rich drink in peace, and everywhere the strong armed against the weak with the formidable power of the law.

All this happens peacefully and without resistance. It is the tranquillity of Ulysses' comrades, shut in the cave of the Cyclops, waiting to be eaten. One must groan and keep silent. Let us draw a veil over these horrifying subjects. I raise my eyes and look into the distance. I see fires and flames, the countryside deserted, towns pillaged. Savages, where are you dragging those unfortunate people? I hear a terrible noise; what an uproar! I draw near; I see a scene of murder, ten thousand butchered men, the dead piled in heaps, the dying trampled under horses' hooves, everywhere the face of death and agony. So this is the fruit of these peaceful institutions! Pity and indignation rise from the bottom of my heart. Barbarous philosopher! Come and read us your book on the field of battle!

Whose stomach would not be turned by these sad subjects? But one is no longer allowed to be human and to plead the cause of humanity. Justice and truth must be bent to serve the most powerful: that is the rule. The people give neither pensions, nor employment, nor chairs, nor places at the Academies; why protect them? Magnanimous Princes, I speak in the name of the literary body; oppress the people with a good conscience; it is from you alone that we expect everything; the people cannot do anything for us.

'How can such a weak voice make itself heard above so much mercenary clamour? Alas! I must keep silent. But is the voice of my heart unable to pierce so sad a silence? No; without entering into odious details which would pass for satire solely because they are true, I will limit myself, as I always do, to examining institutions according to their principles, to correcting if possible the false ideas that have been given us by biased authors, and to ensuring that at least injustice and violence do not shamelessly masquerade as fairness and right.

The first thing I notice, in considering the condition of the human species, is an open contradiction in its constitution which causes it to vacillate incessantly. As individual men we live in a civil state subject to laws; as peoples we each enjoy a natural liberty: this makes our position fundamentally worse than if these distinctions were unknown. For living simultaneously in the social order and in the state of nature we are subjected to the inconveniences of both, without finding security in either. The perfection of the social order consists, it is true, in the conjunction of force and law. But this demands that law guides the use of force; whereas according to the ideas of absolute independence held by Princes, force alone, speaking to the citizens under the name of law and to foreigners under the name of *raison d'État*, removes from the latter the power, and from the former the will to resist, in such a way that everywhere the empty name of justice serves only as a safeguard for violence.

As for what is commonly called international law, because its laws lack any sanction, they are unquestionably mere illusions, even feebler than the law of nature. The latter at least speaks in the heart of individual men; whereas the decisions of international law, having no other guarantee than their usefulness to the person who submits to them, are only respected in so far as interest

175

accords with them. In the mixed condition in which we find ourselves, whichever system we prefer, making too much or too little of it, we have achieved nothing, and are in the worst state of all. That, it seems to me, is the true origin of public disasters.

Let us contrast these ideas for a moment with Hobbes' horrible system, and we will find the very reverse of his absurd doctrine. Far from the state of war being natural to man, war springs from peace, or at least from the precautions that men have taken to ensure a lasting peace. But before entering into this discussion let us try to explain what he . . . [unfinished]

Who could have imagined without shuddering the insane system of a natural war of all against all? What could be stranger than a creature who thought his own welfare depended on the destruction of his whole species! And how could one conceive that such a species, so monstrous and detestable, would last only two generations? Yet that is where one of the finest geniuses who ever lived has been led by his desire, or rather frenzy, to establish despotism and passive obedience. So ferocious a principle was worthy of its object.

The social state which restrains all our national inclinations cannot however extinguish them; in spite of our prejudices and in spite of ourselves, they still speak from the bottom of our hearts and often lead us back to the truth which we abandon for illusions. If this mutual and destructive hostility formed part of our make-up, it would still make itself felt, pushing us back, in spite of ourselves, across all social bonds. A terrible hatred of humanity would gnaw man's heart. He would grieve at the birth of his own children; he would rejoice at the death of his brothers; and if he discovered someone asleep his first reaction would be to kill him.

The goodwill which makes us share in the happiness of our fellow men, the compassion which identifies us with the sufferer and afflicts us with his sorrow, these would be unknown feelings directly contrary to nature. The sufferer would be a monster rather than a sensitive man, worthy of pity; and we would be by nature the kind of person we have difficulty in becoming even in the midst of the depravity which pursues us.

In vain the sophist will say that this mutual enmity is not innate and immediate, but founded on the inevitable competition which arises from the right of each to everything. For the awareness of this supposed right is no more natural to man than the war which it produces.

I have already stated, and I cannot repeat it too often, that the error of Hobbes and the philosophers is to confuse natural man with the man before their eyes, and to transpose into one system a being who can only exist in another. Man desires his own well-being and all that can contribute towards it; that is incontestable. But this well-being is limited by nature to physical necessity; for what does a man lack in order to be happy according to his constitution if he has a healthy spirit and a body free from suffering? He who has nothing desires little; he who commands no one has little ambition. But abundance arouses greed; the more one gets the more one desires. He who has much wants to have all; and the madness of universal monarchy only ever tormented the heart of a great King. Such is the march of nature, such is the development of the passions. A superficial philosopher observes souls that have been kneaded and worked a hundred times in the leaven of society, and thinks he has observed man. But in order to know him well, one must be able to disentangle the natural hierarchy of his feelings, and it is not amongst the inhabitants of a big town that one must look for the first sign of nature imprinted in the human heart.

Thus this analytic method only produces chasms and mysteries in which the wisest understands the least. Ask why morals become corrupted as minds become more enlightened. Unable to find a reason, they will have the audacity to deny the fact. Ask why savages brought amongst us do not share either our passions or our pleasures, and care nothing for the things we so ardently cherish. They will never explain, or explain only by my principles. They know only what they see and have never seen nature. A citizen of London or Paris they understand very well; but they can never understand man.

Fragments on War

1. In order to understand precisely what are the laws of war let us examine closely the nature of the case, and admit only that which necessarily follows. Two men are fighting in the state of nature; there clearly is a condition of war between them. But why are they fighting? Are they set upon eating one another? Even among animals that occurs only between different species. It is the same with men as it is between wolves in that the issue involved in the quarrel is always quite divorced from the lives of the combatants. It of course happens that one of them may be killed in the fight, but his death is the means to victory and not its purpose, because as soon as one admits defeat, the victor grabs hold of the thing in dispute, the fighting stops and the war is over.

One should note that social life surrounds us with a multitude of things which derive more from our imaginings than our needs and to which we are naturally indifferent. So much so that for the most part the issues in war become even more alien than in the state of nature and eventually reach the point where individuals care very little about what goes on during a public war. One takes up arms in order to settle questions of strength, wealth, or prestige and the subject of such matters finishes by being so removed from the lives of citizens that they are neither better nor worse off by being victors or vanquished. It would be odd indeed if a war about this kind of thing had much to do with their lives and that one felt entitled to kill solely to prove one's superior strength.

One kills in order to vanquish, but there is no man so bestial that he seeks victory in order to kill.

2. Now that the state of nature is abolished among us, war no longer exists between individuals and men who on their own account attack others, even where they have received some direct injury, are not treated as enemies, but as outlaws. So true is this, that a subject who, taking literally the terms of a declaration of

war, would wish, without authorization or letters patent to attack his Prince's enemies would be punished or at least should be.

3. Only those peoples soundly established over a long period of time can imagine making war a distinct profession and a special class out of those who practise it. Among a new people where the common interest is still lively all citizens are soldiers in wartime and in peacetime there are no soldiers at all. This is one of the best marks of the youth and vigour of a nation. Men always under arms are necessarily the enemies of all other men. One uses these divisive means only as an instrument against domestic weakness; the first standing troops are in a way the first wrinkles which signal the forthcoming senility of Governments.

4. Thanks to God one no longer sees such things among Europeans. One would be horrified of a Prince who killed his prisoners. Men become outraged even against those who treat prisoners badly and those frightful maxims which revolt one's reason and make all humanity shudder no longer remain known except to lawyers, who without a blush make them the foundations of their political systems and who instead of showing us sovereignty as the source of men's happiness dare to show it as the hope of the defeated.

As one moves from point to point the faulty principle strikes one at every step; one realizes that in arriving at such a grave decision one has no more consulted reason than nature. If I wanted to get to the bottom of the notion of the state of war I would easily show that it could only arise from the free choice of the belligerents, that if one attacked and the other chose not to defend himself there is only violence and aggression, but no state of war and that the state of war being a question of free choice, free and mutual agreement is just as necessary to re-establish peace. Unless one of the adversaries is destroyed war can only be ended between them when both parties quite openly renounce it; in the sense that in virtue of their relation of master to slave they continue in spite of themselves in the state of war. I could even question whether promises extracted by force and designed to avoid death are binding in the state of liberty, and whether all those promises which a prisoner makes to his master in that condition can have any other significance than this: 'I bind myself to obey you so long as you, being the stronger, do not threaten my life'.

There is something else. I should like someone to tell me which of the following considerations should carry the day: solemn and binding commitments to my country, taken in complete freedom, or those which the fear of death itself makes one contract with the victorious enemy. The so called right of slavery to which prisoners of war are subject is limitless. Lawyers decide on this matter specifically. There is nothing, says Grotius, that one cannot with impunity do to such slaves. There is nothing that one cannot command them to do, nothing at all to which one cannot subject them. Now say one forgoes all these possibilities of torment and limits one's demands to insisting that prisoners carry arms against their own country, then I should like to know which duty they must carry out: the free promise which they made to their country or the one which the enemy extracted while weak. Will they disobey their masters or will they slaughter their fellow citizens?

Perhaps someone will dare to tell me that slavery, in subjecting prisoners to their masters, they then and thereby change their condition and, becoming subjects of their new Sovereign, they renounce their old country.

5. First of all, the victor having no more right to make than to carry out this threat, the outcome cannot be lawful. Secondly, if ever promises extracted by force were null then that above all others is null which subjects men to the most far reaching commitment that they can make and which consequently presupposes entire freedom of choice among those who take it. The prior promise which binds us to our country annuls even more firmly the case of a promise binding us to another Sovereign since the first had been made in complete freedom and the second while in chains. In order to know whether one may force a man to become naturalized in a foreign state one must go back to the essential and primary object of political societies which is the happiness of peoples. Now it challenges the law of reason to say to others: 'The way I want to see you happy differs from the way you see it'.

6. When thousands of bellicose peoples have slaughtered their prisoners, when thousands of doctors in the keep of tyrants have justified these crimes, do in truth man's errors matter or their barbarity to justice? Let us not search for what has been done but rather for what should be done and let us dismiss evil and mercenary authorities who end up by making men slaves, evil and miserable.

IMMANUEL KANT

The great German philosopher Kant (1724-1804) turned his attention to international relations on a number of occasions. His essay on 'Perpetual Peace' is by far the most famous of his writings on the subject, but some of his lesser known contributions are also valuable, not only for the light they shed on the essay but for the new themes they present. In the selections which follow, *Perpetual Peace* has been placed in chronological sequence among the three most important of Kant's other contributions so that the full development of his thinking can be traced.

The fascination of Kant's approach is that he combines a very bleak estimate of the existing state of international relations with a profound conviction that these relations must be reformed. For Kant the international world is a savage state of nature in which war, which he considers a barbarous institution, constantly recurs. This savagery springs not from the nature of the state but from the nature of man. Man, as part of what Kant calls the 'sensuous' world is apt to be led by his desires and instincts towards exclusive self-assertion. More than this, man has a deep-seated propensity to *choose* this course of action. Outside the discipline of the state these propensities express themselves without restraint and constant mutual antagonism is the result. Kant has little faith in the ability either of conventional international law or the balance of power to restrain this tendency towards viciousness – though he is perhaps less sceptical in his last writings.

On the other hand Kant also argues that man belongs to a 'supersensuous' world, and is capable through his reason of prescribing ends for himself which by their very nature are capable of fulfilment. These ends derive ultimately from the formal rules of morality contained in the categorical imperative. Perpetual peace, the subordination of international relations to a lawful condition analogous, though not identical, to that of the state, is one such end or 'maxim'.

There is a further twist to Kant's argument, one that is amply documented in the following selections. Because man is capable of prescribing and following his own ends, nature must be presumed to be an area in which, despite appearances, such ends are realizable. Nature, in other words, is not merely a mechanism but a teleological organism, working towards the same end as man himself. Perpetual peace is therefore not solely a moral imperative, but something towards which nature, through such apparent catastrophes as war and violence, is also tending.

Kant's writings on international politics present, in microcosm, his whole philosophy of man, morality, and nature. It is this which gives them their depth, and renders them a standing challenge to those who consider that realism necessarily implies pessimism.

The first three extracts which follow have been taken from *Kant's Principles of Politics including his Essay on Perpetual Peace*, edited and translated by W. Hastie, Edinburgh, 1891. The extracts comprise pp. 15-25, pp. 63-74, and pp. 75-148 of the volume. The bulk of the footnotes, which Hastie omitted, have been translated or summarized by Murray Forsyth. Hastie's titles for the first two extracts have been replaced by Kant's original titles, and there have been some very minor alterations of Hastie's text, where modernity seemed to demand them. The German text used has been Immanuel Kant's *Werke*, ed. Ernst Casirer, Berlin 1922-23. The final extract is from Immanuel Kant: *The Metaphysical Elements of Justice*, translated by John Ladd, copyright 1965, by the Bobbs-Merrill Company, Inc., reprinted by permission of the College Division of the Bobbs-Merrill Company, Inc.

The *Idea for a Universal History from a Cosmo-political Point of View* from which the first extract is taken, was originally published in 1784. It consists of nine propositions, of which the last three have been reprinted here. The second extract forms the last part of Kant's essay *On the Commonplace: That may be right in theory but is useless in practice*. This was originally published in 1793. *Perpetual Peace* was published in 1795, and *The Metaphysical Elements of Justice* in 1797.

Suggested Reading

K. N. Waltz, Kant, Liberalism, and War; in the *American Political Science Review*, Vol. LVI, No 2, June 1962.

P. Hassner, Les Concepts de Guerre et de Paix chez Kant; in *Revue Française de Science Politique*, Vol. II, September 1961.

Idea for a Universal History from a Cosmo-political Point of View

SEVENTH PROPOSITION

The problem of the establishment of a perfect Civil Constitution is dependent on the problem of the regulation of the external relations between the States conformably to Law; and without the solution of this latter problem it cannot be solved.

What avails it to labour at the arrangement of a Commonwealth as a Civil Constitution regulated by law among individual men? The same unsociableness which forced men to it, becomes again the cause of each Commonwealth assuming the attitude of uncontrolled freedom in its external relations, that is, as one State in relation to other States; and consequently, any one State must expect from any other the same sort of evils as oppressed individual men and compelled them to enter into a Civil Union regulated by law. Nature has accordingly again used the unsociableness of men, and even of great societies and political bodies, her creatures of this kind, as a means to work out through their mutual Antagonism a condition of rest and security. She works through wars, through the strain of never relaxed preparation for them and through the necessity which every State is at last compelled to feel within itself, even in the midst of peace, to begin some imperfect efforts to carry out her purpose. And, at last, after many devastations, overthrows, and even complete internal exhaustion of their powers, the nations are driven forward to the goal which Reason might have well impressed upon them, even without so much sad experience. This is none other than the advance out of the lawless state of savages and the entering into a Federation of Nations. It is thus brought about that every State, including even the smallest, may rely for its safety and its rights, not on its own power or its own judgment of Right, but only on this great International Federation (*Foedus Amphictionum*), on its combined power, and on the decision of the common will according to laws. However visionary this idea may appear to be – and it has been ridiculed in the way in which it has been presented by an Abbé de Saint-Pierre or Rousseau (perhaps because they believed its realization to be so near) – it is nevertheless the inevitable issue of the necessity in which men involve one another. For this necessity must compel the Nations to the very resolution – however hard it may appear – to which the savage in his uncivilized state, was so unwillingly compelled, when he had to surrender his brutal liberty and seek rest and security in a Constitution regulated by law. All wars are, accordingly, so many attempts – not, indeed, in the intention of men, but yet according to the purpose of Nature – to bring about new relations between the Nations; and by destruction or at least dismemberment of them all to form new political corporations. These new organizations, again, are not capable of being preserved either in themselves or beside one another, and they must therefore pass in turn through similar new Revolutions, till at last, partly by the best possible arrangement of the Civil Constitution within, and partly by common convention and legislation without, a condition will be attained, which, in the likeness of a Civil Commonwealth and after the manner of an Automaton, will be able to preserve itself.

Three views may be put forward as to the way in which this condition is to be attained. In the first place, it may be held that from an *Epicurean* concourse of causes in action, it is to be expected that the States, like the little particles of matter, will try by their fortuitous conjunctions all sort of formations which will be again destroyed by new collisions, till at last some one constitution will by *chance* succeed in preserving itself in its proper form – a lucky accident which will hardly ever come about! In the second place, it may rather be maintained that Nature here pursues a regular march in carrying our species up from the lower stage of animality to the highest stage of humanity, and that this is done by a compulsive art that is inherent in man, whereby his natural capacities and endowments are developed in perfect regularity through an apparently wild disorder. Or, in the third place, it may even be asserted, that out of all these actions and reactions of men as a whole, nothing at all – or at least nothing rational – will ever be produced; that it will be in the future as it has ever been in the past, and that no one will ever be able to say whether the discord which is so natural to our species, may not be preparing for us, even in this civilized state of society, a hell of evils at the end, nay, that it is not perhaps advancing even now to annihilate again by barbaric devastation, this actual state of society and all the progress hitherto made in civilization – a fate against which there is no guarantee under a government of blind chance, identical as it is with lawless freedom in action, unless a connecting wisdom is covertly assumed to underlie the system of Nature. Now, which of these views is to be adopted, depends entirely on the question, whether it is rational to recognize *harmony and design* in the *parts* of the Constitution of Nature, and to deny them of the *whole*? We have glanced at what has been done by the seemingly purposeless state of savages; how it checked for a time all the natural capacities of our species but at last by the very evils in which it involved mankind, it compelled them to pass from this state, and to enter into a civil Constitution, in which all the germs of humanity could be unfolded. And, in like manner, the barbarian freedom of the States when once they were founded, proceeded in the same way of progress. By the expenditure of all the resources of the Commonwealth in military preparations against each other, by the devastations occasioned by war, and still more by the necessity of holding themselves continually in readiness for it, the full development of the capacities of mankind are undoubtedly retarded in their progress; but, on the other hand, the very evils which thus arise, compel men to find out means against them. A law of Equilibrium is thus discovered for the regulation of the really wholesome antagonism of contiguous States as it springs up out of their freedom; and a united Power, giving emphasis to this law, is constituted, whereby there is introduced a universal condition of public security among the Nations. And that the powers of mankind may not fall asleep, this condition is not entirely free from *danger*; but it is at the same time not without a principle which operates, so as to *equalize* the mutual action and reaction of these powers, that they may not destroy each other. Before the last step of bringing in a universal Union of the States is taken – and accordingly when human nature is only halfway in its progress – it has to endure the hardest evils of all, under the deceptive semblance of outward prosperity; and Rousseau was not so far wrong when he preferred the state of the savages, if the last stage which our race has yet to surmount be left out of view. We are *cultivated* in a high degree by Science and Art. We are *civilized*, even to excess, in the way of all sorts of social forms of politeness and elegance. But there is still much to be done before we can be regarded as moralized. The idea of morality certainly belongs to real Culture; but an application of this idea which extends no farther than the likeness of morality in the sense of honour and external propriety, merely constitutes civilization. So long, however, as States lavish all their resources upon vain and violent schemes of aggrandizement, so long as they continually impede the slow movements of the endeavour to cultivate the newer habits of thought and character on the part of the citizens, and even withdraw from them all the means of furthering it, nothing in the way of moral progress can be expected. A long internal process of improvement is thus required in every Commonwealth as a condition for the higher culture of its citizens. But all apparent good that is not grafted upon a morally good disposition, is nothing but mere illusion and glittering misery. In this condition the Human Race will remain until it shall have worked itself, in the way that has been indicated, out of the existing chaos of its political relations.

EIGHTH PROPOSITION

The history of the human race, viewed as a whole, may be regarded as the realization of a hidden plan of Nature to bring about a political Constitution, internally, and, for this purpose, also externally perfect, as the only state in which the capacities implanted by her in Mankind can be fully developed.

The proposition is a corollary from the preceding proposition. We see by it that philosophy may also have its millennial view, but in this case, the Chiliasm is of such a nature that the very idea of it – although only in a far-off way – may help to further its realization; and such a prospect is, therefore, anything but visionary. The real question is, whether experience discloses anything of such a movement in the purpose of Nature. I can only say *it does a little*; for the movement in this orbit appears to require such a long time till it goes full round that the form of its path and the relation of its parts to the whole, can hardly be determined out of the small portion which the human race has yet passed through in this relation. The determination of this problem is just as difficult and uncertain as it is to calculate from all previous astronomical observations what course our sun, with the whole host of his attendant train, is pursuing in the great system of the fixed stars, although on the ground of the total arrangement of the structure of the universe and the little that has been observed of it, we may infer, confidently enough, to the result of such a movement. Human Nature, however, is so constituted that it cannot be indifferent even in regard to the most distant epoch that may affect our race, if only it can be expected with certainty. And such indifference is the less possible in the case before us when it appears that we might by our own rational arrangements hasten the coming of this joyous period for our descendants. Hence the faintest traces of the approach of this period will be very important to ourselves. Now the States are already involved in the present day in such close relations with each other, that none of them can pause or slacken in its internal civilization without losing power and influence in relation to the rest; and, hence the maintenance, if not the progress, of this end of Nature is, in a manner, secured even by the ambitious designs of the States themselves. Further, Civil Liberty cannot now be easily assailed without inflicting such damage as will be felt in all trades and industries, and especially in commerce; and this would entail a diminution of the powers of the State in external relations. This Liberty, moreover, gradually advances further. But if the citizen is hindered in seeking his prosperity in any way suitable to himself that is consistent with the liberty of others the activity of business is checked generally; and thereby the powers of the whole State, again, are weakened. Hence the restrictions on personal liberty of action are always more and more removed, and universal liberty even in Religion comes to be conceded. And thus it is that notwithstanding the intrusion of many a delusion and caprice, the *spirit of Enlightenment* gradually arises as a great God which the human race must derive even from the selfish purposes of aggrandizement on the part of its rulers, if they understand what is for their own advantage. This Enlightenment, however, and along with it a certain sympathetic interest which the enlightened man cannot avoid taking in the good which he perfectly understands, must by and by pass up to the throne and exert an influence even upon the principles of Government. Thus although our rulers at present have no money to spend on public educational institutions, or in general on all that concerns the highest good of the world – because all their resources are already placed to the account of the next war – yet they will certainly find it to be to their own advantage at least not to hinder the people in their own efforts in this direction, however weak and slow these may be. Finally, the war itself comes to be regarded as a very hazardous and objectionable undertaking, not only from its being so artificial in itself and so uncertain as regards its issue on both sides, but also from the afterpains which the State feels in the ever increasing burdens it entails in the form of national debt – a modern infliction – which it becomes almost impossible to extinguish. And to this is to be added the influence which every political disturbance of any State of our continent – linked as it is so closely to others by the connections of trade – exerts upon all the States and which becomes so observable that they are forced by their common danger, although without lawful authority, to offer themselves as arbiters in the troubles of any such State. In doing so, they are beginning to arrange for a great future political Body, such as the world has never yet seen. Although this political Body may as yet exist only in a rough outline, nevertheless a feeling begins, as it were, to stir in all its members, each of which has a common interest in the maintenance of the whole. And this may well inspire the hope that after many political revolutions and transformations, the highest purpose of Nature will be at last realized in the establishment of a universal *Cosmopolitical Institution*, in the bosom of which all the original capacities and endowments of the human species will be unfolded and developed.

NINTH PROPOSITION

A philosophical attempt to work out the Universal History of the world according to the plan of Nature in its aiming at a perfect Civil Union, must be regarded as possible, and as even capable of helping forward the purpose of Nature.

It seems, at first sight, a strange and even absurd proposal to suggest the composition of a *History* according to the idea of how the course of the world must proceed, if it is to be conformable to certain rational laws. It may well appear that only a *Romance* could be produced from such a point of view. However, if it be assumed that Nature, even in the play of human freedom, does not proceed without plan and design, the idea may well be regarded as practicable; and, although we are too short-sighted to see through the secret mechanism of her constitution, yet the idea may be serviceable as a clue to enable us to penetrate the otherwise planless *Aggregate* of human actions as a whole, and to represent them as constituting a *System*. For the idea may so far be easily verified. Thus, suppose we start from the history of *Greece*, as that by which all the older or contemporaneous History has been preserved, or at least accredited to us.[1] Then, if we study its influence upon the formation and malformation of the political institutions of the Roman people, which swallowed up the Greek States, and if we further follow the influence of the Roman Empire upon the Barbarians who destroyed it in turn, and continue this investigation down to our own day, conjoining with it episodically the political history of other peoples according as the knowledge of them has gradually reached us through these more enlightened nations, we shall discover a regular movement

[1] Only a learned public which has existed without break from its beginning up to the present can accredit ancient history. Beyond such a society everything is *terra incognita*; and the history of peoples who live outside it can only begin from the moment they came into contact with it. This happened to the Jewish people at the time of the Ptolemies when the Bible was translated into Greek; without this, little credence would have been given to their isolated accounts. From that moment, once the starting-point was properly ascertained, their history can be followed. It is the same with all other peoples. The first page of Thucydides, says Hume, is the sole beginning of all true history.

of progress through the political institutions of our Continent, which is probably destined to give laws to all other parts of the world. Applying the same method of study everywhere, both to the internal civil constitutions and laws of the States, and to their external relations to each other, we see how in both relations the good they contained served for a certain period to elevate and glorify particular nations, and with themselves, their arts and sciences – until the defects attaching to their institutions came in time to cause their overthrow. And yet their very ruin leaves always a germ of growing enlightenment behind, which being further developed by every revolution, acts as a preparation for a subsequent higher stage of progress and improvement. Thus, as I believe, we can discover a clue which may serve for more than the explanation of the confused play of human things, or for the art of political prophecy in reference to future changes in States – a use which has been already made of the history of mankind, even although it was regarded as the incoherent effect of an unregulated freedom! Much more than all this is attained by the idea of Human History viewed as founded upon the assumption of a universal plan in Nature. For this idea gives us a new ground of hope, as it opens up to us a consoling view of the future, in which the human species is represented in the far distance as having at last worked itself up to a condition in which all the germs implanted in it by Nature may be fully developed, and its destination here on earth fulfilled. Such a *justification of Nature* – or rather, let us say, of *Providence* – is no insignificant motive for choosing a particular point of view in contemplating the course of the world. For, what avails it, to magnify the glory and wisdom of the creation in the irrational domain of Nature, and to recommend it to devout contemplation, if that part of the great display of the supreme wisdom, which presents the End of it all in the history of the Human Race, is to be viewed as only furnishing perpetual objections to that glory and wisdom? The spectacle of History if thus viewed would compel us to turn away our eyes from it against our will; and the despair of ever finding a perfect rational Purpose in its movement, would reduce us to hope for it, if at all, only in another world.

This Idea of a Universal History is no doubt to a certain extent of an *a priori* character, but it would be a misunderstanding of my object were it imagined that I have any wish to supplant the empirical cultivation of History, or the narration of the actual facts of experience. It is only a thought of what a philosophical mind – which, as such, must be thoroughly versed in History – might be induced to attempt from another standpoint. Besides, the praiseworthy circumstantiality with which our history is now written, may well lead one to raise the question as to how our remote posterity will be able to cope with the burden of history as it will be transmitted to them after a few centuries? They will surely estimate the history of the oldest times, of which the documentary records may have been long lost, only from the point of view of what will interest them, and no doubt this will be what the nations and governments have achieved, or failed to achieve, in the universal world-wide relation. It is well to be giving thought to this relation; and at the same time to draw the attention of ambitious rulers and their servants to the only means by which they can leave an honourable memorial of themselves to latest times. And this may also form a *minor* motive for attempting to produce such a philosophical History.

On the Commonplace : That May Be Correct in Theory but Is Useless in Practice

---

ON THE RELATIONSHIP OF THEORY TO PRACTICE IN INTERNATIONAL LAW VIEWED FROM A UNIVERSAL-PHILANTHROPIC, i.e. COSMO-POLITICAL STANDPOINT[1]
(Against Moses Mendelssohn)

Does the human race, viewed as a whole, appear worthy of being loved; or is it an object which we must look upon with repugnance, so that, while in order to avoid misanthropy, we continue to wish for it all that is good, we yet can never expect good from it, and would rather turn our eyes away from its affairs? The reply to this question will depend on the answer that may be given to this other question; 'Is human nature endowed with capacities from which we can infer that the species will always advance to a better condition, so that the Evil of the present and past times will be lost in the Good of the future? Under such a condition we may indeed love the race, at least when viewed as continually approaching to the Good, but otherwise we might well despise or even hate it, let the affectation of a universal philanthropy – which at most would then be only a benevolent wish, and not a satisfied love – express itself as it may. For, what is and remains bad, especially in the form of an international and mutual violation of the holiest rights of men, cannot but be hated, whatever efforts may be made to constrain the feeling of love towards it. Not that this dislike of human evil would prompt us to inflict evil upon men, but it would at least lead us to have as little to do with them as possible.

[1] Jerusalem, II, 44-77.

Moses Mendelssohn was of this latter opinion; and he has opposed it to his friend Lessing's hypothesis of a 'Divine Education of the Human Race'. It is, in his view,[1] a mere illusion to hold 'that the whole of mankind here below shall always move forwards in the course of time, and thus perfect itself'. He says, 'We see the human race as a whole making oscillations backward and forward; but it has never taken a few steps forwards without soon sliding back with double rapidity to its former state'. This is then the very movement of the stone of Sisyphus; and we might thus suppose, like the Hindoo, that the earth is a place for the expiation of old and forgotten sins. 'The individual man', he continues, 'advances, but mankind, as a whole moves up and down between fixed limits, and maintains through all periods of time about the same stage of morality, the same amount of religion and irreligion, of virtue and vice, of happiness (?) and misery.' These assertions he introduces by saying: 'You would fain find out what are the purposes of Providence with regard to mankind. But form no hypotheses (he had formerly said 'theory'), only look around on what actually happens; and if you can survey the history of all times, upon what has happened from the beginning. This gives facts. This much must have belonged to the purpose of Providence, and must have been approved in the plan of Wisdom, or at least must have been adopted along with it.'

I am of a different opinion. If it is a spectacle worthy of a Divinity to see a virtuous man struggling with adversities and temptation, and yet holding his ground against them, it is a spectacle most unworthy – I will not say of a Divinity, but even of the commonest well-disposed man – to see the human race making a few steps upwards in virtue from one period to another, and soon thereafter falling down again as deep into vice and misery as before. To gaze for a short while upon this tragedy, may be moving and instructive; but the curtain must at last be let fall upon it. For when prolonged in this manner, it becomes a farce; and although the actors may not become weary, being fools, yet the spectator will become tired of it, having enough in one or two

---

[1] It is not immediately apparent how a universal philanthropic assumption leads to a civil constitution for the world (albeit one based on international law), as the sole condition in which those faculties of man which make our species worthy to be loved come to full fruition. This connection will be made clear at the end of the section.

acts, where he has got grounds to infer that this play that comes never to an end is but an eternal repetition of the same thing. The punishment that follows at the close may, indeed, in the case of a mere drama, compensate for the unpleasant feelings by the issue of the whole. But to see numberless vices, even accompanied with occasional virtues, towered and heaped on each other in the world of reality in order that there may be some grand retribution in the end, is – at least according to our ideas – altogether opposed to the morality of a wise Creator and Governor of the world.

I will, therefore, venture to assume that as the human race is continually advancing in civilization and culture as its natural purpose, so it is continually making progress for the better in relation to the moral end of its existence, and that this progress, although it may be sometimes interrupted, will never be entirely broken off or stopped. It is not necessary for me to prove this assumption; the burden of proof lies on its opponents. For I take my stand upon my innate sense of duty in this connection. Every member in the series of generations to which I belong as a man – although possibly not so well equipped with the requisite moral qualifications as I ought to be, and consequently might be – is, in fact prompted by his sense of duty so to act in reference to posterity that they may always become better, and the possibility of this must be assumed. This duty can thus be rightfully transmitted from one member of the generations to another. Now whatever doubts may be drawn from history against my hopes, and were they even of such a kind as, in case of their being demonstrated, might move me to desist from efforts which according to all appearances would be vain, yet so long as this is not made out with complete certainty, I am not entitled to give up the guidance of duty which is clear, and to adopt the prudential rule of not working at the impracticable, since this is not clear but is mere hypothesis. And, however uncertain I may be as to whether we may rightly hope that the human race will attain to a better condition, yet this individual uncertainty cannot detract from the general rule of conduct or from the necessary assumption in the practical relation that such a condition is practicable.

This hope of better times, without which an earnest desire to do something conducive to the common well-being would never have warmed the human heart, has always exercised an influence upon the practical conduct of the well-disposed of mankind; and the good Mendelssohn must also have recognized its power in his own zealous efforts for the enlightenment and prosperity of the nation to which he belonged. For he could not have reasonably hoped by himself alone to have accomplished those objects, unless others after him were to advance further on the same path. In presence of the saddening spectacle, not merely of the evils which oppress the human race from natural causes, but still more of those which men inflict on each other, the heart is still gladdened by the prospect that it may become better in part by our unselfish benevolence, even after we have been long in the grave and have ceased to be able to reap the fruits which we ourselves have sown. Arguments from experience against the success of such endeavours resolved and carried out in hope, are of no avail. For the fact that something has not yet succeeded, is no proof that it will never succeed; nor would such an argument even justify the abandonment of any practical or technical efforts, such as, for example, the attempts to make pleasure excursions in aerostatic balloons. And still less would such conditions justify the abandonment of a moral purpose which, as such, becomes a duty if its realization is not demonstrated to be impossible. Besides all this, many proofs can be given that the human race as a whole, is actually farther advanced in our age towards what is morally better than it ever was before, and is even considerably so when its present condition is compared with what it has been in all former ages, notwithstanding temporary impediments, which being transitory, can prove nothing against the general position. And hence the cry about the continually increasing degeneracy of the race just arises from the fact that, as it stands on a higher stage of morality, it sees so much the further before it; and thus its judgment on what men are in comparison with what they ought to be, becomes – as in our own self-examination – the more secure the more the stages of morality which mankind have already surmounted in the whole course of the world's history as it is now known to us.

The question next arises as to the means by which this continuous progress to the better may be maintained and even hastened. When carefully considered, we soon see that as this process must go on to an incalculable distance of time, it cannot depend so much on what we may do of ourselves, for instance, on the education we give to the younger generation, or on the method by which we may proceed in order to realize it, as on what human nature as such will do *in* and with us, to compel us to move in a track into which we would not readily have betaken ourselves. For, it is from human nature in general, or rather – since supreme wisdom is requisite for the accomplishment of this End – it is from *Providence* alone that we can expect a result which proceeds by relation to the whole and reacts through the whole upon the parts. Men with their *plans* start, on the contrary, only from the parts, and even continue to regard the parts alone, while the whole as such is viewed as too great for them to influence and as attainable by them only in idea. And this holds all the more seeing that, being adverse to each other in their plans, they would hardly be able to unite together in order to influence the whole out of any particular free purpose of their own.

Nevertheless universal violence and the evils arising from it, at last force a people of necessity to resolve to subject themselves to the constraint of public Law, which is the very means that reason itself prescribes; and thus to form and enter into a civil or *political Constitution*. And, in like manner, the evils arising from constant wars by which the States seek to reduce or subdue each other, bring them at last, even against their will, also to enter into a universal or *cosmo-political Constitution*. Or should such a condition of universal peace – as has often been the case with overgrown States – be even more dangerous to liberty on another side than war, by introducing the most terrible despotism, then the evils from which deliverance is sought will compel the introduction of a condition among the nations which does not assume the form of a universal Commonwealth or Empire under one Sovereign but of a FEDERATION regulated by law, according to the *Right of Nations* as concerted in common.

For, the advancing civilization of the several States is accompanied with a growing propensity to enlarge themselves at the cost of others, by fraud or force. And thus wars are multiplied; and greater expenditure is always caused by the necessary maintenance of increased standing armies, kept in a state of readiness and discipline and provided ever and again with more numerous instruments of war. At the same time the prices of all the necessaries of life must go on continually increasing while there can be no hope of a proportionately progressive growth of the metals that represent them. Nor does peace ever last so long that the savings during it would equal the expenditure required for the next war. Against this evil the introduction of national debts is indeed an ingenious resource, but it is one which must annihilate itself in the long run. Under pressure of all these evils, what goodwill ought to have done but did not do, is at last brought about by sheer weakness, so that every State becomes so organized within that it is no longer the Sovereign – to whom war properly costs nothing since he carries it on at the cost of the people–but it is the People on whom the cost falls, who have the deciding voice as to whether there shall be war or no. This is necessarily implied in the realization of the idea of the original Contract. But when the decision of the question of War falls to the people, neither will the desire of aggrandizement nor mere verbal injuries be likely to induce them to put themselves in danger of personal privation and want, by inflicting upon themselves the calamities of war, which the Sovereign in his own person escapes. And thus posterity, no longer oppressed by undeserved burdens, and owing it not to the direct love of others for them, but only to the rational self-love of each age for itself, will be able to make progress even in moral relations. For each Commonwealth, now become unable to injure any other by violence, must maintain itself by Right alone; and it may hope on real grounds that the others being constituted like itself will then come, on occasions of need, to its aid.

This, however, it may be said, is only opinion and mere hypothesis, and it is uncertain, like all theories which aim at stating the only suitable natural cause for a proposed effect that is not wholly in our own power. Further, even regarded as such, the cause suggested, when it is taken in relation to an already existing State, does not contain a principle that is applicable to the Subject so as to compel the production of the effect but is only available through Sovereigns who are free from compulsion. But although it does not lie in the nature of men, according to common experience, to make a voluntary renunciation of their power, yet in pressing circumstances this is not at all impossible. And so it may be regarded as an expression not unsuitable to the moral wishes and hopes of men conscious of their own incapability, when it is said that the circumstances requisite for the end in question are to be expected from *Providence*. For it is to Providence we must look for the realization of the End of *Humanity* in the whole of the species, as furnishing the means for the attainment of the final destination of man, through the free exercise of his powers so far as they can go. For to this End, the purposes of individual men, regarded separately, are directly opposed. Yet even the oppositions of the inclinations from which evil arises, in their mutual antagonism, give free play to Reason and opportunity to subject them all; and so, instead of the Evil which destroys itself, it makes the Good predominant, which when it is more established, will continue thereafter to maintain itself.

Human Nature appears nowhere less amiable than in the relation of whole nations to each other. No State is for a moment secure against another in its independence or its possessions. The will to subdue each other or to reduce their power, is always rampant; and the equipment for defence, which often makes peace even more oppressive and more destructive of internal prosperity than war, can never be relaxed. Against such evils there is no possible remedy other than a system of *International Right* founded upon public laws conjoined with power, to which every State must submit – according to the analogy of the civil or political Right of individuals in any State. For, a lasting universal Peace on the basis of the so-called *Balance of Power in Europe* is a mere chimera. It is like the house described by Swift, which was built by an architect so perfectly in accordance with all the laws of equilibrium, that when a sparrow lighted upon it, it immediately fell. 'But', it may be said, 'the States will never submit to such compulsory laws; and the proposal to institute a universal International State or Union of Nations – a Union under whose power all the separate States shall voluntarily arrange themselves in order to obey its laws – may sound ever so pretty in the theory of an Abbé de Saint-Pierre or a Rousseau, but it is of no value for practical purposes; and as such it has always been laughed at by great Statesmen, and still more by Sovereigns and Rulers, as a childish and pedantic idea fit only for the schools from which it takes its rise.'

For my part, on the contrary, I trust to a theory which is based upon the principle of Right as determining what the relations between men and States *ought to be*; and which lays down to these earthly gods the maxim that they ought so to proceed in their disputes that such a universal International State may be introduced thereby, and to assume it therefore as not only possible in practice but such as may yet be presented in reality. – Nay more, this theory is further to be regarded as founded upon the nature of things, which compels movement in a direction even against the will of man. 'Fata volentem ducunt, nolentem trahunt.' Under the Nature of things, Human Nature is also to be taken into account; and as in Human Nature there is always a living respect for Right and Duty, I neither can nor will regard it as so sunk in evil that the practical moral Reason could ultimately fail to triumph over this evil, even after many of its attempts have failed. And so it is that I would represent Human Nature as worthy to be loved. In the widest cosmo-political relation the position therefore holds good, that what is valid on rational grounds as a Theory, is also valid and good for Practice.

Perpetual Peace : A Philosophical Essay

THE PERPETUAL PEACE

These words were once put by a Dutch innkeeper on his signboard, as a satirical inscription over the representation of a churchyard. We need not enquire whether they hold of men in general, or particularly of the rulers of States who seem never to be satisfied of war, or even only of the Philosophers who dream that sweet dream of Peace. The author of the present Sketch, however, would make one remark by way of reservation in reference to it. It is well known that the practical politician looks down, with great self-complacency, on the theoretical politician, when he comes in the way, as a mere pedant whose empty ideas can bring no danger to the State, proceeding as it does, upon principles derived from experience; and the theorizer may, therefore, be allowed to throw down his eleven skittle-pins at once, while the sagacious Statesman who knows the world, need not, on that account, even give himself a turn! This being so, should any matter of controversy arise between them, the practical Statesman must so far proceed consistently and not scent out a danger for the State behind the opinions of the theoretical thinker, which he has ventured in a good intent publicly to express. By which 'saving clause' the Author will consider himself expressly safeguarded against all malicious interpretation.

First Section

Which contains the preliminary articles of a perpetual peace between states

1. 'No conclusion of Peace shall be held to be valid as such, when it has been made with the secret reservation of the material for a future War.'

For, in that case, it would be a mere truce, or a suspension of hostilities, and not a *Peace*. A Peace properly signifies the end of *all* hostilities; and to qualify it by the addition of the epithet 'perpetual' or 'eternal' is pleonastic and suspicious. All existing causes for a future war – although they were perhaps unknown to the contracting parties at the time – are to be regarded as entirely removed, or annihilated by the Treaty of Peace, even if they could be picked out by the dexterity of an acute interpretation from the terms of documents in the public Archives. There may be a mental reservation of old pretensions or claims with the view of asserting them at a future time, of which, however, neither party makes any mention for the present because they are too exhausted to continue the war, while there remains the evil will to take advantage of the first favourable opportunity for this purpose; but this is illegitimate and belongs to the Jesuitical casuistry of Politics. If we consider the subject of reservation in itself, it is beneath the dignity of the Rulers of States to have to do with it, and, in like manner, the complacent participation in such deductions is beneath the dignity of their Ministers. But if the true glory of the State is placed in the continual increase of its power, by any means whatever – according to certain 'enlightened' notions of national policy – then this judgment will certainly appear to those who adopt that view, to be impractical and pedantic.

2. 'No State having an existence by itself – whether it be small or large – shall be acquirable by another State through inheritance, exchange, purchase or donation.'

A State is not to be regarded as a property or patrimony, like the soil on which it may be settled. It is a society of men, over which no one but itself has the right to rule or to dispose. Like the stem of a tree it has its one root, and to incorporate it as a graft in another State, is to destroy its existence as a moral Person; it is to reduce it to a Thing, and thereby to contradict the idea of the original Compact without which a Right over a people is inconceivable.[1] Everyone knows what danger the prejudice in favour

---

[1] A hereditary kingdom is not a State which can be bequeathed to another State, but one whose right to rule can be transmitted to another physical person. The State thus acquires a ruler, but the ruler does not as such (that is, as already possessing another kingdom) acquire the State.

of thus acquiring States has brought to Europe – for in the other parts of the world it has never been known; and that this has gone on even up to our own times. It was considered that the States might marry one another; and hence, on the one hand, a new kind of industry in the effort to acquire predominance by family alliances, without any expenditure of power; and, on the other hand, to increase, in this way, by new possessions the extent of a Country. Further, the lending of the troops of one State to another on pay, to fight against an enemy not at war with their own State, has arisen from the same erroneous view; for the Subjects of the State are thus used and abused as Things that may be managed at will.

3. 'Standing Armies shall be entirely abolished in the course of time.'

For they threaten other States incessantly with War, by their appearing to be always equipped to enter upon it. Standing armies (*miles perpetuus*) excite the States to outrival each other in the number of their armed men which has no limits. By the expense occasioned thereby, Peace becomes in the long run even more oppressive than a short war; and Standing Armies are thus the cause of aggressive wars undertaken in order to get rid of this burden. Besides, it has to be considered that for men to be hired for pay to kill or to be killed, appears to imply the using of them as mere machines and instruments in the hand of another, although it be the State; and that this cannot be well reconciled with the Right of humanity in our own person. It is quite otherwise, however, as regards the voluntary exercise of the citizens in arms at certain appointed periods; for the object in view is thereby to protect themselves and their country from external attacks. The accumulation of treasure in a State would have the same sort of influence as regular troops, in so far as, being regarded by other States as a threat of war, it might compel them to anticipate such a war by an attack upon the State. For of the three powers known in the State as *the Power of the Army, the Power of external Alliance* and *the Power of Money* the money-power might well become the most reliable instrument of war, did not the difficulty of determining its real force stand in the way of its employment.

4. 'No National Debts shall be contracted in connection with the external affairs of the State.'

No objection can be taken to seeking assistance, either without or within the State, on behalf of the economical administration of the country; such as, for the improvement of highways, or in support of new colonies, or in the establishment of resources against dearth and famine. A loan, whether externally or internally, as a source of aid in such cases is above suspicion. But a Credit System when used by the Powers as a hostile antagonistic instrument against each other, and when the debts under it go on increasing to an excessive extent and yet are always secured for the present (because all the creditors are not to put in their claims at once), is a dangerous money power. This arrangement – the ingenious invention of a commercial people in this century – constitutes, in fact, a treasure for the carrying on of War; it may exceed the treasures of all the other States taken together, and it can only be exhausted by the forthcoming deficit of the taxes – which, however, may be long delayed even by the animation of the national commerce from the reaction of the system upon industry and trade. The facility given by this system for engaging in War, combined with the inclination of Rulers towards it (an inclination which seems to be implanted in human nature) – is, therefore, a great obstacle in the way of a Perpetual Peace. The prohibition of it must be laid down as a Preliminary Article in the conditions of such a Peace, even more strongly on the further ground, that the national bankruptcy, which it inevitably brings at last, would necessarily involve many other States that are without debt in the loss; and this would be a public lesion of these other States. And consequently the other States are justified in allying themselves against such a State and its pretensions.

5. 'No State shall intermeddle by force with the Constitution or Government of another State.'

For what could justify it in doing so? The scandal or offence given by that State to the subjects of another State perhaps? Then the offending State should much rather serve as a warning by the example of the great Evils which people have drawn upon themselves through their lawlessness; and generally a bad example given by one free person to another (as a *scandalum acceptum*), is not a lesion of his Right. But it is a different case where a State has become divided in two by internal disunion, and when each of the parts represents itself as a separate State laying claim to the whole; for, to furnish assistance to one of them under these circumstances might not be reckoned as the intermeddling of an External State with the Constitution of another, as that other is then in a condition of Anarchy. Yet so long as this internal strife is not decided, such an interference on the part of external Powers would be a violation of the Rights of an independent people that is only struggling with an external evil. It would therefore itself be a cause of offence, and would make the Autonomy of all other States insecure.

6. 'No State at war with another shall adopt such modes of hostility as would necessarily render mutual confidence impossible in a future Peace; such as, the employment of Assassins (*percussores*) or Poisoners (*venefici*), the violation of a Capitulation, the instigation of Treason and such like.'

These are dishonourable stratagems. For there must be some trust in the habit and disposition even of an enemy in War, otherwise no Peace could be concluded, and the hostilities would pass into an internecine war of extermination. War, however, is only a melancholy necessity of asserting Right by force – where, as in the state of Nature, there is no common tribunal with the rightful power to adjudicate on causes of quarrel. In such circumstances neither of the two parties can be declared to be an unjust enemy as this presupposes a judicial sentence: but the *issue* of the conflict – as in the 'judgments of God' – has to decide on which side is the Right. As between States, however, a punitive war, according to the principle of punishment, is inconceivable; because there is no relation of subordination between them, as between Superior and Inferior. Hence it follows that a war of extermination, in which the process of annihilation would strike at both parties, and likewise at all Right at the same time, would reach Perpetual Peace only on the final Golgotha of the human race. Such a war, therefore, as well as the use of such means as might lead to it, must be absolutely unallowable. And that the means referred to inevitably lead to that result, is apparent from the fact that when these hellish arts, which are debasing in themselves, are once brought into use, they are not kept long within the limits of war. Such, for instance, is the employment of Spies. In this case it is only the *dishonesty* of others that is employed, and as such practices and habits cannot be exterminated once, they

founded.[1] As regards public Right, the republican principles, therefore, lie originally and essentially, at the basis of the Civil Constitution in all its forms; and the only question for us now is as to whether it is also the only Constitution that can lead to a Perpetual Peace?

Now, in point of fact, the Republican Constitution, in addition to the purity of its origin as arising from the original source of the

[1] Legal (external) freedom cannot be defined, as is customarily done, by the right [Befügnis] to do everything one wants so long as one does not do wrong to anybody else. For what does a right mean: the possibility of acting so long as one does not thereby do wrong to anyone. The definition would thus read: Freedom is the possibility of actions which do no wrong to anyone. One does no wrong (one can do what one wants) only if one does no wrong: consequently it is an empty tautology. My external (legal) freedom should rather be defined as follows: it is the right to obey no external laws other than those to which I could have given my consent.

In the same way external (legal) equality in a state is a relationship between the citizens in which a person cannot legally bind another without himself being bound by the law, and in which he can also be reciprocally bound by the other person. (No explanation is required of the principle of legal dependence as this is already contained in the concept of a state's constitution.)

The validity of these inborn rights [Rechte], which belong necessarily to mankind and are inalienable, is confirmed and raised to a higher level through the principle of the legal relationship of man himself to higher beings (if he imagines such things), for he regards himself as the citizen of a supersensuous world according to the very same axioms. As far as my freedom is concerned, I am not bound by the divine law which I know through reason alone, except in so far as I could have given my consent to it. For I am only able to form a concept of the divine will through the law of freedom of my own reason. With regard to the highest being besides God which I liked to imagine (a great Aeon) the principle of equality provides no reason why, if I do my duty in my position as he does in his, I should solely have the duty of obeying and he that of commanding. The reason why this principle of equality does not pertain to the relationship with God (as the principle of freedom does) is that he is the sole being to whom the concept of duty does not apply.

With respect to the right of equality which applies to all citizens as subjects, the answer to the problem whether hereditary nobility should be allowed reduces itself to this: should the rank ascribed to one citizen over another by the state follow merit or not. Now it is clear that if rank is tied to birth it is very uncertain whether merit (political skill and loyalty) will also follow: it is equivalent to a favourite without any merit being entrusted with command. This is something which the general will of the people would never agree to in an original contract (which is the basic principle of all law). For a nobleman is not necessarily a noble man. As to nobility of office (as one might call the higher ranks of the administration which have to be gained by merit), rank here is not the property of the person but of the office, and equality is not thereby infringed. For when anyone lays down his office he simultaneously lays down his rank and returns to the people.

conception of Right, includes also the prospect of realizing the desired object: Perpetual Peace among the nations. And the reason of this may be stated as follows: According to the Republican Constitution, the consent of the citizens as members of the State is required to determine at any time the question, 'Whether there shall be war or not?' Hence, nothing is more natural than they should be very loth to enter upon so undesirable an undertaking; for in decreeing it they would necessarily be resolving to bring upon themselves all the horrors of War. And, in their case, this implies such consequences as these: to have to fight in their own persons; to supply the costs of the war out of their own property; to have sorrowfully to repair the devastation which it leaves behind; and, as a crowning evil, to have to take upon themselves at the end a burden of debt which will go on embittering peace itself, and which it will be impossible ever to pay off on account of the constant threatening of further impending wars. On the other hand, in a Constitution where the Subject is not a voting member of the State, and which is, therefore, not Republican, the resolution to go to war is a matter of the smallest concern in the world. For, in this case, the Ruler, who, as such, is not a mere citizen but the Owner of the State, need not in the least suffer personally by war, nor has he to sacrifice his pleasures of the table or of the chase or his pleasant places, court-festivals and such like. He can, therefore, resolve for war from insignificant reasons, as if it were but a hunting expedition; and, as regards its propriety, he may leave the justification of it without concern to the diplomatic body, who are always too ready to give their services for that purpose.

The Republican Constitution is not to be confounded with the *Democratic* Constitution. But as this is commonly done, the following remarks must be made in order to guard against this confusion. The various forms of the State (*Civitas*) may be divided either according to the difference of the *Persons* who hold the highest authority in the State, or according to the *mode of the governing* of the people through its supreme Head. The first is properly called the form of the Sovereignty in the State (*forma imperii*). There are only three forms of this kind possible, according as *one* only, or as *some* in connection with each other, or as *all* those constituting the Civil Society combined together may happen to possess the governing power; and thus we have either an AUTOCRACY constituted by the power of a Monarch, or an ARISTOCRACY constituted by the power of the Nobles, or a DEMOCRACY constituted by the power of the People. The second principle of division is taken from the form of the Government (*forma regiminis*); and viewing the Constitution as the act of the common or universal will by which a number of men become a People, it regards the mode in which the State, founding on the Constitution, makes use of its supreme power. In this connection the form of government is either *republican* or *despotic*. Republicanism regarded as the constitutive principle of a State is the political severance of the Executive Power of the Government from the Legislative Power. Despotism is in principle the irresponsible executive administration of the State by laws laid down and enacted by the same power that administers them; and consequently the Ruler so far exercises his own private will as if it were the public Will. Of the three forms of the State, a *Democracy*, in the proper sense of the word, is necessarily *a despotism*; because it establishes an Executive power in which All resolve about, and, it may be, also against, any One who is not in accord with it; and consequently the All who thus resolve are really not all; which is a contradiction of the Universal Will with itself and with liberty.

Every form of Government, in fact, which is not *representative*, is properly a spurious form of Government or not a form of Government at all; because the Lawgiver in one and the same person, may, at the same time be the executive administrator of his own Will. And although the other two political constitutions –Autocracy and Aristocracy – are always so far defective in that they afford opportunity for such a mode of government, it is at least possible in their cases that a mode of government may be adopted in conformity with the *spirit* of a representative system. Thus Frederick the Great was wont to say of himself that he was 'merely the highest servant of the State'.[1] But the Democratic Constitution, on the contrary, makes such a spirit impossible; because under it everyone wishes to be master. It may, therefore, be said that the fewer the number of the Rulers or personal Administrators of the power of the State, and the greater the

---

[1] [The high-sounding titles accorded to princes should not be an occasion for pride; rather they should make princes reflect humbly on the immense duties with which God has entrusted them.]

representation embodied in them, so much the more does the political constitution harmonise with the possibility of Republicanism; and such a constitution may hope to raise itself, by gradual reforms, to the Republican Ideal. On this account, it is more difficult to attain to this one perfect constitution according to the principles of Right in an Aristocracy than in a Monarchy, and in a Democracy it is impossible otherwise than by violent revolution. As regards the people, however, the mode of Government is incomparably more important than the form of the Constitution, although the degree of conformity in the Constitution to the end of government is also of much importance.[1] But if the mode of Government is to conform to the idea of Right, it must embody the representative system. For in this system alone is a really republican mode of Government possible; and without it, let the Constitution be what it may, it will be despotic and violent. In none of the ancient so-called 'Republics', was this known; and they necessarily became resolved in consequence into an absolute form of despotism, which is always most bearable when the supreme power is concentrated in a single individual.

11. Second Definitive Article in the conditions of a Perpetual Peace. 'The Right of Nations shall be founded on a Federation of Free States.'

Peoples or nations regarded as States, may be judged like individual men. Now men living in a state of Nature independent of external laws, by their very contiguity to each other, give occasion to mutual injury or lesion. Every people, for the sake of its own security, thus may and ought to demand from any other, that it shall enter along with it into a constitution, similar to the Civil Constitution, in which the Right of each shall be secured. This would give rise to an INTERNATIONAL FEDERATION OF THE PEOPLES. This, however, would not have to take the form of a *State* made up of these Nations. For that would involve a contradiction, since every State, properly so called, contains the relation of a Superior as the lawgiver to an Inferior as the people subject to

---

[1] [Kant rejects Pope's dictum:

'For forms of government let fools contest:
Whate'er is best administered, is best.'

It is either tautologous or wrong. Without a good form or constitution a state which is well administered to-day may run aground tomorrow.]

their laws. Many nations, however, in one State, would constitute only one nation, which is contradictory to the principle assumed, as we are here considering the Right of *Nations* in relation to each other, in so far as they constitute different States and are not to be fused into one.

The attachment of Savages to the lawless liberty of rather being engaged in incessant conflict with each other, than submitting to a legal constraint constituted by themselves, is well known. Hence their preference of wild freedom to rational liberty is looked upon by us with profound contempt, and characterized as barbarism, coarseness, and a brutal degradation of humanity. Thus it might be thought that civilized Nations, being each united into a State, would of necessity make all haste to advance as soon as possible out of any semblance to a condition that is so much condemned. Instead of this, however, we rather find that every *State* founds its Majesty[1] on not being subject to any external legal coercion; and the glory of its Ruler or Head is made to consist in the fact that without his requiring to encounter any danger himself, many thousands stand ready to be sacrificed at his command for a cause which may be no concern of theirs.[2] Thus the difference between the white savages of Europe and the red savages of America, consists mainly in this: that while some tribes of the latter have been entirely eaten up by their enemies, the former know how to make a better use of the vanquished than to eat them, by rather adding them to the number of their subjects, and thereby increasing the multitude of their instruments and means for still more extensive wars.

The depravity of human nature is exhibited without disguise in the unrestrained relations of the Nations to each other, whereas in the legalized state of Civil Society it is greatly veiled under the constraint of government. In view of it, we may well wonder that the word 'RIGHT' has not yet been entirely banished from the policy of war as pedantic, and that no State has as yet ventured to declare itself publicly in favour of that doctrine. For Grotius, Pufendorf, Vattel and the others – miserable comforters all of them

---

[1] The majesty of a *people* or *nation* is an erroneous and absurd expression.

[2] Thus a Bulgarian Prince when the Greek Emperor was desirous to bring his quarrel with him to an end by a duel, gave his answer by saying: 'A smith who has tongs will not pluck the glowing iron out of the coals with his hands'.

– are still always quoted cordially for the *justification* of an out-break of war, although their philosophically or diplomatically composed codes have not, nor could have, the slightest *legal* force, since the States as such stand under no common legal constraint; and there is not an example of a State having been ever moved to desist from its purpose by arguments, although armed with testimonies of such important men. Yet the homage which every State thus renders – at least in words – to the conception of Right still proves that there is to be found in man a higher and greater moral capacity, though it may slumber for a time; and it shows that this capacity will yet attain the mastery over the evil principle in him (the existence of which cannot be denied) and makes him hope for the same from others. For the word 'Right' would otherwise never enter into the vocabulary of States desirous to go to war with each other, unless it were merely to make a jest of it, in the manner of the Gallic prince who declared that 'it is the prerogative of the strong to make the weak obey them'.

The means by which States prosecute their Rights at present can never be by a form of process – as if there were an external tribunal – but can only be by War; but even the favourable issue of war in *victory* will not decide a matter of Right. A treaty of Peace may, indeed, put an end to a particular war, yet not to the general condition of war, in which a pretext can always be found for new hostilities. Nor can such a pretext under these circum-stances be regarded as 'unjust' for in that state of society, every nation is the judge of its own cause. At the same time, the position which, according to the Right of nature, holds of men in a lawless condition that 'they ought to advance out of that condition', cannot according to the Right of Nations be directly applied to States; because as States they have already within themselves a legal Constitution and have thus outgrown the coercive Right of others to bring them under a wider legal constitution according to conceptions of Right. And yet Reason on the throne of the highest moral law-giving power, absolutely condemns War as a mode or Right, and, on the contrary, makes the state of Peace an immediate duty. But the state of Peace cannot be founded or secured without a compact of the Nations with each other. Hence there must be a compact of a special kind which may be called a PACIFIC FEDERATION (*foedus pacificum*), and which would be distinguished from a mere treaty or *Compact of Peace* (*pactum pacis*) in that the latter merely puts an end to one war whereas the former would seek to put an end to all wars for ever. This Federation will not aim at the acquisition of any of the political powers of a State, but merely at the preservation and guarantee for itself, and likewise for the other confederated States, of the liberty that is proper to a State; and this would not require these States to subject themselves for this purpose – as is the case with men in the state of nature – to public laws and to coercion under them. The practicability and objective realization of this idea of *Federalism*, inasmuch as it has to spread itself over all States and thereby lead to Perpetual Peace, may be easily shown. For if happy circumstances bring it about that a powerful and enlightened people form themselves into a Republic – which by its very nature must be disposed in favour of Perpetual Peace – this will furnish a centre of federative union for other States to attach themselves to, and thus to secure the conditions of Liberty among all States, according to the idea of the Right of Nations. And such a Union would extend wider and wider, in the course of time, by the addition of further connections of this kind.

It is intelligible that a People should say: 'There shall be no war among us: for we will form ourselves into a State and constitute of ourselves a supreme legislative, governing and judicial Power which will peacefully settle our differences'. But if this State says: 'There shall be no war between me and other States, although I recognize no supreme legislative power which will secure me my Right and whose Right I will also secure'; then there is no intelligible basis upon which any security for such Rights could be founded unless it were a surrogate of the union embodied in Civil Society. And this can be nothing but *a free Federation of the States*, which Reason must necessarily connect with the idea of the Right of Nations if there is anything further to be thought in connection with it.

The notion of a *Right to go to war*, cannot be properly conceived as an element in the Right of Nations. For it would be equivalent to a Right to determine what is just not by universal external laws limiting the freedom of every individual alike, but through one-sided maxims that operate by means of force. If such a right be conceivable at all it would amount, in fact, to this: that in the case of men who are so disposed it is quite right for them to destroy and devour each other, and thus to find Perpetual Peace only in the wide grave which is to cover all the abomination of the deeds of violence and their authors! For States viewed in relation to each other, there can be only one way, according to reason, of emerging from that lawless condition which contains nothing but occasions of war. Just as in the case of individual men, Reason would drive them to give up their savage lawless freedom, to accommodate themselves to public coercive laws, and thus to form an ever-growing STATE OF NATIONS, such as would at last embrace all the Nations of the Earth. But as the Nations, according to their ideas of international Right, will not have such a positive rational system, and consequently reject in fact (*in thesi*) what is right in theory (*in hypothesi*), it cannot be realised in this pure form. Hence instead of the positive idea of a *Universal Republic* – if all is not to be lost – we shall have as result only the *negative* surrogate of a *Federation of the States* averting war, subsisting in an external union, and always extending itself over the world. And thus the current of those inclinations and passions of men which are antagonistic to Right and productive of war, may be checked, although there will still be a danger of their breaking out betimes. For as Virgil puts it:

'Furor,
Impius intus fremit horridus ore cruento'.[1]

III. Third Definitive Article in the conditions of a Perpetual Peace. 'The Rights of men as Citizens of the world in a cosmo-political system, shall be restricted to conditions of universal Hospitality.'

In this as in the previous Articles, the question is not about a relation of Philanthropy, but one of Right. 'Hospitality' here indicates the Right of a stranger in consequence of his arrival on the soil of another country, not to be treated by its citizens as an enemy. As a stranger he may be turned away, if this can be done without involving his death; but so long as he conducts himself peacefully in the place where he may happen to be, he is not to be dealt with in a hostile way. The stranger may not lay claim to be

---

[1] [Kant considers that nations should not merely give thanks at the end of wars: they should also ask forgiveness for continuing to settle problems by means which are barbarous and cannot obtain the rights of a single state.]

entertained *by right as a Guest* – for this would require a special friendly compact to make him for a certain time the member of a household – he may only claim a *Right of Resort* or of visitation. All men are entitled to present themselves thus to society in virtue of their Right to the common possession of the surface of the earth, to no part of which anyone had originally more right than another; and upon which, from its being a globe, they cannot scatter themselves to infinite distances, but must at last bear to live side by side with each other. Uninhabitable portions of this surface are formed by seas and deserts; these present barriers to the fellowship of men in society; but they are of such a nature that the *ship* or the *camel*, 'the ship of the desert', makes it possible for men to approach each other over these unappropriated regions, and thus to turn the Right which the human species have in common to the surface of the earth, into a means for social intercourse. The inhospitality practised, for instance, on the Barbary coasts, of plundering ships in the neighbouring seas and making slaves of stranded mariners, or that of the sandy deserts, as practised by Arab Badouins who regard their access to nomadic tribes as constituting a right to plunder them, is thus contrary to the Right of Nature. But this Right of Hospitality as vested in strangers arriving in another State, does not extend further than the conditions of the *possibility of entering into social intercourse* with the inhabitants of the country. In this way distant continents may enter into peaceful relations with each other. These may at last become publicly regulated by law, and thus the human race may be always brought nearer to a Cosmo-political Constitution.

If we compare the barbarian instances of inhospitality referred to with the inhuman behaviour of civilized, and especially the commercial States of our Continent, the injustice practised by them in their first contact with foreign lands and peoples, fills us even with horror, the mere *visiting* of such peoples being regarded by them as equivalent to a *conquest*. America, the Negro Lands, the Spice Islands, the Cape of Good Hope, etc., on being dis-covered, were treated as countries that belonged to nobody; for the Aboriginal inhabitants were reckoned as nothing. In the East Indies, under the pretext of intending merely to plant commercial settlements, the Europeans introduced foreign troops, and with them oppression of the Natives, instigation of the different States to widespread wars, famine, sedition, perfidy, and all the litany of evils that can oppress the human race.

China[1] and Japan, having had experience of such guests, therefore, did wisely in limiting their intercourse. China only permitted access to her coasts but not entrance into the country. Japan restricted access to one European people, the Dutch, and they were even treated like prisoners, by being excluded from social intercourse with the Natives. The worst (or, regarded from the standpoint of a moral judge, the best) of all this is that no satisfaction is derived from this violence, as all these commercial Societies are at present on the verge of ruin. The Sugar Islands – that seat of the cruellest and completest slavery – have thrown up no real profit, but have been only indirectly of account, and that in no praiseworthy relation. They have only furnished sailors for ships of war, and have thereby contributed to the carrying on of wars in Europe. And all this has been done by nations who make a great ado about their piety, and who while drinking up iniquity like water, would have themselves regarded as the very elect of the orthodox Faith.

But the social relations between the various Peoples of the world, in narrower or wider circles, have now advanced everywhere so far that a violation of Right in *one* place of the earth, is felt *all* over it. Hence the idea of a Cosmo-political Right of the whole Human Race, is no phantastic or overstrained mode of representing Right, but is a necessary completion of the unwritten Code which carries national and international Right to a consummation in the Public Right of Mankind. Thus the whole system leads to the conclusion of a Perpetual Peace among the Nations. And it is only under the conditions now laid down that men may flatter themselves with the belief that they are making a continual approach to its realization.

First supplement

Of the guarantee of perpetual peace
The guarantee of Perpetual Peace is furnished by no less a power than the great Artist Nature herself: *Natura Daedala rerum.*

[1] [Kant examines the etymology of the name China, and the links between Tibet and Europe.]

The mechanical course of Nature visibly exhibits a design to bring forth concord out of the discord of men, even against their will. This power as a cause working by laws which are unknown to us, is commonly called *Fate*; but in view of the design manifested in the course of the world, it is to be regarded as the deep wisdom of a Higher Cause directed towards the realization of the final purpose of the human race, and predetermining the course of the world by relation to it, and as such we call it *Providence*.[1]

[1] The mechanism of nature, to which man as a sensuous being belongs, reveals a form which is fundamental to its existence. We cannot conceive of this form except by subordinating it to the pre-ordained purpose of a world creator. This predestination we call in general (divine) providence. In so far as it was laid down at the beginning of the world we call it founding providence (*providentia conditrix; semel iussit, semper parent*, Augustine), but in so far as it regulates the course of nature according to general purposive laws it is called governing providence (*providentia gubernatrix*). When it produces particular ends, which cannot be foreseen by men but only conjectured from the result, it is called guiding providence (*providentia directrix*). Finally when particular events embody divine purposes it is no longer called providence but dispensation (*directio extraordinaria*). However, because the latter events are in fact but not name miracles, it is a foolish presumption on man's part to want to interpret them. For it is absurd and full of self-conceit, however pious and humble the language that may be used, to deduce from a single event a particular principle of the effective cause, or to see the event as a purpose and not as the purely mechanical corollary of a purpose completely unknown to us.

Equally false and self-contradictory is the classification of providence, regarded *materialiter*, as it relates to objects in the world, into universal and particular. For example, providence is said to show concern for the preservation of species of creatures, but to leave individuals to chance. It is contradictory because providence is called universal precisely in order that nothing shall be considered exempt from it.

Presumably the classification was meant to be of providence regarded *formaliter*, according to the way in which its intentions are executed, i.e. the regular and the exceptional. An example of regularity is the annual death and rebirth of nature in accordance with the change of seasons. An exceptional occurrence is the way in which timber is carried by sea currents to arctic coasts, where it cannot grow, in order to supply the inhabitants who could not live without it. Although we can explain satisfactorily the physico-mechanical causes of these events (e.g. by reference to the wooded banks of rivers in temperate lands, the falling of trees into the rivers, and then their being carried along by the Gulf Stream), we must not overlook the teleological causes which indicate the concern of an intelligence governing nature.

As for the idea, common in the Schools, of divine intervention or co-operation (*concursus*) to bring about an event in the sensuous world, this must be abandoned. For to try to join dissimilars (*gryphes iungere equis*), and to let that which is itself the perfect cause of changes in the world supplement its own predetermining providence (which must thus have been inadequate) during the course of the world, is first of all self-contradictory. We do this when we say, for example, that

This power we do not indeed perceive externally in the artistic formations of Nature, nor can we even *infer* from them to it; but as in all referring of the form of things to final causes generally, we not only can, but must conjoin this thought with them in order to make their possibility conceivable after the analogy of the operations of human art. The relation and accord of these things to the moral purpose which reason immediately prescribes to us, can only be represented by an idea which theoretically indeed transcends our experience, but which is practically determinable and is well founded in reality. Such for example is the idea of a Perpetual Peace being a duty when the mechanism of nature is regarded as conducing to its realisation. The employment of the term 'Nature' rather than 'Providence' for the designation of this power is more proper and more modest in view of the limits of human reason, when we are dealing with it merely from the theoretical and not from the religious point of view. For human reason, when dealing with the relation of efforts to their causes, must keep within the limits of possible experience; and to speak of Providence as knowable by us in this relation would be putting on Icarian wings with presumptuous rashness in order to approach the mystery of His unfathomable purposes.

Before determining this guarantee more exactly, it will be necessary to look first at that state of things arranged by nature for those who live and act upon the stage of her great theatre, which ultimately gives the guarantee of Peace. Thereafter we shall consider the manner in which this guarantee is furnished.

next to God the doctor cured the patient, as if he had been acting as an assistant. For *causa solitaria non iuvat*. God is the creator of the doctor and all his medicine, so if one wants to ascend to the highest first cause, of which we can have no theoretical knowledge, then the whole effect must be ascribed to Him. Alternatively we can ascribe it entirely to the doctor, in so far as we follow up the event as part of the natural order, to be explained by the terrestrial chain of causes. Secondly, this mode of thinking destroys all definite principles for judging an effect.

But from a moral and practical point of view, which is directed solely at the supersensuous, the concept of divine *concursus* is quite legitimate and even necessary. It is so, for example, when we believe that God will supply our own lack of righteousness through means that are unknowable to us, if only our conviction is sincere, and that we should not relax in our striving after the good. But it is self-evident that no one should attempt to explain a good act (as an event in the world) from such a *concursus*. This would presume theoretical knowledge of the supersensuous, and is hence absurd.

The provisory arrangements of nature in this relation consist mainly in these three things: 1st, she has provided so that men shall be able to live in all parts of the earth: 2nd she has scattered them everywhere by means of war so that they might populate even the most inhospitable regions; and 3rd, by this same means she has compelled them to enter into relations more or less rightful with one another. The facts that come here into view are truly wonderful. Thus in the cold, icy wastes around the Arctic Ocean there grows the moss which the reindeer scrapes forth from beneath the snow in order that it may itself become food, or that it may be yoked to the sledge of the Ostiak or the Samojan. And in like manner, the wildernesses of sand, barren though they be, do yet contain the camel which appears to have been created for travelling through them, in order that they might not be left unutilized. Still more distinctly does design appear when we come to know how, along with the fur-clad animals on the shores of the Arctic Ocean, there are seals, walruses and whales that furnish food by their flesh, and warmth and light by their fat to the inhabitants around. But most of all does the provident care of nature excite our admiration by the driftwood which it brings to the treeless shores, even when it is not well known whence it comes; and yet without this material the dwellers in the region could neither construct their canoes, nor their arms, nor huts for their abode; and this too under such conditions as compel them to carry on war against the wild beasts, so that they have to live at peace with each other. Moreover, it is remarkable that it was probably nothing but war that drove men into different regions. And the first instrument of war which man appropriated to himself from among all the animals was the horse, which he had learned to tame and to domesticate in the early period of the populating of the earth; for the elephant belongs to the later period of the luxury which arose with established States. In like manner, the art of cultivating certain grasses called 'cereals', which are now no longer recognizable by us in their original condition, as well as the multiplication and improvement of species of fruits by transplanting and grafting them, could arise only under the conditions of regulated States when property in the soil had been rendered secure. These arts could only arise after men who had been previously existing in lawless freedom, had advanced from the mode of life of the hunter,[1] the fisher, and the shepherd to that of the cultivator of the land. Then in connection with the life of the agriculturist, salt and iron were discovered which were perhaps the first articles that were sought far and near, and which entered into the commercial intercourse of different peoples. Thereby they would be first brought into a *peaceful relation* to one another; and thus the most distant of them would come to mutual understanding, sociability and pacific intercourse.

Now as nature has provided so that men *could* thus be able to live everywhere on the earth, she has likewise at the same time despotically willed that they *shall* live everywhere upon it, although against their own inclination and even without any idea of duty being connected with this determination through a moral law. On the contrary she has chosen War as the means of attaining to this end. In point of fact, we see certain peoples whose unity of descent is made known by the unity of their language, far divided from each other. Thus the Samojades on the Arctic Ocean are of the same race as other tribes speaking a similar language a thousand miles away from them in the Altaian Mountains: another race of Mongolian origin equipped with horses and of a warlike character having pressed in between them and having thus driven the former apart from the latter into the most inhospitable regions, whither their own inclination would certainly never have carried them.[2] In like manner, the Finns in the northernmost tract of Europe, where they are called Lapps, have been separated by as great a distance from the Hungarians who are affiliated to them in language, by the intrusion of Gothic and Sarmatian races. Nor can anything else but war well account for the presence in the far north of America of the Eskimo, a race entirely distinct from all the American tribes, and perhaps descended from early European adventurers; and the same may be said of the Pesherae who have been driven into Tierra del Fuego, in the far south of America. Nature has thus used War as the means of getting the earth everywhere populated. War, however, requires no special motive for its explanation; it appears to be ingrafted on human

[1] [Kant considers hunting the way of life most opposed to a civilized constitution.]

[2] [Kant believes that nature will always provide the necessities of life for the people of the Arctic. If the sea failed to bring timber, they would obtain it through trade.]

nature and is even regarded as noble in itself, man being stimulated to it by the love of glory without regard to selfish interests. Thus martial courage, not only among the American savages but even among Europeans in the age of chivalry, was considered to be of great value in itself, not merely in time of war – as was right enough – but just because it *was* war; and thus war was often entered upon merely to show off this quality. An inherent dignity was thus attached to war itself, so that even philosophers have glorified it as giving a certain nobleness to humanity, unmindful of the Greek saying that 'War is bad in that it makes more bad people than it takes away'. So much then in reference to what nature does in carrying out her own design in regard to the Human Race as a class of her creatures.

The question then arises, as to what is the essential meaning and aim of this design of a Perpetual Peace. It may be put thus: 'What does Nature do in this respect with reference to the end which man's own reason presents to him as a duty; and, consequently, what does she do for the furtherance of his moral purpose in life? And, further, how does she guarantee that what man ought to do according to the laws of his freedom, and yet does not do, shall be done by him without prejudice to his freedom even by a certain constraint of nature; and how does she secure this in all three relationships of Public Right as Political Right, International Right and Cosmopolitan Right?' When I say of nature that she *wills* a certain thing to be done, I do not mean that she imposes upon us a duty to do it, for only the Practical Reason as essentially free from constraint can do this; but I mean that she does it herself whether we be willing or not. '*Fata volentem ducunt, nolentem trahunt.*'

1. Even if a people were not compelled by internal discord to submit to the coercion of public laws, War as an external influence would effect this. For, according to the arrangement of nature already indicated, every people finds another pressing upon it in its neighbourhood, and it must form itself internally into a State in order to be equipped as a *Power* so as to defend itself. Now the Republican Constitution is the only one which perfectly corresponds to the Rights of man; but it is at the same time the most difficult to found, and still more so to maintain. So much is this the case that many have asserted that the realization of a true

Republic would be like a State formed by angels, because men with their selfish inclinations are incapable of carrying out a constitution of so sublime a form. In these circumstances, then nature comes to the aid of the rational and universal will of man, which, however honoured in itself, is impotent in practice; and it does this just by means of these selfish inclinations. Thus it comes that the chief interest turns only upon a very good organization of the State, which is certainly within the power of man, whereby the powers of the human will shall be so directed in relation to each other, that the one will check the destructive effects of the other, or nullify them; and hence the result will be as regards reason the same as if these forces did not exist when their evil effects are thus neutralized; and man, although not possessed of real moral goodness, yet becomes constrained to be a good citizen.

The problem of the institution of a State, however hard it may appear, would not be insoluble even for a race of devils, assuming only that they have intelligence, and it may be put as follows: 'A multitude of rational beings all requiring laws in common for their own preservation, and yet of such a nature that each of them is inclined secretly to except himself from their sway, have to be put under order, and a constitution has to be established among them so that, although they may be antagonistic to one another in their private sentiments, they have yet to be so organized that, in their public relations, their conduct will have the same result as if they had no such bad sentiments.'

Such a problem must be *capable of solution*. For it does not turn directly upon the moral improvement of men, but only upon the mechanism of nature: and the problem is to know how men can use the conditions of nature in order so to regulate the antagonism of the hostile sentiments at work among the people that the individuals composing it shall have to compel each other to submit to common compulsory laws, and that there shall thus be brought about a state of peace in which the laws will have full power. This process may be seen going on in the actually existing, although still very imperfectly organized States. For in their external relations to one another, they already approach what the idea of Right prescribes, although the essential principle of Morality is certainly not the cause of it; and indeed a good political constitution is not so much to be expected from that principle but rather conversely the good moral culture of a people from such a constitution.

Hence the mechanism of nature as it works through selfish inclinations which are externally and naturally antagonistic in their operation to each other, may be used by reason as a means of making way for the realization of her own end by the application of a Rule of Right, and thereby of furthering and securing Peace both internal and external, so far as it may lie within the power of the State to do so. It may then be said that Nature irresistibly wills that Right shall at last obtain the supremacy. What men may here neglect to do will at length be done of itself, although through much inconvenience, and as Bouterwek says:

> Bend but the reed too strong, it breaks;
> Who wills too much, but nothing makes.

2. The idea of International Right presupposes the separation of several neighbouring States that are independent of each other; and such a condition of things is of itself already one of war. unless by their federated union they can prevent the outbreak of hostilities. Such a condition of things is, however, better, according to the idea of reason, than the fusion of all the States into a Universal Monarchy by one Power that has outgrown the rest and subjected them to its sway. This is so because the laws lose always something of their definiteness as the range of a government becomes enlarged; and soulless despotism when it has choked the seeds of good, at length lapses into anarchy. Nevertheless there is a desire on the part of every State, or its Sovereign, to attain to a lasting condition of Peace by subjecting the whole world, were it possible to its sway. But nature *wills* it otherwise. She employs two means to prevent the peoples from intermingling, and to keep them apart. These are the differences of their Languages and of their Religions,[1] which bring with them a certain tendency to mutual hatred, and furnish pretexts for war. However, as civilization increases, there is a gradual approach of men to greater unanimity in principles, and to a mutual understanding of the conditions of peace even in view of these differences. This pacific spirit, unlike that despotism which revels upon the

---

[1] [By difference of religion Kant means different historical faiths; behind these faiths there is only one religion valid for all men in all ages.]

grave of liberty, is developed and secured, not by the weakening of all the separate powers of the States, but by an equilibrium which is brought forth and guaranteed through their rivalry with each other.

3. Nature wisely separates the nations which the will of each State, even according to the principles of International Right, would fain combine into one by fraud or force. But on the other hand, she again unites the nations whom the idea of a universal Cosmopolitan Right would not have secured from violence and war by regard to their mutual interests. This is effected by the commercial spirit which cannot exist along with war, and which sooner or later controls every people. Among all the means of power subordinate to the regulation of the State, the power of money is the most reliable, and thus the States find themselves driven not directly from motives of morality. Hence, wherever war threatens to break out in the world, the States have an interest to avert it by mediations, just as if they stood in a constant league with each other for this purpose. Thus great combinations with a view to war can but very rarely occur from the very nature of things, and still more rarely can they succeed.

In this way Nature guarantees the conditions of Perpetual Peace by the mechanism involved in our human inclinations themselves; and although this is not realized with a guarantee that is sufficient to enable us to *prophesy* the future theoretically, yet the security involved is sufficient for all practical relations. And thus it becomes a duty to labour for the realization of this purpose as not at all chimerical in itself.

Second Supplement

Secret article relating to Perpetual Peace

A Secret Article in transactions relating to Public Right when viewed objectively or as to its matter is a contradiction. Viewed subjectively, however, and considered in reference to the quality of the Person who dictates it it is possible that there may be a secret contained in it which it may not be compatible with his dignity to have publicly announced as originating with him.

The only Article of this kind is contained in the following proposition: '*The maxims of the philosophers regarding the conditions*

*of the possibility of a public peace, shall be taken into consideration
by the States that are armed for war'.*

It appears, however, to detract from the dignity of the legislative authority of a State – to which we must naturally attribute
the highest wisdom – to have to seek for instruction regarding the
principles of their practical relations to the other States from
subjects even though they be philosophers. Hence the State will
rather encourage them *silently,* making a secret of the matter,
than deal with them directly. This amounts to saying that it will
allow them to speak forth freely and publicly their universal
maxims regarding the carrying on of war and the establishment
of peace; for this they will do of themselves if they are not prohibited from doing it. Nor is there any particular agreement of
the States with one another required in this connection in order
to their harmonising on this point; for it lies already in the
obligations imposed by the common human Reason as a moral
lawgiver. It is not however meant that the State must give a
preference to the principles of the philosopher over the dictates
of the jurist, who is a representative of the political authority; it
is only meant that the philosopher ought to be *heard.* The jurist,
who has taken for his symbol the scales of right and the sword
of justice, commonly uses the latter not merely to keep away
all foreign influences from the former, but (should the one scale
not sink) to throw his sword into it; and then *Vae victis!* The
jurist, who is not at the same time a moral philosopher, is under
the greatest temptation to do this, because the function of his
office is only to apply existing laws, and not to enquire whether
they may be in need of improvement. And further he reckons
this really lower order of his faculty as belonging by its functions
to a higher rank, because it is accompanied with power; as holds
also of the other two faculties of Medicine and Divinity. Philosophy
thus stands on a very humble stage below these allied authorities.
Hence it is said of Philosophy that she is the *handmaid* of Theology;
and the same has been said of her relation to Medicine and Law.
But it is not easy to see, as has been remarked 'whether she bears
the torch before these gracious ladies, or carries their train'.

That 'Kings will philosophise or philosophers become kings',
is not to be expected. Nor indeed is it to be desired, because the
possession of power inevitably corrupts the free judgment of

reason. But kings or king-like nations, who govern themselves according to laws of equality, should not allow the philosophers as a class to disappear, or to be silenced: rather should they be allowed to speak forth their maxims publicly. Nay, this is even indispensable to both for the mutual enlightenment of their functions. Nor should this process of communicating enlightenment be jealously regarded as a kind of Propagandism, because as a class the philosophers are by their nature incapable of combining into political clubs and factions.

Appendix

On the discordance between morals and politics in reference to perpetual peace

The science of Morals relates directly to practice in the objective inasmuch as it is a system of unconditionally authoritative laws, in accordance with which we *ought* to act. It is therefore a manifest absurdity, after admitting the authority of this conception of duty, to assert, notwithstanding, that we *cannot* so act; for, were it so, this conception would have no value. '*Ultra posse nemo obligatur*'. Hence there can be no conflict between Political Philosophy as the practical science of right, and Moral Philosophy as the theoretical science of right; and consequently there can be no opposition in this relation between practice and theory. An opposition can only arise between them when the science of morals is regarded as a general *doctrine of prudence* or expediency, or a theory of the maxims by which we are to choose the means most conducive for the attainment of useful and advantageous objects; and this amounts to denying generally that there is a Science of Morals. Politics may be regarded as saying, '*be wise* (i.e. prudent) *as serpents*'; Morals adds as a limiting condition, '*and harmless* (i.e. guileless) *as doves*'. If the two maxims cannot co-exist in one commandment, there is really an incongruity between Politics and Morals; but, if the two can be combined throughout, any idea of antagonism between them is absurd, and any question about harmonizing them, as if they were in conflict, need not be even raised. It is true that the saying '*Honesty is the best policy*', contains a theory which unhappily is very often contradicted by practice; and yet the equally theoretical proposition, '*Honesty is better than policy'*, is infinitely removed above all objection, and it is even to be held that honesty or honour is the indispensable condition of all true policy. The tutelary divinity who is the guardian of the boundaries of morals, does not yield to the Jupiter who is the limiting divinity of force, for he still stands under the sway of fate. In other words, reason is not sufficiently enlightened to foresee the series of the pre-determining causes, which, with certainty, would enable it to predict the happy or unhappy consequences that would follow from the conduct of men according to the mechanism of Nature, however much our wishes and hopes may be directed to it. But what we have to do in order to continue on the path of duty according to rules of wisdom, reason shows us everywhere clearly enough in the light of the final End which we have to pursue.

The practical man, however, who regards morals as a mere theory, rejects our generous hopes of attaining to that end, even while admitting the distinction between *ought* to be and what *can* be. He founds his unbelief specially upon the fact that he pretends to be able to foresee from the nature of man that man will never resolve to do what is required to bring about the result that leads to Perpetual Peace. Now it is admitted that the voluntary determination of all individual men to live under a legal constitution according to principles of liberty, when viewed as a distributive unity made up of the wills of all, is not sufficient to attain to this end, but all must will the realisation of this condition through the collective unity of their wills, in order that the solution of so difficult a problem may be attained; for such a collective unity is required in order that civil society may take form as a whole. Further, a uniting cause must supervene upon this diversity in the particular wills of all, in order to educe such a common will from them, as they could not individually attain. Hence, in the realization of that idea in practice, no other beginning of a social state of right can be reckoned upon, than one that is brought about by force; and upon such compulsion, Public Right is afterwards founded. This condition certainly leads us from the outset to expect great divergences in actual experience from the idea of right as apprehended in theory. For the moral sentiment of the lawgiver cannot be relied upon in this connection to the extent of assuming that, after the chaotic mass has been united into a people, he will then leave it to themselves to bring about a legal constitution by their common will. This amounts to saying that, when anyone has once got the power in his hands, he will not allow the people to prescribe laws for him. Similarly, a State which has once entered into possession of its power so as to be subject to no external laws, will not bring itself to submit to the judgment of other States as to how it shall seek to maintain its rights in relation to them; and even a continent, when it realizes its superiority to another which may not be at all in its way, will not neglect to use the means of strengthening its own power, even by spoliation or conquest. Thus it appears that all the theoretical plans relating to the realization of the ends of right, whether it be National Right, or International Right, or Cosmopolitical Right, dissolve into empty, unrealisable ideals, and only practice, founded upon the empirical principles of human nature and considering nothing in the world too low for furnishing guidance for its maxims, can hope to find a sure foundation for its system of political expediency.

Now, certainly, if there is no freedom nor any moral law founded upon it, so that all that happens or can happen is a mere mechanism of nature, this would hold true, under that supposition; and Politics viewed as the art of applying the mechanical arrangements of Nature to the government of men, would constitute the whole of practical wisdom, and the conception of right would be an empty and unreal thought. But, on the other hand, it may be the case that it is indispensably necessary to combine the arrangements of nature with the method of politics, and even to raise them to the position of conditions limiting its practice, and on this ground the possibility of uniting them must be admitted. I can thus easily enough think of a *moral politician*, as one who holds the principles of political expediency in such a way that they can co-exist with morals; but I cannot conceive of a political moralist who fashions a system of morality for himself so as to make it subordinate and subservient to the interest of the statesman. The moral politician will adopt the following as his principle: 'If certain defects which could not be prevented, are found in the political constitution, or in the relations of the State, it becomes a duty especially for the heads of the State to apply themselves to correct them as soon as possible, and to improve the constitution so that it may be brought into conformity with natural

right, which is presented to them as a model in the idea of reason.'
Now it would manifestly be contrary to that political expediency
which is in agreement with morals, to destroy the existing bonds
of National and Cosmopolitical Union before there was a better
constitution ready to take its place; and hence it would be absurd to
demand that every imperfection in the constitution should be at
once violently removed. It may, however, be reasonably required
that the maxim of the necessity of such an alteration should be
consciously recognized by the supreme Power, in order that it
may continue to make constant approximation to the end of
realizing the constitution that is best according to the laws of
right. A State may thus *govern* itself even in a republican manner,
although it may still possess a constitution grounded upon
despotic power. And this may go on until the people gradually
become capable of being influenced by the mere idea of the
authority of the law, as if it possessed the physical power of the
State: and consequently come to be capable of legislating for themselves, which is the mode of government originally founded upon
right. But if, through the violence of a *revolution* caused by the
evils in the constitution, a more lawful constitution were attained
even in a wrong way, it would no longer be proper to hold it
permissible to bring back the people again to the old constitution,
although every one who took part in the revolution by violence,
or intrigue, may have been subjected by law to the penalties
attached to rebels. As regards the external relations of the States,
however, it may be a despotic one, and is likely therefore to be
the stronger in relation to external enemies, so long at least as
that State runs a danger of being suddenly swallowed by other
States. Hence when any such proposal is made, it must at least
be allowed to defer the execution of it till a more opportune
time.[1]

[1] The permissive laws of reason allow public law tainted with injustice to
continue until a complete and total change either develops of its own accord, or
is brought about by peaceful means. For a legal constitution, even if it is scarcely
just, is better than none at all. Precipitate reform would bring about the latter
condition, i.e. anarchy. Political wisdom will therefore make it a duty to improve
the present situation in accordance with the ideal of public law. It will not,
however, use revolutions brought about by nature herself to justify still greater
oppression. Rather it will consider them as a call by nature for fundamental
reforms designed to bring about a legal constitution based on the principles of
freedom, for this is the only lasting constitution.

It may well be that those moralists who are inclined to despotism and who are deficient in practice, may often come into opposition with political prudence, by measures which have been precipitately adopted and overestimated; but experience will gradually bring them from this position of antagonism to nature into a better groove. On the other hand, those politicians who are guided by morality, may make improvement impossible by embellishing principles of government that are contrary to right, on the pretext that human nature is not capable of realizing good according to the idea prescribed by reason, and thus they may do their best to perpetuate violations of right. Instead of dealing with practice in this prudential way, they take up certain practical measures and only consider how these are to be impressed upon the ruling Power in order that their private interest may not be baulked, and how the people, and, if possible, the whole world, may be delivered up to this interest. This is the manner of the mere professional jurists (acting after the fashion of a tradesman rather than of a legislator), when they betake themselves to politics. For, as it is not their business to refine upon legislation itself, but only to carry out the existing laws of the country, every legal constitution as it exists, and any subsequent one taking its place, when it is altered by the higher Power, will always appear to them to be the best; and everything will be regarded as in proper mechanical order. This dexterity of being able to sit upright on any saddle, may fill them with the conceit that they are likewise able to judge about the principles of a political constitution which will be in accordance with the ideas of right, and which, therefore, will be rational and not merely empirical in itself. And, in addition to this, they may put much importance upon their knowledge of *men*, which may indeed be expected, because they have to do with many of them, without their yet truly knowing the nature of man, and what can be made of it, for which a higher standpoint of human observation is required. Now, if, provided with such ideas, they address themselves to the subject of political and international right as prescribed by reason, they cannot do otherwise than carry the spirit of chicane with them in thus stepping beyond their sphere. For they will naturally continue to follow their usual method of mechanically applying compulsory laws that have been despotically laid down, whereas the conceptions of reason will only recognize a lawful compulsion which is in accordance with principles of freedom and by which a rightly existing political constitution only becomes possible. The politician, who thus professes to be wholly practical, accordingly believes that he is able to solve the problem in question by ignoring this rational idea, and proceeding merely by experience seeing that it shows how the previously existing constitutions have been established and in what respects even the best of them may have been contrary to right.

The Maxims which he adopts for his guidance, although he may not give them open expression or avowal, run out into something like the following sophistical proposition:

1. *Fac et excusa.* Seize the opportunity that is favourable for taking into your own possession what is either a right of the State over the people, or over a neighbouring State; and the justification of the act will be much more easily and gracefully presented after the fact so as to palliate its violence. This holds especially in the first case, where the supreme power in the State is also the legislative authority which must be obeyed without reasoning about it, as it is not held that it is desirable to think out convincing reasons first and then to await the counter reasons afterwards. This very hardihood gives a certain appearance of internal conviction of the rightfulness of the act, and the divinity of success (*bonus eventus*) becomes then the best advocate of the cause.

2. *Si fecisti, nega.* What you may have wrongly done yourself, such as may even bring the people to despair and to rebellion, should be denied as being any fault of yours; and, on the other hand, assert that it was owing to the refractoriness of the subjects; or, in the case of an aggression upon a neighbouring State, say that it was the fault of human nature; for, if others are not anticipated by violence, we may safely calculate that they will anticipate us and appropriate what is ours.

3. *Divide et impera.* That is to say, there are certain privileged heads among the people who have chosen you merely for their sovereign as *primus inter pares.* See, then, that you embroil them with each other and put them at variance with the people; next, work upon the latter by holding out the prospect of greater liberty; and everything will then depend upon your absolute will.

Or again, if it be a question about other States, then exciting of suspicion and disagreement among them, is a pretty safe means of subjecting them to yourself, one after the other, under the pretence of assisting the weaker.

It is true that nobody is now taken in by those political maxims, as they are universally understood. This is not so because men have become ashamed of them, as if their injustice was much too evident. The Great Powers are never put to shame before the judgment of the common people, as they are only concerned about one another. And as regards these principles, it is not the fact of their becoming known, but only their failing of success that causes shame; for, as regards the morality of their maxims, they are all at one. Hence there is nothing left but the standpoint of *political* honour upon which they can safely count; and this just comes to a question of the aggrandisement of their power in whatever way they may be able to do so.[1]

With all these serpentine windings of this immoral doctrine of expediency, the idea is still maintained of educing a state of Peace among men from the warlike elements of the state of Nature. And so much at least becomes clear that men can as little escape from the conception of right in their private as in their public relations; and that they do not venture to found

---

[1] Even if one doubts whether wickedness is rooted in the nature of men living together in a state, and plausibly ascribes the unlawful aspects of their character to the insufficient development of civilisation (or rawness), this wickedness reveals itself blatantly and incontestably in the external relations of states. Within each state it is veiled by the force of civil laws, in that the citizens' inclination towards mutual violence is powerfully restrained by a greater force, namely that of the government. Not only does this give the whole a moral veneer (*causae non causae*) but it also facilitates the development of the moral disposition towards direct respect for the law by barring the outbreak of unlawful inclinations.

For each person believes that he would revere and faithfully follow the concept of law if only he could rely on others doing the same, and this the government in part ensures. Thus a big step (though not yet a moral step) is taken towards morality, which consists of obedience to this idea of obligation for its own sake, without any thought of reciprocity.

But because each man has a high opinion of himself and thus presupposes an evil disposition on the part of everyone else, they all judge one another as being in reality of little worth. (We need not discuss how this comes about, though man's nature as a free being cannot be held responsible.) But because respect for the concept of law, which man can never entirely throw off, solemnly sanctions the theory that he is able to conform to it, everyone sees that he, for his part, must act according to it, however others may act.

politics openly on the mere manipulations of expediency, or to renounce all obedience to the conception of public right, as is most strikingly seen in the sphere of international right. On the contrary, they allow all proper honour to this conception in itself, although they may have to devise a hundred evasions and palliations in order to escape from it in practice, and to attribute to a subtle state-craft the authority of the origin and the bond of all right. It will be well to put an end to this sophistry, if not to the injustice it veneers, and to bring the false advocates of the mighty ones of the world to confess that it is not in the interest of Right but of Might that they speak, and in a tone, too, as if they had themselves acquired the right to command. In order to do so it is necessary to point out the deception by which they mislead themselves and others. In their attempt to discover and exhibit the supreme principle from which the tendency towards a Perpetual Peace takes its rise, they try to show that all the evil which comes in the way of it, springs from the fact that the political moralist begins just where the moral politician properly ends; and thus by subordinating their principles to their end – or as the common saying goes, by putting the cart before the horse – the politician frustrates his own intention of bringing Politics into accordance with Morals.

But in order to bring practical philosophy into harmony with itself, it is necessary first of all to decide a preliminary question. That question is: Whether, in dealing with problems of the Practical Reason we ought to begin from its *material* Principle, as the end which is the object of the activity of the will, or from its *formal* Principle, as that which is founded merely upon freedom in its external relation. This formal principle is expressed as follows: 'Act so that thou canst will that thy maxim shall become a universal Law whatever may be its End'.

It cannot be doubted that the latter principle must take the precedence; for, as a principle of right, it has unconditional necessity, whereas the former is obligatory only under the presumption of the empirical conditions of the proposed end so existing that it can be realised: and if the end, as in the case of Perpetual Peace, should also be a duty, the duty would itself have to be deduced from the formal Principle which regulates external action. Now the material principle is the principle of the *political moralist*, and it reduces the question of national, international, and universal Right to the level of a mere *technical* problem. On the other hand, the formal principle is the principle of the *moral politician*, and the question of right becomes with him a moral problem. Their different methods of procedure are thus wide as the poles asunder, in regard to the problem of bringing about Perpetual Peace which, in the view of the moralist, is not merely to be desired as a physical good, but also as a state of things arising out of the recognition of duty.

The solution of the problem in question by the method of political expediency, requires much knowledge of nature in order to be able to employ her mechanical arrangements for bringing about the end in view, and yet the result of them is wholly uncertain so far as regards the realisation of Perpetual Peace. This holds true whichever of the three departments of public right we consider. It is uncertain under any circumstances, whether the people would be better kept in obedience. and at the same time, in prosperity, by severe treatment or by alluring baits of vanity; whether they would be better kept in order by the sovereignty of a single individual or by a combination of several heads; whether this would be best secured merely by an official nobility or by the exercise of popular power within the constitution; and also whether any such result, if attained, could be upheld for long. There are examples of the opposite result presented in history by all the different forms of Government, with the exception of genuine Republicanism only, which system, however, can alone be accepted by a moral politician. A form of International Right professedly established upon statutes devised by foreign ministers, is still more uncertain; for it is in fact but a thing of words without substantial reality and it rests upon compacts which, in the very act of their ratification, admit the secret reservation of the right to transgress them. On the other hand, the solution of the problem by the method of true political wisdom presses forward, so to speak, of itself; it becomes apparent to every one; it brings all artifice to nought; and it leads straight to the proper end. However, it must be accompanied with a prudent warning that it is not to be brought about in a precipitate manner, nor with violence, but it must be unceasingly approached as the favour of circumstances will allow.

All this may be summed up in the exhortation: 'Seek ye first the Kingdom of pure Practical Reason and its *righteousness*, and then will your object, the benefit of Perpetual Peace, be added unto you'.

For the principle of morals has this peculiarity in itself, and it applies to the principles of public right, and consequently pertains to the system of politics that is knowable *a priori*, that the less it makes conduct depend upon the proposed end and the physical or moral advantage related to it, so much the more does it nevertheless coincide in general with these. The reason of this is that it is precisely the universal will as it is given *a priori*, whether in one people or in the relation of different peoples to each other, which alone determines what is just and right among men. This union of the will of all, however, when it proceeds in practice consistently, can also serve as the purely natural cause of the effect intended, and thus realise the idea of right. Thus it is a principle of moral politics that a people ought to unite into a State only according to conceptions of liberty and equality as forms of right, and this principle is not founded upon prudence but upon duty. Political moralists, on the other hand, deserve no hearing, however much they may rationalize about the natural mechanism of a multitude of men conjoined in society, which, if a fact, would weaken those principles and frustrate their purpose; or however much they may seek to prove their assertion by adducing examples of badly organized constitutions in ancient and modern times, such as democracies without a system of representation. And this has to be particularly noted, since such a pernicious theory tends of itself to bring about the evil which it foretells; for according to it, man is thrown into one class with the other living machines, which only need the consciousness of their not being free creatures to become, in their own judgment, the most miserable of all beings.

Fiat justitia, pereat mundus. This proverbial saying may indeed sound somewhat pompous, and yet it is true. It may be popularly rendered thus: Let righteousness prevail though all the knaves in the world should perish for it. It is thus a bold principle of Right cutting through all the crooked ways that are shaped by intrigue or force. It must not, however, be misunderstood as allowing anyone to exercise his own right with the utmost severity, which would be contrary to ethical duty. It is to be understood as signifying the obligation incumbent upon those in power, not to refuse anyone his right, or to take from it, out of favour of sympathy towards others. This requires above all; an internal political constitution, arranged according to pure principles of right, and further, the union of it with other neighbouring or distant States, so as to attain a legal settlement of their disputes by a constitution that would be analogous to a universal State. This proposition just means that political maxims must not start from the prosperity and happiness that are to be expected in each State from following them, nor from the end which each of them makes the object of its will as the highest empirical principle of politics; but they must proceed from the pure conception of the duty of Right or Justice, as an obligatory principle given *a priori* by pure reason. And this is to be held whatever may be the physical consequences which follow from adopting these political principles. The world will certainly not perish from the fact that the number of the wicked thus becomes less. Moral evil has this quality inseparable from its nature that, in carrying out its purposes, it is antagonistic and destructive to itself, especially in relation to such others as are also under its sway; and hence it must give place to the moral principle of goodness, although the progress to this may be slow.

There is therefore objectively in theory no antagonism at all between morals and politics. But subjectively, in consequence of the selfish propensity of men (which however, as not grounded upon rational maxims cannot properly be called practice) such an antagonism is found and it will perhaps always continue to exist because it serves as a whet to virtue. According to the principle *tu ne cede malis sed contra audentior ito*, the true courage of virtue in this case does not consist so much in setting itself with fixed purpose to meet the evils and sacrifices which must thus be encountered but rather in facing and overcoming the wiles of the far more dangerous, lying, treacherous, yet sophistical principle of evil in ourselves, which holds up the weakness of human nature as a justification of every transgression of right.

In fact, the political moralist may say that the ruler and people, or nations and nations, do no wrong to *each other* if they enter on a mutual war by violence or cunning, although they do wrong

236

generally in refusing to respect the conception of right and justice which alone could establish peace for all time. For since the one transgresses his duty towards the other who cherishes just as wrong a sentiment towards him, it may be said that nothing but what is just happens to both of them when they exhaust each other, yet so that there still remains some of their race to carry on this play of force to the most distant times that the latest posterity may take a warning example from them. In all this, indeed, there is a justification of the Providence that rules the course of the world; for the moral principle in man is never extinguished, and his reason, pragmatically trained to realize the ideas of right according to this principle, grows without ceasing through its constantly advancing culture, while the guilt of such transgressions also comes more clearly into light. Yet the process of creation by which such a brood of corrupt beings has been put upon the earth, can apparently be justified by no theodicy or theory of Providence, if we assume that it never will be better, nor can be better, with the human race. But such a standpoint of judgment is really much too high for us to assume, as if we could be entitled theoretically to apply our notions of wisdom to the supreme and unfathomable Power. We shall thus be inevitably driven to a position of despair in consequence of such reasonings, if we do not admit that the pure principles of right and justice have objective reality and that they can be realized in fact. Accordingly, we must hold that these principles are to be treated from the standpoint of the people in the State, and likewise from the relations of the States to one another, let the advocates of empirical politics object to this view as they may. A true political philosophy, therefore, cannot advance a step without first paying homage to the principles of morals; and, although politics taken by itself is a difficult art, yet its union with morals removes it from the difficulties of art. For this combination of them cuts in two the knots which politics alone cannot untie, whenever they come into conflict with each other.

The rights of men must, therefore, be regarded as holy, however great may be the sacrifice which the maintenance of them lays upon the ruling power. We cannot divide right into halves, or devise a modified condition of right intermediate between justice and utility. Rather must all politics bow the knee before the principle of right; but in doing so it may well cherish the hope that it will yet attain, however slowly, to that stage of progress at which it will shine forth with lasting splendour.

Of the accordance of politics with morals according to the
transcendental conception of public right

We may think of Public Right in a formal way after abstracting from all the matters to which it is applied in details, such as the different relations of men in the State, or of the States to each other, as presented in experience; and this is the way in which jurists usually think of it. But apart from the *matter* of public right, there remains only the *form of publicity*, the possibility of which is implied in every expression of right; for without such publicity there would be no justice, this being thinkable only as what is publicly declarable, and hence, without this publicity, there would be no right as right is only administered or distributed by it.

This character of publicity must belong to every mode of right; and, as it can easily be judged whether it can therefore be combined with the principles of an agent, it furnishes a criterion, which is at once presented *a priori* in reason and which it is easy to use in experience. Where it cannot be combined with the principles of an agent, the falsity and wrongness of a pretended right can thus be immediately recognised, as if by an experiment of the pure reason.

Abstraction being thus made from everything empirical that is contained in the conceptions of national and international right (such as the evil disposition of human nature which makes coercion necessary), the following proposition arises, and it may be called the *transcendental formula* of Public Right.

'All actions relating to the rights of other men are wrong, if their maxim is not compatible with publicity.'

This principle is not to be regarded merely as *ethical*, and as belonging only to the doctrine of virtue, but it is also to be regarded as *juridical* and as pertaining to the rights of men. For a maxim cannot be a right maxim which is such that I cannot allow it to be *published* without thereby at the same time frustrating my own intention, which would necessarily have to be kept entirely secret in order that it might succeed, and which I could not *publicly* confess to be mine without inevitably arousing thereby the resistance of all men against my purpose. It is clear that this necessary and universal opposition of all against me on self evident grounds, can arise from nothing else than the injustice which such a maxim threatens to everyone. Further, it is a merely negative maxim in so far as it only serves as a means of making known what is not right and just towards others. It is like an axiom which is certain without demonstration. And, besides all this, it is easily applicable as may be seen from the following examples and illustrations of Public Right.

1. *Public Right of the State.* As regards the right of the State, and in particular its internal right, we may look at the application of this formulated principle to a question which many hold it difficult to answer, but which the transcendental principle of Publicity quite easily resolves. The question we refer to is as to *whether insurrection is a right means for a people to adopt in order to throw off the oppressive power of a so-called tyrant? Non titulo sed exercitio talis.* The rights of the people are violated in the case supposed, and no wrong would be done to the tyrant by his dethronement. Of this latter position there may be no doubt, and yet it is wrong in the highest degree, on the part of the subjects, to pursue their rights in this way; and if they did so they would have as little right on their side to complain of injustice should they fail in this conflict and were afterwards subjected to the severest punishment in consequence.

In this case much may indeed be advanced for and against either position if the attempt is made to establish it by a dogmatic deduction of the principles of right. The transcendental principle of the Publicity of public right can alone spare us all this prolixity of discussion. For, according to that principle the people would only have to ask themselves before the institution of the civil contract whether it would dare to make the maxim of the proposal of an occasional insurrection publicly known. We easily see that were it made a condition at the founding of a political constitution that force was in certain circumstances to be exercised against the supreme authority, the people would have to arrogate to themselves the right of power over that authority. But were it so, that would no longer be the supreme authority, or if both powers were made a condition in the constitution of the State, the establishment of such an authority would really not be possible, although this was the intention of the people. The wrongness of rebellion therefore appears plain from the fact that the maxim upon which it would proceed, *were it to be publicly professed as such*, would make its own purpose impossible. It would therefore necessarily have to be kept secret. This latter condition, however, would not be at all necessary on the part of the head of the State. The sovereign power may freely announce that every form of insurrection or revolt will be punished with the death of the ringleaders, however the latter may believe that it was the sovereign who first violated the fundamental law. For if the sovereign is conscious of possessing *irresistible* supreme power (and this must be assumed in every civil constitution, because he who has not power enough to protect any member of the people against every other has no right to command him), he need have no anxiety about frustrating his own purpose by the publication of his maxim. And it is quite consistent with this position to hold that, if the people succeed in a rebellion the sovereign must then return to the position of a subject. But he will not then be entitled to begin a new rebellion with a view to his own restoration; and neither should he have to fear that he will be called to account for his former administration.

2. *International Right.* There can only be a system of International Right on the assumption that there is really a state of right as the external condition under which right can become real among men. And this is so because, *as* public right, it already implies the publication of a common will assigning to every one what is his own. This *status juridicus* must arise out of some sort of compact which, unlike that from which a State springs, cannot be founded upon compulsory laws, but it may, in all cases, assume the form of a permanent *free association*; and this we have already indicated as assuming the form of a Federation of the different States. Without some jural organization to connect the different persons, moral or physical, in an active form, and therefore in the state of nature, there can be no other right but private right. Here again comes in a conflict of Politics with Morals when the latter is regarded as a doctrine of right; and the criterion of the publicity of maxims again finds an easy application to it, but only on the condition that the States are bound by a compact

with the object only of maintaining themselves in peace with each other, and not at all in the intention of acquiring new possessions. The following instances of antinomies arising between Politics and Morals may be here given along with their solution.

(1) 'If one State has promised something to another, whether it be assistance or a cession of country, or subsidies, or such like, the question may arise as to whether in a case on which the well being of the State is dependent, it may withdraw from keeping its promise, on the ground that it would have itself to be regarded as a double person; first as a *sovereign*, from being responsible to no one in the State, and, secondly, merely as the highest political *official*, from having to give account to the State; and then the conclusion is drawn that what it had become responsible for in the first quality, it may be discharged from in the second.' But if the sovereign of a State should proclaim openly such a maxim it is evident that every other State would naturally avoid it, or would unite with others to resist such pretensions; and this proves that politics, with all its craftiness, would frustrate its own purpose by such an application of the principle of publicity; and consequently any such maxim must be wrong.

(2) 'If a neighbouring Power that has grown formidable by its aggrandisement, excites anxiety, it may be asked whether, because it is able, it will also resolve to oppress others, and whether this gives to the less powerful States a right to make a united attack upon it, although it may as yet have committed no injury?' A State which would affirmatively *proclaim* such a maxim, would only bring about more certainly and rapidly the evil that is dreaded. For the greater power would anticipate the lesser; and, as regards their union, it would be but a weak bundle of reeds against it, if it knew how to practise the rule *divide et impera*. Such a maxim of political prudence if publicly declared, would therefore necessarily frustrate its own purpose; and it is consequently wrong.

(3) 'If a small State, by its geographical position divides the territorial unity of a greater State which requires this unity for its own preservation, is such a State not entitled to subject the smaller State to itself, and unite it to its own territory?' Here again it is easily seen that the greater State cannot possibly let the maxim of such a procedure be previously known; for

either the lesser States would combine early against it, or other powerful States would contend with it for this prize, and so the maxim would make itself impracticable by its very publicity. This would be a sign of the wrongness of the maxim, and it would be so in a very high degree; for the smallness of the object of an injustice does not prevent the injustice manifested by it from being very great.

3. *Cosmopolitical Right.* As regards Cosmopolitical Right, I may pass over it in silence here, because on account of its analogy with International Right its maxims may, in a similar manner, be easily indicated and estimated.

The principle of the incompatibility of certain maxims of International Right with their publicity, thus furnishes us with a good criterion relative to the *non-agreement* of Politics with Morals viewed as the Science of right. But it is necessary also to be informed as to the condition under which its maxims *agree* with the Right of Nations. For it cannot be inferred conversely, that those maxims which are compatible with publicity are on that account also right, because he who has a decided supremacy does not need to conceal his maxims. The condition of the possibility of a Right of Nations generally, is that there does exist a prior *state of right.* For without this there is no public right, but every kind of right which could be thought as existing without it (as in the state of nature) is merely private right. Now we have seen above that a federative union of States, having for its sole object the removal of war, is the only condition compatible with their freedom, and in which their rights can have existence in common. Hence the agreement of Politics with Morals is only possible in this connection, by means of a federative union, a union which is also necessarily and really involved *a priori* in the principles of right. And all public policy can have a rightful basis only by the establishment of such a union in its greatest possible extent; and apart from this end, ingenuity is but unwisdom and disguised injustice. Yet there is such an ingenuity, and its bastard policy has a casuistry of its own that might defy the best Jesuit school to outrival it. It has its *mental reservation,* as in the composition of public treaties by using such expressions as may at will be interpreted to suit the occasion and in any interest such as the distinction between the *status quo* of fact and the *status quo* of right.

Again it has its probabilism, when it construes evil intentions in others, or even the probabilities of their possible superiority into a justifiable reason for undermining other peaceful States. And, finally it has its *philosophical sin* (*peccadillo* or *bagatelle*) when it maintains that the absorption of a small State is an easily pardonable triviality, if a much larger State thereby gains to the supposed greater advantage of the whole.[1]

A pretext of all this is furnished by the double-dealing of Politics in relation to Morals, according as it employs one or other of its departments for its own purposes. No, in fact, both philanthropy and respect for the rights of men are obligatory as duties. But the former is only a *conditional* duty, the latter is unconditioned and absolutely imperative; and he who would give himself up to the sweet feeling of well-doing, must first be fully assured that he has not transgressed it. Now Politics easily accords with Morals in the former sense (as Ethics) by making it incumbent on men to give up their right to their superiors, but it is otherwise when Morals is taken in the second sense (as Jurisprudence or the Science of Right) before which politics must bow the knee. Here Politics finds it advisable not to trust at all to any compact, but rather to take away from right all reality, and to reduce all duties to mere benevolence. This artifice of a mode of policy that shuns the light would be easily frustrated by publicity being given to such maxims, if it only dared allow the philosophers to give publicity to their maxims.

From this point of view, I shall now propose another principle of Public Right which is at once transcendental and affirmative, and whose formula would be as follows:

'All Maxims which require Publicity in order that they may not fail of their end, are in accordance with both right and politics united with each other.'

For if these maxims can only attain their end by publicity, they must be conformable to the common end of the public, which is happiness; and it is the special problem of politics to put itself into agreement with the public, and to make the people contented with their condition. But if this end is to be attained

---

[1] [Kant reproves the writer Christian Garve for approving the union of politics and morality but at the same time admitting that he cannot meet all the objections to it.]

only by publicity, as the means of removing all distrust of political maxims, these maxims must also be in harmony with the right of the public; for the union of the ends of all is only possible in the harmony established by right. I must, however, defer the further development and explanation of this principle till another occasion. But it may be already seen that it is a transcendental formula from the fact that all the empirical conditions of happiness, as the matter of the law, are removed from it; and it merely has regard to the form of a universal legislation.

If it is a duty to realize a state of public right, and if at the same time there is a well-grounded hope of its being realized – although it may only be by an approximation that advances *ad infinitum* – then Perpetual Peace is destined historically to follow those measures which have hitherto been falsely called Peace Treaties, and which have been in reality mere armistices. Perpetual Peace is, therefore, no empty idea, but a task which, by a gradual process of implementation, is coming always nearer its goal; and it may be hoped that progress towards it will be made with ever-increasing rapidity in the times to come.

The Metaphysical Elements of Justice

THE LAW OF NATIONS

[Definition of the Law of Nations]
Those individual human beings who make up a nation[1] can, as
natives of the country, be represented as the offspring of a common
ancestry (*congeniti*), although this is, of course, only a kind of
analogy and is not strictly true. If, however, we interpret this
relationship in an intellectual and juridical sense, a Nation bears
a resemblance to a family (*gens, natio*) whose members (citizens)
are by birth equal to one another, having been born of a common
mother (*the republic*). As such, they regard those who might
happen to live next to them in a state of nature as social inferiors
and consequently will not mingle or marry with them, even
though the latter (the savages) think that they themselves are
superior by virtue of the lawless freedom that they have chosen.
People who live thus in a state of nature constitute primitive
societies [*Völkerschaften*], rather than states.

Our present concern, however, is with the Law governing the
relations among states [rather than among peoples or societies],
although it has been given the name of the Law of Nations [*Völker-
recht*]. (The expression 'the Law of Nations' is therefore a mis-
nomer, and the Law concerned should more properly be called
'the Law of states' – *jus publicum civitatum.*)

Under the Law of Nations, a state is regarded as a moral
person living with and in opposition to another state in a condition of natural freedom, which itself is a condition of continual
war. [Accordingly, the Law of Nations is concerned with those
rights of a state that involve war in one way or another. These
rights consist] partly of the right to make war, partly of rights

---

[1] [The German *Volk* can be translated by either 'people' or 'nation'. In general,
I shall use 'nation' when the relations among nations are involved and 'people'
where the internal relations among the people and the state and its officials are
involved. The reader should be warned, however, against attributing connota-
tions of 'nationalism' to Kant's use of *Volk*.]

during a war, and partly of rights after a war, namely, the right to compel each other to abandon the state of war and to establish a constitution that will guarantee an enduring peace. The principal difference between the state of nature that exists among individuals or families (in their relationship to one another) and that which exists among nations as such is that the Law of Nations is concerned, not only with the relationship of one state to another, but also with relationships of individuals in one state to individuals in another and of an individual to another whole state. But this difference between the Law of Nations and the Law of individuals in a state of nature does not imply any [special] qualifications that are not easily deductible from the concept of the latter.

[*The elements of the Law of Nations*]
The elements of the Law of Nations are as follows:

(1) With regard to their external relationship to one another, states are naturally in a nonjuridical condition (like lawless savages).

(2) This condition is a state of war (the right of the stronger), even though there may not be an actual war or continuous fighting (hostility). Nevertheless (inasmuch as neither side wants to have it better), it is still a condition that is in the highest degree unjust, and it is a condition that states adjoining one another are obligated to abandon.

(3) A league of Nations in accordance with the Idea of an original social contract is necessary, not, indeed, in order to meddle in one another's internal dissensions, but in order to afford protection against external aggression.

(4) But this alliance must not involve a sovereign authority (as in a civil constitution), but only a confederation. Such an alliance can be renounced at any time and therefore must be renewed from time to time. This is a right that follows as a corollary *in subsidium* from another right, which is original, namely, the right to protect oneself against the danger of becoming involved in an actual war among the adherents of the confederation (*foedus Amphictyonum*).[1]

---

[1] [An amphictyonic league was a league of neighbouring states or tribes in ancient Greece that was formed for religious purposes and mutual protection. The most famous of these was the Theban amphictyony (sixth century B.C.).]

[*The right of going to war in relation to the state's own subjects*]
In connection with the original right of free states in a state of
nature to wage war against one another (in order perhaps to
establish a condition closer to the juridical state of affairs), the
first question that arises is: What right does the state have over
its own subjects in the war? May it employ them in the war, use
their goods, or even expend their lives, regardless of their personal judgment as to whether they want to go to war? May the
sovereign send them into the war through his supreme command
[alone]?

It might seem that his right to do so could be easily demonstrated from the right that a person has to do whatever he wants
to do with what belongs to him, that is, with what he owns. But
everyone indisputably owns whatever he himself has sub-
stantially made [*der Substanz nach*, that is, something that he has
actually brought into existence and has not merely changed].
This is the Deduction of this right as it would be formulated
by a mere jurist. [Let us now examine the argument in more
detail.]

In any country, there are, of course, various products of nature
that nevertheless, because of their abundance, must be regarded
as artifacts (*artefacta*) of the state, inasmuch as the land would
not have produced so much had there been no state or powerful
government, but the inhabitants had, instead, remained in a
state of nature. For example, because of shortage of feed or beasts
of prey, hens (the most useful species of bird), sheep, swine,
cattle, and the like would either not exist at all in the country
in which I live or would be exceedingly rare if there were no
government to safeguard the acquisitions and possessions of its
inhabitants. The same is true of the number of people [in a
country], for [without a government] it can only remain small, just
as it is in the American wilderness; indeed, the people would
still remain small in numbers even if we were to assume that they
are much more industrious [than those who live under a govern-
ment] (as, of course, they are not). The inhabitants of such a
country would be very sparse, since they would be unable to
spread themselves out on the land with their households, because
of the danger of devastation by other men, by savages, or by

beasts of prey. Consequently, under such circumstances, there would be no adequate means of livelihood for such a great number of people as now populate a country. Inasmuch as crops (for example, potatoes) and domestic animals are products of human labour, at least as far as their quantity is concerned, we can say that they may be used, consumed, or destroyed (killed). In the same vein, it might seem that we could say that the supreme authority in the state, the sovereign, also has the right to lead his subjects into a war as though it were a hunting expedition and to march them on to a field of battle as though it were a pleasure excursion on the grounds that they are for the most part products of his own activity.

This kind of argument for a right (which in all likelihood hovers darkly in the minds of monarchs) is indeed valid with respect to animals, which can be owned by human beings, but it absolutely cannot be applied to a human being, and especially not to a citizen. A citizen must always be regarded as a co-legislative member of the state (that is, not merely as a means, but at the same time as an end in itself), and as such he must give his free consent through his representatives, not only to the waging of war in general, but also to any particular declaration of war. It is only under this limiting condition that the state may demand and dispose of a citizen's services if they involve being exposed to danger.

Therefore we shall have to derive the right in question from the duty of the sovereign to the people (rather than conversely). [Moreover, if this right is exercised], we must be certain that the people have given their consent, and, in this respect, even though they may be passive (in the sense that they merely comply), they are also still active autonomously and themselves represent the sovereign.

[*The right of going to war in relation to other states*]
In the state of nature among states, the right to go to war (to commence hostilities) constitutes the permitted means by which one state prosecutes its right against another. In other words, a state is permitted to employ violent measures to secure redress when it believes that it has been injured by another state, inas-

much as, in the state of nature, this cannot be accomplished through a judicial process (which is the only means by which such disputes are settled under a juridical condition of affairs). [The offences for which remedy may be sought in this way include,] not only actual injury (through first aggression, which is to be distinguished from first hostilities), but also threats. We may consider a threat to exist if another state engages in military preparations, and this is the basis of the right of preventive war (*ius praeventionis*). Or even the mere menacing increase of power (*potentia tremenda*) of another state (through the acquisition of new territory) can be regarded as a threat, inasmuch as the mere existence of a superior power is itself injurious to a lesser power, and this makes an attack on the former undoubtedly legitimate in a state of nature. On this is founded the right to preserve a balance of power among all states that are contiguous to one another and act on one another.

Among these overt attacks that provide grounds for the exercise of the right to go to war, acts of retaliation (*retorsio*) must be included, that is, acts by which one nation seeks through self-help to gain redress for an injury done to it without attempting to obtain compensation (through peaceful means). In its form, this procedure is much like starting a war without declaring war beforehand. If, however, one wants to find any justice or rights in a state of war, then something analogous to a contract must be presupposed, namely, the acceptance of the declaration of war by the other party, so that it can be assumed that both parties wish to pursue their rights in this fashion.

[Rights during a war]

The question of justice and rights during a war presents the greatest difficulty, inasmuch as it is difficult without contradicting oneself even to form any concept of such a right and to think of there being any law in a condition that is itself lawless (*inter arma silent leges*). If there is any justice and right under such circumstances, it must be as follows: The war must be conducted according to such principles as will not preclude the possibility of abandoning the state of nature existing among states (in their external relations) and of entering into a juridical condition.

No war between independent states can be a punitive one (*bellum punitivum*), for punishment takes place only where there is a relationship of superior (*imperantis*) to a subject (*subditum*), and no such relationship exists between states. Nor can any war be one of extermination (*bellum internecinum*) or a war of subjugation (*bellum subjugatorium*), inasmuch as such wars result in the elimination of a state as a moral being by absorbing its people into one mass with the people of the conqueror or by reducing them to slavery. It is not that the state's use of such measures, if they were necessary to achieve peace, would in themselves contradict the rights of a state, but the Idea of the Law of Nations only involves the concept of an antagonism that is in accordance with the principles of external freedom, that is to say, it permits the use of force only to maintain and preserve one's property and not as a means of acquisition of the kind that would result in the aggrandizement of one state becoming a threat to another.

To a state against which a war is being fought, defensive measures of every kind except those that would make a subject of that state unfit to be a citizen are allowed. If it were to employ such measures, it would thereby make itself unfit to be considered a person in relation to other states in the eyes of the Law of Nations (and as such to participate in equal rights with the other states). Among such forbidden measures are the following: employing its subjects as spies and using them, or even foreigners, as assassins or poisoners (we should also include here so-called guerrillas [*Scharfschützen*], who wait for individuals in ambush) or just using them to spread false rumours; in a word, it is forbidden to employ any such treacherous measures as would destroy the mutual faith that is required if any enduring peace is to be established in the future.

During a war, although it is permissible to impose exactions and contributions on a vanquished enemy, it is still not permissible to plunder the people, that is, to seize forcibly the belongings of individuals (because that would be robbery, inasmuch as it was not the conquered people themselves who waged the war, but the state to which they were subject and which waged the war through them). Furthermore, receipts should be given for any requisitions that are made, so that in the peace that follows the burden that was imposed on the country or province can be equitably distributed.

[*Rights after a war*]

Justice and rights after a war, that is, at the time the peace treaty is concluded and in relation to the consequences of the treaty, consist in the following: The victor lays down the conditions, and these are customarily drawn up in a peace treaty, to which the vanquished power is supposed to agree and which leads to the conclusion of the peace. In laying down these conditions, the victor makes no pretence of appealing to a right against his opponent that is based on some supposed injury from him, but, leaving such questions unanswered, he rests his case on his strength [*Gewalt*] alone. It follows that the conqueror cannot request compensation for the costs of the war, inasmuch as, in doing so, he would have to admit that the waging of war on the part of his opponent was unjust [*ungerecht*]. Even if he thinks that this is a good argument, he still cannot use it here, because in doing so, he would be declaring that the war was a punitive one, and, in waging a punitive war, he himself would in turn be committing an offence against his opponent. [On the conclusion of peace] there should be an exchange (with no ransom) of prisoners of war without regard to the equality of the numbers of prisoners released by each side.

Neither a conquered state nor its citizens lose their civil freedom as a result of the capture of their country in the sense that the former is degraded to the status of a colony or the latter to that of slaves. It could be otherwise only if the war had been a punitive one, which is self-contradictory. A colony or province consists of people who, indeed, have their own constitution, legislation, and land. In this land, those people who belong to another state are aliens, even if their state has executive authority over the people in the colony or province. Such a state is called the 'mother state'. The 'daughter state' is subject to the 'mother state', but it rules itself (through its own parliament, which is usually presided over by a viceroy [*civitas hybrida*]). Such a relation existed between Athens and the various islands and now exists between Great Britain and Ireland.

It is even less possible to base slavery on the conquest of a people through war and to derive its legitimacy from this fact, for this would require us to assume that the war was a punitive one. Least of all would hereditary slaves based on conquest be possible; indeed it would be quite absurd, inasmuch as the guilt from a person's crime cannot be inherited.

That a general amnesty should be included in a peace treaty is already implied in the concept of the latter.

[The rights of peace]

The rights of peace are as follows: (1) the right to remain at peace when there is a war in the vicinity, that is, the right of neutrality; (2) the right to secure for oneself the continuation of a peace that has been concluded, that is, the right of guarantee; (3) the right to form reciprocal alliances with other states (confederations) for common defence against any possible attacks from without or from within; but this does not include the right to form a league for aggression and internal aggrandizement.

[The right of the state against an unjust enemy]

There is no limit to the rights of a state against an unjust enemy [ungerechter Feind][1] (in respect to quantity or degree, although there are limits with respect to quality or kind). In other words, although an injured state may not use every means at its disposal in order to defend what belongs to it, it may use those means that are allowable in any amount or degree that it is able to do so. But what, then is an unjust enemy according to concepts of the Law of nations, which holds that every state is a judge in its own cause as in a state of nature in general? An unjust enemy is someone whose publicly expressed Will (whether by words or by deeds) discloses a maxim that, if made into a universal rule, would make peace among nations impossible and would perpetuate the state of nature forever. An example of this would be the violation of public treaties, which, it can be assumed, is a matter that concerns every nation, inasmuch as their freedom is thereby threatened. And so all nations are called upon to unite against this mischief and to take away from the malefactor the power of committing it. But this does not include [the right of] causing a state at the same time to disappear from the face of the earth, so that its land will be distributed among the others. That would be an injustice against the people, who cannot lose their original

[1] [In this paragraph, I have translated ungerecht and Ungerechtigkeit by 'unjust' and 'injustice' respectively.]

right to unite into a commonwealth. They may be required, however, to adopt a new constitution that by its nature will be unfavourable to the passion for war.

As a matter of fact, the expression 'an unjust enemy in a state of nature' is a redundancy, for the state of nature is itself a condition of legal injustice. A just enemy would be one to whom I would do an injustice if I resisted him; but in that case he would also not be my enemy.

[*The establishment of enduring peace*]

Inasmuch as the state of nature among nations, just like that among individual men, is a condition that should be abandoned in favour of entering a lawful condition, all the rights of Nations and all the external property of Nations that can be acquired or preserved through war are merely provisional before this change takes place; only through the establishment of a universal union of states (in analogy to the union that makes a people into a state) can these rights become peremptory and a true state of peace be achieved. Because, however, such a state composed of nations would extend over vast regions, it would be too large to govern, and consequently the protection of each of its members would, in the end, be impossible, with the result that the multitude of such corporations would lead back to a state of war. It follows that perpetual peace (the ultimate goal of all of the Law of nations) is, of course, an Idea that cannot be realized. But the basic political principles that aim at this Idea by instructing us to enter such alliances of states as a means of continually approaching it closer are themselves feasible, inasmuch as continually attempting to approach this Idea is a requirement grounded in duty and in the rights of men and states.

Such a union of several states whose purpose is to preserve peace may be called the 'permanent congress of states'. Any neighbouring state is free to join such a congress. We have an example of such a congress (at least as far as the [legal] formalities of the Law of nations relating to the preservation of peace are concerned) in the assembly of states-general at The Hague in the first half of this [the eighteenth] century. To this assembly, the ministers of most European courts and even of the smallest republics brought their complaints about the hostilities carried out by one against another. Thus, all of Europe thought of itself as a single federated state, which was supposed to fulfil the function of judicial arbitrator in these public disputes. Later, however, instead of this, the Law of Nations disappeared from the cabinets [of those states] and survived only in books, or, after force had already been employed, it was relegated as a [useless] form of deduction to the darkness of the archives.

A congress, in the sense intended here, is merely a free and essentially arbitrary [*willkürliche*] combination of various states that can be dissolved at any time. As such, it should not be confused with a union (such as that of the American states) that is founded on a political constitution and which therefore cannot be dissolved. Only through the latter kind of union can the Idea of the kind of public Law of Nations that should be established become a reality, so that Nations will settle their differences in a civilized way by judicial process, rather than in the barbaric way (of savages), namely, through war.

WORLD LAW

[*The world community*]
The rational Idea of a peaceful, even if not friendly, universal community of all nations on earth that can come into mutual active relations with one another is not a philanthropic (ethical) principle, but a juridical one [*rechtliches Prinzip*]. From the fact that nature has enclosed all nations within a limited boundary (because of the spherical shape of the earth on which they live, as a *globus terraqueous*), it follows that any piece of land that is possessed by an inhabitant of the earth and on which he lives is only a part of a determinate whole, and, as such, everyone can be conceived as originally having a right to it. Accordingly, all nations originally hold a community of the land, although it is not a juridical community of possession (*communio*), and therefore of use, or community of ownership of the same. The kind of community that they hold is that of possible physical interaction (*commercium*), that is, a community that involves a universal relationship of each to all the others such that they can offer to trade with one another; consequently, they have a right to attempt to trade with a foreigner without his being justified in regarding

anyone who attempts it as an enemy. These rights and duties, in so far as they involve a possible unification of all nations for the purpose of establishing certain universal laws regarding their intercourse with one another, may be called world Law (*ius cosmopoliticum*) [*das weltbürgerliche Recht*].

It might appear that oceans make a community of Nations impossible. But this is not so, for, thanks to navigation, they provide the most favourable natural condition for commerce, which is even more likely when the coastlines are close to one another (as they are in the Mediterranean Sea). Nevertheless, frequent visits to strange coasts and, even more, the founding of colonies that are linked with a mother country provide an occasion for doing evil and violence to some place on our globe that will be felt everywhere. The fact that such abuse is possible does not nullify the right of a citizen of the earth to attempt [to establish] a community with everyone and to visit all the regions of the earth for this purpose. This right still does not, however, involve the right to colonize the land of another nation, for this requires a special contract.

At this point, the following question might be raised: Where lands have been newly discovered, may a nation settle and take possession of land in the neighbourhood of a people who have already settled in that region, even without obtaining their consent?

If such a settlement takes place far enough away from the place where the first people live so that there will be no encroachment on their use of the land, then the right to do so is indubitable. If, however, the people are shepherding or hunting tribes (like the Hottentots, the Tongas, or most of the American Indians) whose livelihood depends on large, wild tracts of land, such settlement should not be undertaken through violence, but only through a contract. Moreover, any such contract must not take advantage of the ignorance of the inhabitants in regard to the cession of their territory. Against this view, it might seem that there is ample justification for the use of violent means in this kind of situation because of the good for mankind that results from it. On the one hand, it is a means of bringing culture to primitive peoples (this is like the excuse that Büsching[1] offers for

---

[1] [Anton Friedrich Büsching (1724-1793), German theologian and geographer. He wrote many works, principally on geography, of which the main one was the

the bloody introduction of Christianity into Germany), or, on the other hand, it is a means by which it is possible to clean out vagrants and criminals from one's own country, who, it is hoped, will improve themselves or their children in some other part of the world (like New Holland). Nevertheless, all these good intentions still cannot wash away the stains of injustice [*Ungerechtigkeit*] from the use of such means. Here, one might object that, had there been such scruples about using violence to start the erection of a lawful state of society, then perhaps the whole world would still be in a lawless condition. But such an argument will not succeed in invalidating the conditions of justice any more than does the excuse offered by revolutionaries, namely, that, when constitutions are evil, it is proper for the people to reform them by violent means, and so generally to be unjust once and for all, in order thereafter to establish legal justice on a foundation that is so much more secure and to cause it to flourish.

[*Conclusion: perpetual peace*]
If one cannot prove that a certain thing exists, he can try to prove that it does not exist. If he succeeds in doing neither (as frequently happens), he can still ask whether he has any interest in accepting a conjecture that one or the other is true (hypothetically) and, if there is such an interest, whether it is a theoretical or a practical interest. Thus, from a theoretical point of view, we form a conjecture in order to explain a certain phenomenon (for example, for an astronomer, the phenomenon to be explained might be the retrograde motion of the planets). Or, on the other hand, from the practical point of view, we form a conjecture in order to attain some end; such an end may be either pragmatic (purely technological) or moral. If it is a moral end, it is one that duty requires us to adopt as a maxim. Now, it is evident that [although duty may require us to adopt an end as our maxim] it does not require us to conjecture (*suppositio*) the feasibility of the end in the sense in which such a conjecture is a purely theoretical judgment, and a problematic one as well, for there can be no obligation to do this (to believe something). What duty requires is that we act in accordance with the Idea of such an end, even if there is not the

Erdbeschreibung, a description of the earth, in seven parts, He is often regarded as the founder of modern statistical geography.]

slightest theoretical probability that it is feasible, as long as its impossibility cannot be demonstrated either.

Now, moral-practical reasons within us voices its irresistible veto: *There shall be no war*, either between thee and me in a state of nature or among states, which are still in a lawless condition in their external relations with one another, even though internally they are not. This is not the way in which anyone should prosecute his rights. Accordingly, there is no longer any question as to whether perpetual peace is a reality or a fiction and whether we deceive ourselves if we assume in a theoretical judgment that it is real. We must, however, act *as though* perpetual peace were a reality, which perhaps it is not, by working for its establishment and for the kind of constitution that seems best adapted for bringing it about (perhaps republicanism in every state). By this means [we may hope to] bring an end to the abominable practice of war, which up to now has been the chief purpose for which every state, without exception, has adapted its institutions. Even if the realization of this goal of abolishing war were always to remain just a pious wish, we still would certainly not be deceiving ourselves by adopting the maxim of working for it with unrelenting perseverance. Indeed, we have a duty to do so, and to assume that the moral law within us might deceive us would give rise to the disgusting wish to dispense with reason altogether and to conceive of ourselves and our principles as thrown in together with all the other species of animals under the same mechanism of nature.

As a matter of fact, it can be said that the establishment of a universal and enduring peace is not just a part, but rather constitutes the whole of the ultimate purpose of Law [*Rechtslehre*] within the bounds of pure reason. When a number of men live together in the same vicinity, a state of peace is the only condition under which the security of property is guaranteed by laws, that is, when they live together under a constitution. Furthermore, the rule involved here is not a standard of conduct for others that is based on the experience of those who have hitherto found it most to their advantage. On the contrary, it must be derived *a priori* through reason from the Idea of a juridical association of men under public laws in general. In fact, every [empirical] example is deceptive (and can be used only to illustrate but not to prove

257

[a principle]), and so a metaphysics is most certainly required. Even those who deride metaphysics still acknowledge its necessity when they say, for instance, as they often do: 'The best constitution is one in which the power is exercised, not by men, but by the laws.' What could be more sublimely metaphysical than this Idea? Yet it is an Idea that by their own admission possesses the most authentic objective reality, as can be easily shown in particular instances if need be. No attempt should be made, however, to realize this Idea precipitously through revolutionary methods, that is, by the violent overthrow of a previously existing imperfect and corrupt [government] (for in that case there would be an intervening moment when the entire juridical state of affairs would be annihilated). Instead, the Idea should be attempted and carried out through gradual reform according to fixed principles. Only in this way is it possible to approach continually closer to the highest political good – perpetual peace.

HENRY BROUGHAM

Lord Brougham (1778-1868), a radical in English politics who took office as Lord Chancellor in the early 1830s, wrote upon the balance of power when still a young man in his mid-twenties. The essay on the balance of power must be regarded as complementary to the work of Friedrich Gentz which follows it in this selection of writings in international theory. The essay by Lord Brougham lacks the consistency and coherence of Gentz's analysis of the balance, but it stands as an interesting forerunner to the Prussian's contribution since it appeared in 1803, three years before the *Fragment upon the Present State of the Political Balance of Europe*. Although Gentz defines and defends the idea of a European balance more lucidly, Lord Brougham carefully pinpoints the key elements – 'the perpetual attention to foreign affairs', 'the constant watchfulness', 'the unceasing care which it dictates of nations most remotely situated'. It is this awareness of the significance of the balance of power which led Cobden, in the essay included later in this selection, to link the name of Brougham to those of Vattel and Gentz, the principal exponents of the theory. The extract by Lord Brougham is therefore most appropriately read in conjunction with those by Gentz. Lord Brougham's essay, 'Balance of Power', is taken from *Works of Henry Lord Brougham*, vol. VIII, 'Dissertations – Historical and Political', Edinburgh, 1872, pp. 1-18.

Suggested Reading

A. Aspinall, *Lord Brougham and the Whig Party*, 1939.

Balance of Power

The balance of power, and the general system of international relations which has grown up in modern Europe, have afforded to one class of politicians a perpetual subject of ridicule and invective, and to another class the constant opportunity of defending or attacking every measure, of discussing or affecting to discuss, every political subject, by a reference to certain terms of art and abstract ideas, of which it is fair to suspect that they little understood the meaning and the force.

Of these reasoners or declaimers, the former sect are undoubtedly the most dangerous. The refinements of modern policy which have sprung from the progressive improvement of the species, and have, in their turn, secured that progress, and accelerated its pace, are in no danger of being either perverted or brought into disrepute by the petulance of pretended Statesmen. But the sophistries and cavils which political sceptics and innovators have founded, partly on a misconception of the theory, and partly on a misstatement of the facts, tend directly to a degradation of the system in the eyes of superficial reasoners, and may ultimately renew a state of things, from which the unassisted efforts of natural heroism might be altogether unable to redeem any one community.

The attacks of those men have, moreover, been extremely inconsistent and contradictory. While, at one time, they maintain that the idea of a political equilibrium is pregnant with every species of absurdity, and would produce, if acted upon in the affairs of nations, those very evils which the system is extolled for preventing: at another time, they tell us that the notion is simple and obvious; that it arises naturally out of the passions of men; that it is no refinement of modern statesmen, but has influenced the councils of princes and commonwealths in all ages of the world. Now – the balance of power is an unintelligible jargon, invented to cover every scheme; to furnish pretexts for every act of national injustice; to lull the jealousy of the people in any emergency; or to excite their alarms upon any occasion. Now – it is useless and superfluous; an interference with the natural order of things; or an attempt to effect that which would happen at any rate. Now – it is pernicious in the extreme; the parent of wars and offensive alliances; the exciting cause of national violence; the watchword of ambitious princes and destroying commonwealths; a refinement only of injustice; and a system of nothing but treachery or caprice. It is very manifest, without any argument, that the system of modern policy cannot be liable to all those accusations at once, and that the declaimers, who have used such language with respect to it, must have been talking of very different things at different times. But as the foreign policy of nations was never, at any period of modern history, so interesting as at present, we shall proceed to offer a few observations upon that system which has often been so little understood, and is still the subject of such great misrepresentation.

The national jealousy, by which at all times the European states are animated, and which ranges them on different sides in each public crisis, has been denominated, not a principle of policy, but a national emotion. Nations, it is said, like the individuals who compose them, are moved by caprice, and actuated by passions; excited to contention by envy and hatred; soothed to reconciliation when exhausted by the efforts of their enmity; leagued in friendship by the dictates of an interested prudence; united together by the thirst of plunder; or combined for the gratification of some common revenge. The principle (we are told) which has been pompously called the great spring of civilized policy, is perhaps nothing more than a systematic indulgence of those natural feelings which impel the savage to attack his more wealthy neighbour, or unite rival hordes in a temporary friendship, when invaded by a powerful and common enemy. The policy (it is added) which we have heard extolled as the grand arcanum of modern statesmen, and dignified with the title of a system, is nothing more than the natural result of a conflict between desire of conquest and the desire of security, refined on by ingenious men, and spun into a regular theory.

These remarks are partly true, and partly unfounded. It is true, that nations are guided by human councils, and subject, of course, to the passions and caprices of men; but it is no less certain, that the more regularly any system of government is established, the more will men of sober minds acquire a weight in the management of affairs; and that the longer the art of administering the concerns of empires is practised, prudence will gain the greater ascendancy over passion. It is true that the dictates of feelings not always amiable, and often outrageous, are frequently, more than any impulse of reason, the springs which actuate the operations of states; but it is equally true, that in all animals the passions themselves are implanted for the wisest of purposes; that instinct is the principle to which, more than reason, the preservation of life, and the maintenance of order in the universe, must be ascribed; and that national councils may be operating what no foresight could combine, while they appear to be swayed only by prejudice and passion. The existence of rude states is indeed frequently preserved, and their civilization insured by the operation of principles, to assist the development of which is the great pride of the most learned and skilful statesmen; yet, the want of this assistance in those rude times, and the absence of a constant superintendence and control, which renders the popular feelings useful in one case and harmless in another, is certainly the cause of that instability of national power, and those perpetual changes in dominion – those constant broils, and that state of unceasing insecurity, to which we may attribute the many revolutions in the situation of savage communities, and the long continuance of their barbarism.

That the system which we are now considering has oftentimes been abused, no one can deny. What human institution can defend itself from this charge? But many of the evils which are ascribed to the principle in question, have been owing only to an erroneous conception of its nature. Many of them have arisen, from failing to carry the line of policy recommended by it, to the lengths which it enjoins; and, in not a few instances, those events which have been deemed pernicious, would have proved altogether fatal, had not its influence modified and controlled them. We are desired, with no small appearance of triumph, to view the history of the last century, and to mark the manifold wars which the balancing system produced; the various intrigues to which it gave rise; the destructive conquests of which it furnished the pretext; and the national catastrophies which it could not avert. But had it not been for that wholesome jealousy of rival neighbours, which modern politicians have learned to cherish, how many conquests and changes of dominion would have taken place, instead of wars, in which some lives were lost, not, perhaps, the most valuable in the community, and some superfluous millions were squandered! How many fair portions of the globe might have been deluged in blood, instead of some hundreds of sailors fighting harmlessly on the barren plains of the ocean, and some thousands of soldiers carrying on a scientific, and regular, and quiet system of warfare in countries set apart for the purpose, and resorted to as the arena where the disputes of nations might be determined! We may indeed look to the history of the last century as the proudest era in the annals of the species; the period most distinguished for learning, and skill, and industry; for the milder virtues, and for common sense; for refinement in government, and an equal diffusion of liberty; above all, for that perfect knowledge of the arts of administration, which has established certain general rules of conduct among nations; has prevented the overthrow of empires, and the absorption of weak states into the bodies of devouring neighbours, has set bounds to the march of conquest, and rendered the unsheathing of the sword the last measure; whereas, in other times, it was always resorted to in the first instance.

In the beginning of that century, we saw the gigantic power of France humbled by a coalition of princes, each resolved to undergo immediate loss, and run a great present risk, in order to prevent the greater chance of ruin at the distance of a few years. In ancient times the Stadtholder would have been more jealous of Great Britain or Austria than of France. The Great Monarch, like Caesar, would have found a Divitiacus in the heart of the Empire. By splitting the neighbouring potentates into adverse factions, and fighting one against the other, he would, in a few years, have subjugated the whole. No power would then have conceived that common prudence required an immediate sacrifice of peace, in order to ward off a distant peril. All would have waited quietly till the invasion came on; then, fighting with a desperate, but an insulted valour, all would have been conquered in detail by the ambitious enemy of Europe; and the story of the Roman Empire would have been renewed, when submission to foreign power, and loss of liberty, and interruption of peaceful pursuits, were no longer the phantoms of vulgar terror, or the themes of idle declamation, but real, and imminent, and inevitable calamities.

In the middle of the century, we indeed saw an ancient crown despoiled of its hereditary provinces; and the neighbouring states in vain attempting to crush the new-born energies of the Prussian power. It is, however, extremely doubtful whether the principles of an enlightened policy would not have favoured the rise of a state whose professed and natural object was the balancing of the Imperial House, and the protection of the smaller princes of the empire, against the preponderating, and formerly absolute, sway of the Austrian monarchs. And, at any rate, admitting the other powers to have been actuated by no such views, it is clear that the success of the Silesian usurpation must be attributed to the actual dereliction of the balancing system, and not to its inefficacy; for both in the Silesian and in the Seven-Years War,[1] the part of Prussia was openly espoused by some of the great powers, in the former, by France and Bavaria; in the latter, first by England, and then by Russia herself. The preservation and accurate adjustment of the balance might perhaps have required some such event as the acquisition which Prussia actually made; but if the immediate object of the system, the maintenance of the established division of power, was held to be a more important consideration, it is clear that the part of Prussia ought not to have been taken by France and Bavaria, in the one case, or by England and Russia in the other, until the usurped dominions of Austria had been restored; and then the allies of that power ought instantly to have deserted her, if she did not remain satisfied with the fruits of their interference.

Soon after the Seven-Years War was terminated, the dismemberment of an ancient European kingdom was projected by the powers who had been most exhausted in the Silesian contest, and who wished to indemnify themselves for their losses at the expense of the Poles. The success of this most iniquitous transaction, although it only demonstrates that the modern system has

---

[1] It is well known that the peace of Dresden was only a truce; that the war of 1756 owed its origin to the causes of the former contest; and that the possession of Silesia was only secured by the peace of Hubertsburgh.

not been carried to its proper length – that it is incapable of changing the nature of men, or disarming the ambition and rapacity of princes – has been always quoted by a certain set of politicians, as an irrefragable proof of the futility and inefficacy of the great principle of modern politics. That calamitous event is indeed a sufficient proof, that the statesmen of Europe had for a while forgotten their most sacred principles, and that the princes who did not interfere to prevent it were blind to their best interests. It serves, therefore, to show us what would be the situation of the world, were the maxims of ancient times to be revived, and the salutary system of modern Europe to lose its influence over the councils of states; but, for this very reason, the partition of Poland cannot, with any truth, be said to prove the inefficacy of those principles, by acting in direct opposition to which, the great powers of Europe permitted it to happen. If, however, the policy of the neighbouring states provided no check to the injustice of the partitioning powers, the influence of the balancing system upon the conduct of those parties themselves, was productive of important and beneficial effects. Had the ancient maxims of national indifference and insulation prevailed in the cabinets of princes at the crisis of Polish affairs in 1772, the distracted state of that unhappy country would indeed have called in the interference of foreign force. But this interference would have proceeded from one quarter alone. Poland would have been overwhelmed, and its vast resources appropriated, by one only of the conterminous powers, probably by the Russian empire, which would thus have suddenly acquired a preponderance fatal to the rest of Europe; and, without receiving any check in the proportional aggrandizement of the neighbouring states, would have been enabled to stretch its arm into the very heart of the great western commonwealth. But the prevalence of that national jealousy, and anxious attention to the affairs of other states, which is the master principle of the modern system, prevented the usurpation of Russia, even at the moment when she was actually mistress of the kingdom, garrisoned the capital with her troops, and ruled the national councils by a viceroy, under the name of ambassador. With all these circumstances in her favour, she was not even the first proposer of the partition. Her natural enemies, Austria and Prussia, actually gained a greater share of the spoil, and, instead of being the first victims of her extended empire, as they infallibly would have been in ancient times, they have themselves acquired, at the same moment, an increase of resources, which enables them effectually to withstand the force of her augmented power.

Although, then, it is extremely absurd to adduce the partition of Poland as an instance of the balancing system (after the manner of the Prussian statesmen)[1] it is equally erroneous to assert that it proves the inefficacy of that system, or to deny that the rest of Europe has been saved by the influence upon the parties in the usurpation, of those principles which should have led the other great powers of Europe to prevent it. It is scarcely necessary to remark, that in asserting the injustice and impolicy of the transaction upon a great scale, we are looking to the effects of the balancing system in maintaining the independence of the weaker states. The case of Poland at present is perhaps one of the very few instances which have ever occurred, of a nation being placed in such unnatural circumstances of embarrassment, turbulence, and degradation of every sort, that scarce any change of affairs could render it worse, and scarce any revolution by domestic violence, or foreign invasion, could fail to alter it for the better. Setting apart the high-sounding phrases of patriotism and national spirit, and the feelings of admiration which the very natural emotions of pity have taught us to couple with the name of Poland, it is impossible for a sober-minded observer not to perceive, that ages of the most debasing servitude had utterly disqualified the Polish boors for enjoying the privileges of free subjects; that a lifetime divided between unceasing tumult in public, and the revellings of a boisterous, barbarous hospitality, had unfitted the rest of the state for co-operating in the formation of a constitution which would possess either energy or regularity; and that the greater part of the country has gained from a dismemberment, lamented by those who had no experience of its necessity.

The memorable events which took place at the close of the

---

[1] Count Hertzberg (the King's first minister in 1772), in a speculative essay on this subject, gives the partition as an opposite case of the balancing system. It was made, he says, 'Selon les principes d'une balance dont les trois puissances partageantes étaient convenues entre elles'. *Mém.*, Vol., i, p. 296.

eighteenth century, it is almost needless to observe, were the immediate consequence of an adherence to the principles of the modern system of international policy. The internal state of France would never have alarmed the neighbouring nations in ancient times. Without anxiety, they would have seen the overthrow of all regular government, the progress of Jacobin contagion, and the development of those popular energies which armed a people, devoted exclusively to war, with resistless power to accomplish the grand object of their demagogues, the overthrow of altars and thrones, and the establishment of universal empire. Far from combining to resist the progress of the new horde, they would have split into factions, and assisted its destructive course. No efforts to check it would have been thought of, until all resistance was too late; nor would those modern Gauls have found hostility effectual to oppose them from the Manlius of any capital in Europe. That this has not been the fate of everything refined and valuable in Europe, is owing to the degree to which the maxims of the balancing system began to produce their usual effects at the very moment when the first changes took place in France. But that much injury has been done; that many independent states have been humbled; that some powers have been overwhelmed; and that melancholy changes have been effected in the distribution of dominion – has been owing to the unprincipled ambition of certain princes, and the taint of disaffection in the people of some countries, which have, together, prevented the modern system of external policy from being followed out, and have given to the common enemy of national independence an advantage proportioned to the neglect of those sound and necessary principles.

It is not, then, to the last century that we can appeal as affording arguments against the balance of power. That eventful period in the history of mankind has been marked by the formation of vast schemes, which either by their success may allure, or by their failure may warn, future statesmen to cling still closer to those maxims of conduct which are necessary to the preservation of liberty and peace.

The remarks which have been frequently made on the knowledge of the ancients, in this branch of policy, are for the most part just. Mr Hume, so far as we know, is the first who stated this point, in an essay replete with acute observation, and distinguished by accuracy of classical illustration, but mingled also with some injurious perversions of facts in more recent history; and with the misstatement, in one or two points of the great system itself, which he appears to treat with disrespect.[1] The celebrated passage in Polybius, which has so often been quoted,[2] is indeed a distinct statement of one general principle in that system; and the orations of Demosthenes contain some discussions of the most delicate parts of the theory – discussions which, from the events of his time, we may be assured were but imperfectly comprehended in those early ages.[3] But the number of discoveries or inventions which have been suddenly made in any branch of knowledge, is small indeed. All the more important steps in the progress of the human mind may rather be termed improvements than inventions: they are refinements upon methods formerly known – generalizations of ideas previously conceived. By how many small and slowly following steps was the true nature of the planetary motions brought to light! By how many insensible gradations did that theory receive its explanation from the great law of gravitation, which, constantly and universally acting, keeps each body in its place, and preserves the arrangement of the whole system. In like manner has that theory of political expediency been gradually unfolded, and its parts refined, which regulates the mutual actions of the European nations; subject each to the influence of others, however remote; connects all together by a common principle; regulates the motions of the whole; and confining within narrow limits whatever deviations may occur in any direction, maintains the order and stability of the vast complicated system. As the newly-discovered planets are found to obey the same law that keeps the rest in their orbits; so the powers, which frequently arise in the European world, immediately fall into their places, and conform to the same principles that fix the positions and direct the movements of the ancient states. And as, even in this enlightened age, we have not yet succeeded in discovering the whole extent of the planetary law, or in reducing certain apparent

[1] 'Essay on the Balance of Power'.
[2] *Polyb.*, Book 1, Chap. 83.
[3] Particularly the famous speech 'Pro Megalopolitanis'—*passim*. The knowledge of the ancients on this subject is treated at large in a subsequent dissertation.

irregularities, of the system to the common principles; so, in these days of political improvement, we have not attained the utmost refinements of international policy, and have still to lament the irregularities which continue to disturb the arrangement of the European commonwealth.

It is not, then, in the mere plan of forming offensive or defensive alliances; or in the principle of attacking a neighbour in order to weaken his power, before he has betrayed hostile views; or in the policy of defending a rival, in order to stay, in proper time, the progress of a common enemy; it is not in these simple maxims that the modern system consists. These are, indeed, the elements, the great and leading parts of the theory; they are its most prominent features; they are maxims dictated by the plainest and coarsest view of political expediency: but they do not form the whole system; nor does the knowledge of them (for it cannot be pretended that ancient states were in possession of anything beyond the speculative knowledge of them) comprehend an acquaintance with the profounder and more subtle parts of modern policy. The grand and distinguishing feature of the balancing theory, is the systematic form to which it reduces those plain and obvious principles of national conduct; the perpetual attention to foreign affairs which it inculcates; the constant watchfulness which it prescribes over every movement in all parts of the system; the subjection in which it tends to place all national passions and antipathies to the views of remote expediency; the unceasing care which it dictates of nations most remotely situated, and apparently unconnected with ourselves; the general union, which it has effected, of all the European powers in one connecting system – obeying certain laws, and actuated, for the most part, by a common principle; in fine, as a consequence of the whole, the right of mutual inspection, now universally recognized among civilized states, in the appointment of public envoys and residents. This is the balancing theory. It was as much unknown to Athens and Rome, as the Keplerian or Newtonian laws were concealed from Plato and Cicero, who certainly knew the effect of gravitation upon terrestrial bodies. It has arisen, in the progress of science, out of the circumstances of modern Europe – the greater extent and nearer equality of the contiguous states – the more constant intercourse of the different nations with each other. We have been told by historians,[1] that the principle of the balance of power was a discovery made at the end of the fifteenth century by the Italian politicians, in consequence of the invasion of Charles VIII. Against such statements as this, it is perfectly fair to adduce the arguments of Mr Hume and others, who have traced in ancient times, vastly more refined notions of policy than any that dictated the Italian defensive league. It was, in truth, not to any such single event, that the balancing system owed either its origin, or its refinement; but to the progress of society, which placed the whole states of Europe in the same relative situation in which the states of Italy were at that period, and taught them not to wait for an actual invasion, but to see a Charles at all times in every prince or commonwealth that should manifest the least desire of change.

The circumstances of the European states, by promoting national intercourse, have been singularly favourable to the development of those principles of easy and constant union. Consolidated into one system of provincial government under the empire of Rome, they were separated by the same causes, and nearly at the same time. Reduced by a people whose character and manners were never effaced by the most rapid conquests, or most remote emigrations, they were formed into divisions under constitutions of the same nature, peculiarly calculated to preserve the uniformity of customs, which originally marked the whole. The progress of political government has been similar in all, from the dominion of the nobles to the tyranny of the prince, and, in these latter times, to the freedom of the people. That spirit of commercial intercourse, which produces a perpetual connection, little known in the ancient world, has conspired with the similarity of situation, and the resemblance of manners, to render Europe a united whole within itself, almost separated from the rest of the world; a great federacy, acknowledging, indeed, no common chief; but united by certain common principles, and obeying one system of international law.

It is from these natural sources, through this gradual progress, and not suddenly from any accidental occurrences in the fifteenth century, or from the cabinets of particular statesmen, that we must deduce the refined system of interference, which has regulated,

[1] Robertson's *Charles V*, Vol. i.

for so long a time, the councils of Europe in foreign affairs; and we are to consider the union of the Italian states against the invasion of Charles, merely as a symptom of the same progressive improvement, which has since taken place in the other parts of Europe.

The question of the propriety of a nation interfering with those concerns of its neighbours, which have only a remote connection with its own interests, may be stated in two different forms; either as a general question applicable to any state, or in its particular reference to the situation of a nation placed in certain circumstances. Thus many politicians, who have no hesitation in recommending the balancing system to such powers as Austria and Prussia, placed in the heart of Europe, and surrounded by many other states of various complexions and magnitudes, are yet of opinion, that the situation of Great Britain is very different; that she is, by nature, insulated from the rest of Europe; that she can defend herself against any invasion, by means of her natural barrier and internal resources; and that she ought not to sacrifice the improvement of these resources, and the means of maintaining peace, to the vain wish of holding the European balance, and embroiling herself in the stormy politics of foreign states. Without entering fully into the discussion of this great national question, we may remark, that so long as Great Britain is engaged in a commercial intercourse with other nations; so long as her insular situation only serves to promote and extend those commercial relations; so long as other states possess a large portion of sea-coast, engage in a wide commercial circle, and are acquiring a navy of formidable power; so long as Britain interferes with them in other quarters of the globe, where her dominions are the most valuable and extensive – it is an abuse of language to talk of her being separated from the continent of Europe by the straits of Dover. The transport of an army by sea is often more easy than the march over a considerable tract of land. The fate of a naval engagement is generally more quick, decisive, and dependent upon fortune, than the siege of barrier towns, or the forcing of mountainous passes; and the elements may, by retaining the British fleets in Plymouth or Portsmouth, while they waft the enemy's squadron from Brest or the Texel, destroy in a moment that bulwark to which we vainly intrusted the national defence, and render utterly useless the whole *natural force* (as it is termed) of the country, which, after a change of weather, may display, triumphantly, its flags over every sea in Europe, while the Consular legions are revelling in the plunder of the Bank, or burning all the dockyards in the kingdom. To say that England may trust to her fleets, then, is to recommend a full reliance upon the chance of a single battle, or the event of a sea-chase; to inculcate a silly confidence in good fortune, and to advise that the fate of Great Britain should be committed to the changes of the elements, the shifting of a wind, or the settling of a fog. It is to her armies that every nation, insular or continental, must look for her sure and *natural defence*. But although it would be absurd to recommend, that the internal resources of a country should be neglected, either in order to favour its naval force, or in order to commit its defence to the movements of intrigue, and the efforts of foreign policy; yet he would be an equally dangerous counsellor who should advise us to neglect those means of preventing war, and of rendering it harmless when it does occur, which are only to be found in a compliance with the principles of the balancing system.

When the different nations of Europe placed their whole glory in the splendour of their warlike renown, and attended only to the improvement of their military resources, every person of free rank was a soldier, and devoted his life to the profession of arms. But as soon as the arts of peace acquired an ascendancy, and other fame beside that of martial deeds was sought after, war became an object of dread, as deranging the main operations of society, and exposing the national independence to unforeseen casualties and dangers. Instead of being followed for its own sake, it was now only resorted to as a necessary evil, to avoid a greater risk. The first great consequence of this change in the occupations and character of men, was the separation of the military from the civil professions; the intrusting a small class in each community with the defence of the rest; the adoption of standing armies, one of the most important improvements in the art of government, with which history has made us acquainted. As this great change has disarmed war of its greatest dangers, so another change, equally important, has arisen out of it, rendered wars much less frequent, and confined their influence to a small portion of the centre of the Continent. The European powers have formed a species of general law, which supersedes, in most instances, an appeal to the sword, by rendering such an appeal fatal to any power that may infringe upon the code; by uniting the forces of the rest inevitably against each delinquent; by agreeing, that any project of violating a neighbour's integrity shall be prevented or avenged, not according to the resources of this neighbour, but according to the full resources of all the other members of the European community; and by constantly watching over the state of public affairs even in profound peace. Such, at least, would be the balancing system, carried to its full extent; and such is the state of refinement towards which it is constantly tending. The division of labour, too, and the separation of the military profession, has been carried by some of the richer nations to a still greater extent than the mere embodying of standing armies. Those states which are the most injured by the operations of war, are also the richest in superfluous stock. They have contrived a species of pecuniary commutation of war, similar to the commutation of military service, which paved the way for the introduction of standing armies; they have managed to turn off the battle from their gates by paying less wealthy allies for fighting in their cause at a safe distance. The operations of war are in this manner rendered more harmless and a foundation is laid for their gradual disuse. A few millions that can be spared are sacrificed, and a few lives; the arts of peace continue to flourish, sometimes with increased prosperity; and the policy of preferring to purchase defeat, if need be, at a distance rather than victory at home – of paying allies for being vanquished, rather than gain triumphs on our own ground – has been amply rewarded by the safety, increased resources, and real addition of power, which result from an enjoyment of all the substantial blessings of peace, with the only real advantages of necessary warfare.

Such are the general outlines of the modern system, founded upon the preservation of a balance of power. The science which professes to discuss the general principles of this system, and their particular application in detail to the actual situation of the European powers, is, consequently, next to jurisprudence, the most important that can occupy the attention of the statesman. It has, however, been alleged, that this is an inquiry reducible to no general or fixed principles; that it does not deserve the name of science; that it depends on the caprices of a few individuals, and variations in their views or measures, occasioned by accidental occurrences. Mr Hume, in particular, at the very time when he recommends the drawing of our conclusions on subjects of domestic policy as fine as it is possible, adds 'that in these affairs, the inferences rest on the concurrence of a multitude of causes, not as in foreign politics, upon accidents, and chances, and the caprices of a few persons'.[1] It may, however, be observed, that the very same general arguments, so irresistibly stated by this acute and profound writer, to prove that politics may be reduced to a science,[2] apply as well to the foreign as to the domestic policy of a state.

[1] *Political Essays.*   [2] Essay III.

FRIEDRICH VON GENTZ

The *Fragments upon the Present State of the Political Balance of Europe* was published in 1806, a year of acute crisis in the history of Europe and of Gentz's own country. This was the year of the defeat of Prussia by Napoleon at Jena and Auerstädt. For this reason Gentz's work seems closely related to the events of his time. Yet in the course of his analysis of the European scene of 1806 Gentz developed a theory of the working of a 'balance of power'.

Gentz (1764-1832) was a Prussian civil servant and author of numerous essays on contemporary affairs. His interest in international politics came after his transfer to the Prussian *Kriegsrat* in 1793, a year in which he was also much impressed by Burke's *Reflections on the Revolution in France*, translating this work into German. Until about 1800 Gentz was an advocate of neutrality, urging this policy to King Frederick William III, and his arguments followed a pacifist tone, stressing that no positive advantage was worth the cost of war. The precise point at which Gentz changed his views remains uncertain, but he became an advocate of war against France in the interests of maintaining the 'balance of power'. He particularly attacked the position of the Comte d'Hauterive who had claimed that international law could only exist as a result of the domination of Europe by one state (*De l'état de la France à la fin de l'an VIII*). Such a law and international order were attainable in Gentz's view by the application of a 'balance of power'. It was at this point that the *Fragments* appeared.

Gentz preferred to call the 'balance of power' *counterpoise*, and this more accurately describes the notion which had recommended itself to statesmen since the sixteenth century, and had characterized their policies in so far as there had been neither a 'universal dominion' nor a constant condition of war among the states of Europe during these centuries. On the contrary, Gentz argues, the states had managed to remain in existence, with the exception of a few and these had disappeared as a result of the clumsy application (or neglect) of the 'balance of power'. In this connection he discusses the case of Poland at some length. One of the consequences of this notion of 'counterpoise' was that wars in the interests of maintaining the 'balance' were necessary and to be carefully distinguished from those fought with a view to destroying the European structure, like those of Napoleon. Another consequence was that there was a point at which intervention in the affairs of another state was necessary (and therefore justified) in order to maintain the balanced existence of the structure. Gentz studied the relationships between states, rather than the foreign policies of separate states, but in a manner which led him to a conservative position. He was the champion of the *status quo*, but he realized that the *status quo* would itself change, that it was a concept and not always embodied in a defined state of affairs. Once Poland had been partitioned, however reprehensible that act might have been, the *status quo* had been changed and a new international order created which in turn had to be preserved:'This event belongs entirely to history. It is in every sense of the word concluded; its results have passed into the province of right and order, into the constitution of Europe, as it is recognized, prescribed, and established by treaties, into that system which has been consecrated by the public sanction of nations.'

The extracts below are taken from the translation of the *Fragments upon the Present State of the Political Balance of Europe*, London, 1806, pp. xxi-xxv and xxviii-xxxi of the Introduction, and pp. 55-91 and 101-116.

Principal events relevant to Gentz's *Fragments upon the Present State of the Political Balance of Europe*:

1772 First partition of Poland.

1793 Second partition of Poland.

1795 Third and final partition of Poland. Prussia withdrawn from war with France.

1801 Treaty of Lunéville between France and Austria. French frontier along the Rhine, and new republics created, Batavia, Helvetia, Cisalpine and Ligurian republics.

1804 War of the third coalition against France, comprising Austria, Russia, Prussia, Sweden, Naples and Great Britain.

1805 Battle of Austerlitz, and treaty between Austria and France at Pressburg.

1806 Defeat of Prussia at Jena and Auerstädt.

1807 Peace of Tilsit between France and Russia.

Suggested Reading

G. Mann, *Friedrich von Gentz: Secretary of Europe*, 1946.
P. R. Sweet, *Friedrich von Gentz: Defender of the Old Order*, 1941.

Introduction

[Gentz is here attacking those who viewed the threat of French domination of Europe with indifference, or with satisfaction. The 'evil' to which he refers later in the same sentence is precisely 'the ignominious fall of the European commonwealth' in the face of Napoleon's armies.]

The word-mongers of the *indifferent* party, rich in dispiriting encouragements, and desolating consolations, in order to soothe the discontent of their own contemporaries, at one time represent the evil as unavoidable, and at another they describe the advantages which are still left us. 'Now,' say they, 'that Europe by an irresistible destiny is reduced to a situation in which hardly a shred of its ancient political constitution is left, it is no longer worthwhile to treat or fight about it. Experience has clearly demonstrated, that every attempt to stem the torrent of destruction has been attended with a contrary effect; when power has attained a certain pitch it is madness to resist; in such a case wisdom prescribes to us to capitulate on the best possible terms, and instead of defending the entrenchments, an early surrender, deference to the will of the conqueror, assiduity in courting his favour, so that all that can be saved may be saved. Besides our lot, taken even in its most threatening aspect, is far from being intolerable. The balance of power among states has always been a chimera; in all times the weak have received laws from the strong; whether the law is pronounced by one individual, or twenty, is the same to him whose fortune it is to obey. To live under the sceptre of a stranger, and to see all the appurtenances of an independent constitution swallowed up in the vortex of a prodigious monarchy, where everything is engorged, and mingled, and sunk, and forgotten, has, to be sure, something repulsive in it; but in whatever hands the chief authority may be placed, there will always be local regents, and whether these be men of ancient race, or upstarts, whether they be called presidents, or prefects, or stadholders, or electors, or Kings; of what consequence is this to the subjects? No one can be robbed of those things which he values the most, his house, his land, a part (who will be insatiable!) of his hereditary or acquired fortune; and let the worst happen, no despot can disturb what constitutes the real enjoyments of this passing life, the pleasures of the table, and of love, music, the theatre, good instructive reading, a friendly game at cards, a comfortable restoring sleep. The rest consists merely of accessories of imaginary, rather than real goods, which are not to be rejected, it is true, when they can be obtained by moderate exertion, or even by temporary sacrifices; but which we should cease to pursue as soon as they endanger the possession of more substantial advantages, the enjoyments of which is always sufficient to console us for the want of the others.'

Every person must perceive after a moment's reflection, that it would be a fruitless undertaking to combat such a system with argument. For between what lies within its sphere, and what lies without it, a common basis is wanting, without which no discussion can lead to any right conclusions. Must it be formally demonstrated that every member of a state, however low and insignificant he may be, besides the common wants of life has other desires of a higher nature, among which national honour, a respected name, an independent constitution, a fixed and well assured interest in the political system, hold a principal place? These truths must be felt, and those who are insensible to them can never be convinced of them by argument. When a people or a generation is so far degraded by egotism, by unworthy maxims, and by a low and contracted manner of thinking, as to have lost all sense of public interest, to consider the country as a name without a meaning, to weigh the value of an independent existence in the same balance with the commonest benefits, and to view the loss of liberty, and honour, as an event of indifference; then it is no longer time to appeal to the nobler feelings; slavery is complete before the oppressor has appeared; the state is dissolved before being the object of violence; and when the first trying catastrophe arrives, those who were no longer able to endure the light of the sun will be delivered over to the minister of darkness. But if reason and experience compel us to pronounce that indifference to the public good, which characterizes a very great proportion of the people of our time, an incurable evil; what are we to think of another error, which, though less frequent, is still more revolting than that, (for it would be going too far to call it more destructive), I mean the *satisfaction* with which some amongst us hail the dissolution of all the old constitutions, the more than half finished, and soon to be completed, subjection of Europe! Here it is not grounds of consolation which they offer us to sweeten a bitter and inevitable destiny; it is formal congratulations, it is a call to joy and exultation. One informs us with philosophical profundity, that what in appearance is so frightful, if considered in a just point of view, is the best and most convenient way to attain an everlasting peace; war, the only evil – for human wisdom will ere long get the better of earthquakes, pestilence, and famine – will soon vanish from the earth, when everything is subjected to one master. Another is of opinion, not quite without ground, if the conclusion followed from the premises – that the old political body is become so weak, the joints which unite the different members so feeble, and the spirit which animated the whole so exhausted, impotent and scant, that its dissolution should not occasion much regret; but on the contrary, as opening a better prospect for futurity, that it is more to be wished for than deprecated. The vigorous creative hand of one individual of an absolute sovereign will restore to everything life and youth. A third dwells on the greatness of the man, whom Providence has chosen to govern the world according to his will; when the struggle is once finished, and every obstructing obstacle removed, then will his mighty genius put us again in possession of what we have lost, and convert united Europe into a scene of comfort and abundance, of splendour and bliss. The public hear this language, not indeed with unqualified confidence, but without any symptom of disgust; and in the minds of most people, there is something which predisposes them favourably to receive it. They pant after repose. They think it impossible but the present painful, embroiled, and tumultous state of things, must tend to a speedy and determinate issue; leading either to the re-establishment of order, or to the completion of that disorder, where everything must begin anew. But as the road which conducts to the former of these results is much more long and rugged than that which leads to the latter, they accustom themselves, by little and little, to consider the very abyss of evil as a sort of haven in which their hopes repose; and thus become familiar with the most criminal wishes, of which they were originally quite unaware.

Such a temper of mind as that here described we cannot be expected to combat. In so far as it has obtained an ascendant among the great mass of the people, it originated either in childish credulity, or in dark despair.

CHAPTER I

THE TRUE ACCEPTATION OF A
BALANCE OF POWER

What is usually termed a balance of power, is that constitution subsisting among neighbouring states more or less connected with one another; by virtue of which no one among them can injure the independence or the essential rights of another, without meeting with effectual resistance on some side, and consequently exposing itself to danger.

The allusion in the term to corporeal objects has given occasion to various misconceptions. It has been represented that those who recognize the principles of a combination among states founded on an equal balance of power, had in view the most perfect possible *equality* or *equalization* of powers, and required that the different states composing a great political league should, in respect of extent, population, riches, resources, and so forth, be exactly measured, squared and rounded by a common standard. Out of this false hypothesis, according as it has been applied by credulity or scepticism to the relations between states, have sprung two opposite errors, the one almost as hurtful as the other. Those who adopted that imaginary principle in its full extent, were thereby led to believe that in every case in which a state gains an accession of strength, either by external acquisitions, or by the development of its internal resources, the rest must oppose, and contend with it till they have either obtained an equivalent or reduced it to its former situation. A different set justly persuaded of the impossibility of such a system have, on the other hand, declared the whole idea of a political balance to be a chimera invented by dreamers, and artfully made use of by designing men as a pretext for disputes, injustice and violence. The former of these errors would banish peace from earth; the latter would open the most desirable prospects to every state which, under the influence of ambition, aspired to universal dominion.

Both errors proceed from the same mixture of ideas, which, in the province of the interior economy of states, have produced all the visionary and airy theories of *civil liberty*, and the failure of all the practical attempts to carry them into execution. In every well ordered state the collective body of citizens, and in every well ordered commonwealth of nations the collective body of states should be *equal in rights*, (that is) their *rights* should be *equally respected*; but it by no means follows that they should have the *same rights*, that is, *rights of equal quality and value*. True *equality*, and the other equality attainable by legitimate means, consists, in both cases, in this, that the smallest as well as the greatest is secured in the possession of *his right*, and that it can neither be forced from him nor encroached upon by *lawless* power.

As it is a fundamental principle in every well-organized state, and the triumph of its constitution, that a multitude of persons in the greatest degree unequal in rights and powers, in talents and capacities, in acquired and inherited possessions, so happily exist together under common laws, and a common government, that no one can arbitrarily thrust himself into his neighbour's sphere; and that the poorest can as little be molested in the enjoyment of his cottage and his field, as the richest can be in the possession of his palace and domains; so the proper character of a union of states, such as has existed in modern Europe, and the triumph of its constitution, is, that a certain number of states, possessing various degrees of power and wealth, shall each remain untroubled within its own confines, under the protection of a common league, and that, that state whose whole territory is encircled by the walls of a single town, shall be held as sacred by its neighbours as any other, whose possessions and power extends over lands and seas.

But as the best constitution of a single state which can be devised by man never completely answers its purpose, and always leaves room for individual acts of violence, oppression, injustice; in the same manner the most perfect federal constitution is never sufficiently strong to prevent every attack of a more powerful state on the rights of a less powerful. Nay more, if the conditions are in other respects equal, a league between states will, in a certain proportion, be more defective in protecting the independence and security of its members, than a single state is in defending the legal equality and security of its citizens. The security of the citizens of a single state rests upon the unity of its legislation and administration. The laws all proceed from one central point, their maintenance is the work of one and the same authority, and those who are disposed to infringe them can be checked at the outset by legal coercion; or those who have actually transgressed them, can be made responsible to a tribunal of justice. The law which binds states together consists in their mutual compacts; and as these, from the endless diversity of the relations out of which they spring, are susceptible of an infinite number of differences in their principle, spirit, and character, the nature of their origin excludes, in the strict sense of the word, a higher common sanction. Among independent nations there is neither an executive nor a judicial power; to create the one or the other has been long a fruitless, pious wish, and the object of many a vain, well-meaning effort. But what the nature of these relations prevented from ever being perfectly accomplished was, at least, obtained in approximation; and in the general political system of modern Europe the problem was as happily solved as could be expected from the endeavours of men, and the application of human wisdom.

There was formed among the states of this quarter of the globe an extensive social commonwealth, of which the characteristic object was the preservation and reciprocal guarantee of the rights of all its members. From the time that this respectable object came to be distinctly and clearly recognized, the necessary eternal conditions, on which it was attainable, unfolded themselves by degrees. Men were soon aware that there were certain fundamental principles, arising out of the proportional power of each of the component parts to the whole, without the constant influence of which order could not be secured; and the following maxims were gradually set down as a practical basis, which was not to be deviated from;

That if the states system of Europe is to exist and be maintained by common exertions, no one of its members must ever become so powerful as to be able to coerce all the rest put together;

That if that system is not merely to exist, but to be maintained without constant perils and violent concussions; each member which infringes it must be in a condition to be coerced, not only by the collective strength of the other members, but by any majority of them, if not by one individual;

But that to escape the alternate danger of an uninterrupted series of wars, or of an arbitrary oppression of the weaker members in every short interval of peace; *the fear* of awakening common vengeance, must of itself be sufficient to keep every one within the bounds of moderation; and

That if ever a European state attempted by unlawful enterprizes to attain to a degree of power, (or had in fact attained it), which enabled it to defy the danger of a union of several of its neighbours, or even an alliance of the whole, such a state should be treated as a common enemy; and that if, on the other hand, it had acquired that degree of force by an accidental concurrence of circumstances, and without any acts of violence, when ever it appeared upon the public theatre, no means which political wisdom could devise for the purpose of diminishing its power, should be neglected or untried.

These maxims contain the only intelligible theory of a balance of power in the political world.[1]

The original equality of the parties in such a union as is here described is not an accidental circumstance, much less a casual evil; but is in a certain degree to be considered as the previous condition and foundation of the whole system.[2] It is not *how much power* one or other possess, but whether he possess it in such a manner that he cannot with impunity encroach upon that of the rest; which is the true question to be answered, in order to enable us to judge at every given moment of the proportion between individual parts and of the general sufficiency of the structure: hence even a subsequent increase of that original necessary inequality, provided it has not sprung from sources, or been intro-

---

[1] It perhaps would have been with more propriety called a system of *counterpoise*. For perhaps the highest of its results is not so much a perfect *equipoise* as a constant alternate *vacillation* in the scales of the balance, which, from the application of *counterweights*, is prevented from ever passing certain limits.

[2] Had the surface of the globe been divided into equal parts, no such union would ever have taken place; and an eternal war of each against the whole is probably the only event we should have heard of.

duced by practices, which contravene one of the fundamental maxims above-mentioned, may be in itself blameless.

It is only when a state with open wantonness, or under fictitious pretences and titles artificially invented, proceeds to such enter-prizes as immediately, or in their unavoidable consequences, pre-pare the way for the subjugation of its weaker neighbours, and for perpetual danger to the stronger, that conformably to sound conceptions of the general interest of the commonwealth, a rupture of the balance is to be apprehended; it is only then that several should unite together to prevent the decided preponderance of one individual power.

By this system, which has been acted upon since the beginning of the sixteenth century, with more or less good fortune, but with great constancy, and often with uncommon prudence; at first more in a practical way, and, as it were from political instinct, afterwards with clear, reflecting, and methodical constancy, two great results were obtained, in the midst of a tumultuous assemblage of the most decisive events. The one was, that no person succeeded in prescribing laws to Europe, and that (till our times), all apprehen-sion, even of the return of a universal dominion, was gradually banished from every mind. The other, that the political constitu-tion, as it was framed in the sixteenth century, remained so entire in all its members till the end of the eighteenth, (when all ancient ordinances were abolished), that none of the independent powers, which originally belonged to the confederacy, had lost their political existence.

How these two important results were obtained, amid cares and dangers of various sorts, amid many storms and tempests, to the credit of the European statemanship, and to the no small advantage of humanity, is to be learnt in the history of that period.[1] It was only at the commencement of this period, before experience and deeper observation had spoiled the phantom of its terrors, that the possibility of an universal monarchy obtained belief.[2] But wiser

---

[1] Few writers have illustrated modern history in this point of view with more learning and ingenuity than Mr Ancillon, in his *Tableau des Révolutions du Systéme Politique de l'Europe*.

[2] The extent of the possessions of Charles V had suggested the idea of such an event, and had given it a certain importance; but it has never been made even probable that this monarch entertained this project, or pursued it under any form. Posterior to his time, when the power of the house of Austria was

men afterwards perceived, that though a complete universal dominion, such as the Romans established, might on sufficient grounds be declared impossible in modern Europe, this was by no means the only danger: they perceived that by extraordinary circumstances, and by neglecting to oppose the proper obstacles, one great kingdom or another might attain such a degree of preponderance as might gradually draw upon the whole system, if not immediate sudden destruction, at least the loss of its independance; as might change substantive parts of its territory (under whatever title it might be), into provinces of the principal state; as might convert regents into vassals, and whatever other evils might arise out of such a constitution, they clearly and with utter abhorrence recognized in its eventual establishment, the unavoidable ruin of the smaller, the oppression and degradation of the greater, and the constant peril of the middling states.

But by the arrangements adopted by the statesmen of better times, and less by individual measures than by the general vigilance, alertness, energy, and true political spirit which guided them at every step, they succeeded in most successfully solving their second problem, in preserving inviolate the whole structure committed to their care, even in its lowest compartments, and in protecting with eminent dexterity those weaker parts which were in danger from time to time of being undermined. It is certainly a remarkable occurrence, that in the course of three most eventful centuries, amid so many bloody wars, so various and decisive negotiations, so frequent changes of power, so great and extended revolutions, amid a general anarchy of all social, civil, religious, and political relations, not one independent state was annihilated by violent means. Neither Switzerland, nor Holland, nor any spiritual nor temporal German prince, nor the most insignificant imperial town, nor Venice, nor Genoa, nor the small Italian republics, though surrounded on all sides by states of gigantic

divided into two separate branches, it was indeed attempted to revive the terror, but it was merely an artifice of hostile powers. It is remarkable that Hume, one of the most dispassionate, soberest, and most impartial of our modern historians, pointedly maintains that the house of Austria, particularly from the scattered situation of its provinces, was by no means so well calculated to establish a universal monarchy as France, 'which possessed all the advantages of the Austrian powers, and laboured under none of its defects'. See 'Essay on the Balance of Power' in Hume's *Essays and Treatises*, Vol. i.

greatness, nor Malta left to itself, nor the weak, though flourishing Geneva pressed by France on one side, and Savoy on the other; nor even the power of Savoy, at one time threatened by Austria, at another by France; nor Portugal, enclosed on all sides by the Spanish territory; nor Sweden, nor Denmark, both endangered by the prodigious extension and aggrandizement of the Russian and Prussian powers; not one of all these states disappeared. Several of them certainly maintained themselves by their own courage and strength, or by superior wisdom, or by the recollection of those achievements by means of which in earlier times they had attained to independance and dignity. But the greater part of them, if not all, would, to the vast prejudice of the whole, have gone to ruin, had they not been supported and protected by the general interest of Europe, and those great enlightened principles, by which that interest was conducted.

The whole of this excellent system has now at length, like all the works of man, seen the hour of its fall approach; and it has sunk under those maladies which gradually prove fatal to all the productions of the moral world, *abuse of form* on one hand, and *apathy of spirit* on the other. How this has happened will be shown in the following chapters, and, at the same time, we shall conscientiously enquire, whether because much is lost, and much irretrievably lost, we should on that account, with cowardly indifference, give up that which still remains; or, whether we ought not rather to do our utmost to save what can yet be saved, and from the ruins of the old building to rear a new and more substantial edifice?

CHAPTER II

OF THE SHOCK GIVEN TO THE BALANCE OF POWER BY THE INTRODUCTION OF THE PARTITION SYSTEM

In the physical world, a system, the operations of which are regulated by weights and counterweights, can only be shaken by one or more of these losing their original power, and thus producing the preponderance of the others, and the ruin of the machine. A similar system, when applied to human relations, is exposed, besides that now mentioned, to another danger. As its powers in this case are endowed with freedom, a part of these may combine to the prejudice of the rest, and effect what would have been impossible for any one singly to have produced, the ruin of the devoted member, and thus the destruction of the whole machine.

A system of political counterpoise, has both in its structure and operations, a remarkable analogy with what, in the internal economy of states, is called a mixed constitution, or constitutional balance. When this, as in England for example, has attained to the highest pitch of perfection of which it is susceptible; when everything is arranged and constituted in the wisest manner, when none of the different powers of which it is composed can surpass the bounds of their respective spheres, or in any way transgress their limits without encountering a repelling force, there is yet another danger which baffles all human skill to avoid. As the divided powers must necessarily act in concert for good and salutary purposes, they can also, in extraordinary cases, voluntarily combine for bad ones; and thus, what would have been impossible for any one singly to operate had the principles of mutual counteraction continued, may be effected by a fatal understanding between them, to the prejudice of the state, and the ruin of its constitution.

In precisely the same manner it is possible that the members of a great confederacy, which, in the natural course of things, should act as a counterpoise the one to the other; and in times of common danger, by common measures of prevention, oppose the preponderance of one individual, may be misled by extraordinary conjectures, may unite for the oppression, humiliation, or annihilation of a weaker member, and thus employ for the purpose of attack and destruction the same powers which were destined for protection and preservation. To such a perversion of a system grounded in wisdom, and calculated for beneficial purposes, by the constant action and reaction of reciprocal limitation; to such an *abuse of form* the partition system is indebted for its origin.

The possibility of an abuse of this kind arose so clearly out of the particular construction of the European national league, that, as it strikes us at present, a mind reflecting on futurity must have dreaded the contingency of the evil long before its approach. But in all human things there are certain outrageous extremes, it would seem, which even the mind most capable of combination does not take into its calculation till the evil actually arrive, brought on as it were by a fatal influence of the stars; such is the case with that unfortunate perversion by which the most salutary political principle was converted into a tool of unrighteousness. It was not known, it was not counted upon, it was scarce ever dreaded, when in the year 1772 the partition of Poland took place.

This event belongs entirely to history. It is in every sense of the word concluded; its results have passed into the province of right and order, into the constitution of Europe, as it is recognized, prescribed, and established by treaties, into that system which has been consecrated by the public sanction of nations. Besides this, its authors and those who took a part in it have disappeared from the theatre, posterity now pronounces judgment on their transactions. If we regard them with a rigorous eye, it is not only for the purpose of ascertaining with correctness the causes of the shock sustained by the social constitution of Europe, and of the means of remedying the evil, we are actuated by another and more pressing motive. The partition of Poland is now pleaded as a just pretence for completely overturning what still remains of the old constitution, and forcibly and violently knocking to the ground its pillars and supporters. It is explicitly maintained, not merely by private writers, who must first clear the path, but by the French government and its immediate acknowledged organs, that France is justified even now in demanding idemnity for what the neighbouring powers gained by the partition of Poland, and that by just analogy, as they carried their plans into execution without the consent of France, so France must pursue its advantage, without regarding their remonstrances, wherever it can carry its arms. In order to strip this pretence of everything which has a tendency to blind the weak, to mislead the wise, to encourage and to favour the enemies of the public weal, it is proper and necessary attentively to consider it. In great transactions like these, a contempt of all little aids and an undisguised representation of truth is always the surest way to one's object. With the more frankness and sincerity that we pronounce upon past injustice, so much more undoubted is our right not to spare those who have called it back into existence for the purpose of building upon it a new and more extended system of iniquity and still wider devastation.

What rendered the project of a partition of Poland so incomparably more destructive to the higher interests of Europe than any former acts of violence of apparently a more aggravated character, was the decisive circumstance of its originating in that very sphere from which was expected to flow nothing but benefits and blessings, security in time of peace, and salvation in periods of danger. An union between several regents had been always considered as a barrier against lawless power, and the passions of an individual oppressor; it now appeared, to the terror of the world! that such an union could be formed for the purpose of bringing about precisely that evil against which it seemed destined as a bulwark of defence. The impression made by this detestable discovery must be still deeper and more painful, when we reflect that the framers of the wicked project, in the whole course of their undertaking, adopted the principle of the political balance as a star to conduct them through it; that they acted conformably to this principle as far as circumstances would admit in the adjustment of their respective interests, and that while they inflicted upon its spirit the most frightful wounds, they borrowed its

attire, its forms, and even its language. *Corruptio optimi pessima.*
To witness such an abuse of the noblest mean which the European
commonwealth possessed for assuring its safety and welfare, was,
in itself, a revolting spectacle; but the malignant character of the
deed was first completely brought to light in its consequences.
The cause of public justice was on all hands abandoned and
betrayed. A horde of jabbering sophists who, at that time in
France, were striving to shake the foundations of all principle, and
to undermine every existing constitution now that the mighty of
the earth had broken into the sanctuary of national right, not
under the impulse of incendiary passions, but deliberately and
systematically turned the most respectable political ideas into
ridicule without fear or reserve. Even among the enlightened and
upright of the time only a few escaped the dreadful contagion.
Notwithstanding that what is purest in its nature may be profaned,
and what is most wholesome may be poisoned – notwithstanding
that the fatal blow which the federal constitution of Europe had
received called upon them the more loudly to unite, to establish
the foundations of the building on a firmer basis, and more
vigorously to exert themselves in its defence, they either gave
themselves up to a comfortless incredulity in the inefficacy of
political maxims, or to a systematic indifference. The multitude
misled by the former, or not sufficiently warned against the latter,
sunk every day deeper in the bottomless void, and became more
and more accustomed to expect their law from violence, and their
salvation from chance. How much this fatal habit of thinking must
have contributed to facilitate crime, and spread desolation, when
at last the evil days arrived when all right was trampled underfoot,
the ruin of all order conspired, and the whole social machine
disjointed and broken, can have escaped only the inconsiderate
observer.

But we have at last suffered enough; ruins heaped on ruins,
disaster on disaster, and a mass of violence and crime, such as no
age ever witnessed, has covered up that old act of injustice. To
bring it again forward to view, for the sake of grounding upon it
new usurpations, is a pretension so repulsive in its nature, that all
Europe must unite in raising its voice against it. This becomes so
much sounder policy, and so much the more a sacred obligation,
because that unhallowed and wicked pretence, after a long interval

of silence is again brought forward at a moment of crisis and great confusion, so that no one can determine where in the course of time it may lead, and whether at last it may not be explicitly declared, that *Europe* must go to ruin because *Poland* has gone to ruin. It is time to set this whole process aside; France alone still rakes up its ashes: let us unite satisfactorily to prove that France has no right in any political discussion, in the defence of any present measure, or in preferring any claim whether in other respects well or ill grounded, to bring what formerly happened in Poland into reckoning and account. By these means at least if we are not able to impose eternal silence upon all present and future sophists, we shall at least set to rest the sound part of public opinion upon this captious question.

I. The fate of Poland is long ago decided, not only in *fact* but in *right*. By a number of treaties of peace and conventions concluded between the partitioning powers, and all the other European states, their old and new possessions are recognized and guaranteed; the former Polish provinces are now so compleatly united and incorporated with their old territory as to make it impossible to separate the one from the other; the reestablishment of Poland is therefore impracticable, either in *fact* or *right*. Had France by the partition of this country been immediately and essentially injured, had it suffered and lost more than the other neighbouring states, had *it* alone lost and suffered by the transaction, had it the justest claims upon indemnity for this loss, and had it not extended its territory a single foot's breadth, were all these suppositions as true as they are collectively false, it would be no less firmly established that after France had kept silence so long, had kept silence on so many great occasions; nay more, after it formally acknowledged and confirmed the present constitution in all its treaties of peace, its right is for ever extinguished, forfeited and cancelled. The French government has lately[1] made the romantic proposal, to appearance indeed by way of joke, but who can mistake the omen! that all the powers should respectively give up what they have acquired for the last fifty years: but if everything is to be settled in this way, and if all that has been transacted and agreed upon for half a century is to be undone and retracted, why not

[1] In an article of the Moniteur of the 24th July, which I shall often have occasion to mention.

go further back? Why not go at least a hundred or a hundred and fifty years back? Thus would France give up Alsace, the three bishoprics of Loraine; or if it kept them, give an equivalent to the Emperor of Germany in Italy. With much about the same right indeed, the King of Sweden might take possession of the states of Denmark, because his ancestors lost Livonia to Russia; or the King of Spain indemnify himself in Portugal for the loss of Holland.

2. But if all that has been concluded, decided, and ratified by the law of nations, still remained in a state of uncertainty, and a negotiation were now, for the first time, to be set on foot on the question of the interest of France in the partition of Poland, there is no enlightened tribunal of public law which would not decree, that the transaction which took place in Poland did not afford the slightest pretence for the smallest aggrandizement of France. Not now to dwell upon that senseless doctrine on which France has oftener than once grounded her late pretensions, because a *first* violated the right of a *second*, a *third* is justifiable in avenging them on a *fourth*; we consider the case merely in its influence on the collective body of states. Could Europe have been indemnified in any way by the gain of France for the loss which it sustained in the partition of Poland! Would not every attempt of this nature instead of healing the wounds rather have irritated them, and made them mortal? If the King of England, in a critical conjuncture, should combine with both his houses of parliament to adopt some unjust and oppressive measure, tending to the ruin of his land; what would we think of the man who should have the audacity to maintain *now* the House of Commons is at liberty to pass the first arbitrary law that may be proposed *without* the consent of either the King or the Lords? The appeals of France to the transactions of Poland have precisely the same degree of logical force; because the system adopted for the common security experienced a violent shock in consequence of an unfortunate combination of certain powers, shall every power be henceforth at liberty to attack it when it shall think proper? Had such a pretension been brought forward immediately after the partition of Poland, the partitioning powers even ought not to have hesitated a moment to take the field to combat it; for though one has been guilty himself of injustice still it is always proper and laudable in him to prevent others from committing similar injustice. It was the

province and duty of France to stifle the project in the birth, and to prevent its execution in every possible way; but after it was completely accomplished, had the French cabinet at that time under pretence of re-establishing the balance of power, attempted the conquest of a neighbouring country, Holland for example, Austria, Prussia, and Russia would not only have neglected their rights, but would have exposed themselves to a new reproach, if they had not employed their force in frustrating the undertaking.

3. In as far as *political* grounds can be separated from grounds of *justice*, it is indisputably certain, that the aggrandizement of France in consequence of the partition of Poland could not *politically* have been either justified or excused. The powers which were, to use the expression, *personally* interested in this event, were the Ottoman Porte, Sweden, and Denmark: in a more distant degree, and as it were in a second instance, on account of its future possible consequences, the German empire, the States of Italy and Switzerland. What France suffered from it, it suffered in the first place as a party in the common interest of Europe, and secondly in virtue of its near connection with those who were the immediate sufferers. The security of France, its proper personal interests, its prosperity, importance and splendour, remained uninjured and untouched. For France had been for more than a century so fortunately rounded, enclosed, and, as it were, perfected, that there was nothing wanting to render it flourishing, nothing that could bring it into danger. Richly endowed with all the gifts of nature and of Heaven, equally well calculated for a military and maritime power, covered from the danger of hostile attack by strong natural boundaries, prodigious fortresses, and the experience of three centuries, envied only by a single power, if by any; feared and beloved by all the rest. France could behold with indifference, as far as its own interests were concerned, the extension of all the European states. It had under Louis XIV more than once made head against the half of Europe (which then did not attack its rights but opposed its ambition); it possessed a century afterwards – who at this time of day can contest it! – more real sources of power, more means of resistance and attack than it ever possessed under Louis XIV. What it might have obtained with these means, by a regular and judicious system of energy, may be clearly seen from what it has been able to effect in a long fit

of feverish delirium. Even its external political relatives were not hurt by the partition of Poland. For the union of the three partitioning powers was manifestly only a passing phenomenon; and what for France, more than anything else, was then the surest ground of its security, and what afterwards has produced its preponderance, and favoured its usurpations – the rivalship between Austria and Prussia – remained unaltered.

4. Hitherto we have only had the first partition in view, but what we have said of this will, with a few alterations, apply also to the second[1]; the result of this also is ratified by public instruments; it also, however unjust it may have been, furnished France with no legitimate ground for extending its dominion at the expence of its neighbours. The only point which, at first sight, appears at all doubtful, is, whether on account of the extent of the territory gained, France was entitled to indemnity in a *political* view. We firmly maintain, and hope that every enlightened statesman will agree with us, that if France were now limited by its old boundaries, its individual interest would not be at all injured by the final dissolution of Poland; that notwithstanding the consequent aggrandizement of the three powers, it was not threatened more than any other state by a contingent league between them; and that it was much less vulnerable than any other in its vital parts, protected as it is from without by the intervention of the neighbouring kingdoms, fortified as it is internally by its wealth, its great and various industry, the military spirit of its inhabitants, and extraordinary resources of every sort which qualify it for the greatest undertakings; and possessing everything, in short, which the warmest and most discerning patriot could wish for to complete the prosperity of his country. But how distant is the hypothesis upon which we maintain this

---

[1] France has so much less reason to complain of the last partition of Poland, that had it not been for her accursed revolution which threw everything into confusion, it would probably never have taken place; besides it must be confessed, without retracting anything that has been said against the principle, it has become, through extraordinary and unexpected conjunctures, a protection for Europe; for it is easier to imagine, than to point out with precision, what would have become of Europe after the frightful turn which the war with France took, after the last treaty of peace and the dreary days that followed this peace, if in the middle of the only three kingdoms which could oppose a dam to stem the torrent of destruction, there had existed a weak, tumultous, distracted state, continually and *necessarily* the theatre of French cabals.

position from the truth! What an increase of territory, of population and revenue, has France acquired in the course of the last ten years? In reference even to an equal distribution of power, though we always protest against this as the true theory of the constitution of a balance of power, it had acquired before the year 1801,[1] in political strength, more than any one of the three partitioning powers gained by its share of Poland. So that when we hear it said on every occasion, 'France has derived less advantage than any European state from the changes which have taken place in the course of the last fifty years', we are in doubt whether this is meant to impose on the simplicity of the reader, or whether it is thrown out by way of banter.

If the division of Poland was the first event which by an *abuse of form* deranged the political balance of Europe, it was likewise one of the first which begot an *apathy of spirit*, and stupid insensibility to the general interest. The silence of France and England, the silence of all Europe, when a measure of so much importance was planned and executed, is almost as astonishing as the event itself. The weakness of the French cabinet toward the conclusion of the reign of Louis XV, throws some light upon the circumstance, but does not sufficiently explain it. No effectual resistance could have been expected from England alone, and still less from the other powers after France declined to interfere. But it will not escape the observation of the historian, that the omission on that occasion of any public measure, of any energetic remonstrance, of any serious protest, nay, even of any expression of disapprobation, was an undubitable symptom of general debility and relaxation.

And yet how unimportant and trifling appear these passing clouds, when compared with that thick darkness in which we are now involved! The preponderance of the mighty league by which the partition of Poland was effected; the surprising novelty of the transaction; the mystery in which it was long wrapped up; the prudence with which it was concerted; the boldness with which it was executed; all taken together explain how those who naturally might have been expected to oppose it, stunned and petrified, as it were, by sudden terror, forgot their allotted parts. The events of the last ten years were stamped with a different character.

[1] Its later unjust and lawless usurpations we shall not here bring under consideration.

CHAPTER III

OF THE DECAY OF POLITICAL FEELING
IN THE COURSE OF THE
REVOLUTION WAR

The transition from the present state of things to another founded upon a balance of power, and leading to a permanent amelioration of the political system, and to durable order and tranquillity, intelligent men have long perceived cannot be brought about, without strenuous exertions and sacrifices of every sort. The first duty obligatory on us in the present circumstances, is to pour forth the most ardent wishes for the successful progress of those arms which have been taken up in our great cause. But in order that we may not want a foundation on which to build for the future, supposing our efforts to be crowned with success, our undivided attention should be directed to what a true political union, a genuine federal constitution presupposes as the necessary conditions of its existence. The system which our ancestors had organized, has been decomposed and annihilated by an *abuse of Form*, and by *languor of Spirit*. It is indispensable for the future constantly to guard against that abuse, and to oppose the return of this languor with vigilance, activity and wisdom; and in the exercise of these virtues alone, we may not only rebuild what has fallen, but secure the durability of the future edifice.

The first care from its very nature belongs to the governments. The experience of the last twenty years has sufficiently demonstrated what disorder in the political system, what extensive fatal consequences, what distrust, what discontent, what coldness between princes and their subjects, what perilous uncertainty in possession, what debilitation of the federal principle, what destructive examples to usurpers, what pretexts for injustice and tyranny have sprung from projects of partition. Every just and conscientious government must first, therefore, set it down as an unchangeable maxim in its own policy, never henceforth to lend an ear to plans which are not founded in the strictest equity. In the next place, though a general code of laws cannot, in the proper sense of the word, be framed for the regulation of a state confederacy, at least no means should be left untried to procure for these maxims a common sanction, and the solemn ratification of treaties. In every considerable alliance,[1] in every treaty of peace, particularly in every congress composed of several considerable powers, the parties must mutually engage themselves not to endeavour to extend their territory by unjust means; and not to enter into any scheme or association directed against the rights or possessions of an independent state, by whatever name it may be called, whether of dividing, of rounding, of concentrating, of uniting, or of indemnifying themselves for other losses. A sort of anathema must also be pronounced by anticipation, against all such as shall project such violations of right, or call upon others to assist them; so that a lively conviction may be again established in the public mind, that when princes and states enter into combinations with one another, their objects always are preservation and protection and defence against common danger, never the attack and invasion of the innocent.

The second care, that of rousing the public spirit, is the common duty of us all; but here also the governments must lead the way. For if they do not set the example, we have no right to expect that, in an age like ours, so distinguished for general culture, for the development of individual talent, for the refined enjoyment of life, for constantly increasing riches, for growing corruption, for the charm of so many private occupations which tempt to a renunciation of those of a more public nature, and which intice individuals to devote their cares exclusively to their own happiness, their own improvement, their own comfort or pleasures,

---

[1] The two Imperial courts, with a wisdom which can never be sufficiently extolled, in their declaration of September 3rd, voluntarily and uncalled upon, declared 'the integrity of Germany and of the Ottoman "power"', to be one of the bases of their union.

people shall again take a hearty and lively interest in the public welfare, depending as it goes upon the existence and preservation of a great political union. But princes, and particularly those of high rank, are created and live expressly for the purpose of managing the high trust of the general interest. For this purpose they must, before all things, be true to that which to them is dearest. Their most sacred duty is never to permit any diminution of their own rights, but to maintain intact the degree of political weight, importance, and influence, which has been consigned to them; and not to tolerate, under any pretence, the introduction of changes into the general system of the political relations and distributions of power in Europe, by which, sooner or later, they might be driven from their proper stations. But they are no less called upon and obligated to watch over, maintain and defend, the independence, security and rights, of their neighbours, their allies and of every acknowledged and legally constituted power; even those of their rivals, and those of their occasional enemies. From the moment that they no longer feel themselves strong enough to prevent the weakest and most inconsiderable state from being injured with impunity, or robbed of its independence by the criminal and arbitrary acts of a stronger, their own thrones become unstable. We must hear of no insulary systems, no indifference to a danger apparently foreign to their own immediate interests, no absolute neutrality, no unconditional seclusion from any important transaction.[1] The fear of involving themselves in endless disputes and continual wars by this policy (the only true and worthy policy) is altogether imaginary, and is suggested by false philanthropy, or ignoble sloth and pusillanimity. The more industry and vigour is employed in checking the first acts of injustice and violence, the less frequent will be the cases in which it will be necessary to march forth to fight against them in the field; the more steadfastly they hold themselves in a state of preparation, the greater reluctance will be felt to challenge them to combat. In a word, the more perfect, harmonious and stable the federal

---

[1] Such expressions as 'the fate of this or that land, of this or that part of Europe, does not concern them'; or 'that they would confine themselves wholly to the maintenance of tranquillity in this or that circle'; or 'that they had done their duty in admitting this or that state within their line of demarkation', etc., should never be heard from a prince or a statesman.

system of the European states, the greater the sensibility each individual discovers to every violation of common rights, the stronger the tie which binds each member to the collective body, the more rarely wars occur.

When proper care is thus taken to consolidate the walls and joisting of the building, then every individual who possesses any powers within himself may, by a judicious application of activity and continued zeal, perfect and complete the edifice; and however unfavourable the times are, education, and instruction, and information derived from conversation, or from books, will even yet effect a great deal. It is not here the question of begetting what is called cosmo-political feeling – whether the Italian be united in affection with the German, the German with the Briton, the Briton with the Russian, and so forth, is a matter about which we have little concern – all that we contend for is, that every one should be zealous to promote the prosperity, the glory, and above all the prosperity of his native land, and that he should see and be persuaded that this first and most important of all objects cannot be attained as long as he remains indifferent whether others stand or fall. A conviction of the necessity, and a sense of the excellence of a federal system, will always accompany the existence of true patriotism. Let this sentiment only be cherished and culti-vated; and projects of universal dominion will be banished from the earth.

It is impossible that the history of our time should pass without producing some beneficial fruits for us and our posterity. Whether Buonaparte, in the recesses of his haughty and gloomy mind, has really conceived the idea of a universal monarchy; under what form he has conceived it; what progress he has made in forming the project, and when, and how he thinks of realizing it, all this futurity will disclose. But so much is clear and certain, that in the course of six frightful years he has been doing, without inter-mission, all that he must do on the very worst supposition, and that he has succeeded in things which seem very unequivocally to prognosticate the most pernicious and desperate issue. Were every thing here to close, were his career to be terminated, were our undertakings to be crowned with complete success, and his star to set forever, is it possible that we could forget what sorrows, what bitterness, what disgrace, what troubles, what convulsions, what a grievous load of present evils, and what anguish for every coming day, was felt throughout the greatest and best part of Europe, from a bare attempt and beginning to effect such a project? and shall we not therefore adopt every expedient which wisdom can devise to prevent the return of these hard trials?

It is necessary above all to recollect that the measures of prevention and security, to which we here alluded, must be the work of a better (and God grant not distant) futurity; *and that this futurity must be acquired by victory*. But in order to be able to give a satisfactory account to ourselves of what we will and must be, it is necessary accurately to know what we at present are. A general review of the existing political relations between France and the other states is, therefore, one of the *desiderata* of the time.

CHAPTER IV

OF THE RELATION BETWEEN FRANCE
AND THE OTHER STATES IN
INTERNAL CONSTITUTION

Conformably to the notion we have given of the genuine accepta-
tion of a political balance in Europe, the internal constitutions of
the respective states come under consideration not *judicially* but
historically. In other words, it cannot be a matter of indifference
to any state to know what is the internal situation of another at
every given point of time; though no one state has the right to
call another to account respecting the constitution it has chosen
to adopt. For though the internal constitution has an immediate
influence upon the strength or weakness of a state, the federal
system is not grounded upon degrees of power, but upon the
external limitations of this power. The state which is not prevented
by any external consideration from oppressing a weaker, is always,
however weak it may be, *too strong* for the interest of the whole;
the state which can be made to respect the rights of the weakest,
though perhaps in itself the most powerful of all, is *not too
powerful*.

There is only a single case in which the principle of the balance
of power can make it a duty, in the whole state confederacy, to
exercise an immediate influence on the internal relations of a
kingdom, namely, when by a mortal distemper in the vital parts
of this kingdom, by a violent overthrow of its government, by a
dissolution of all social ties, a cessation (though perhaps only a
momentary one) of political existence ensues; for besides that in
such a case of pressing urgency, the principals in the league are
collectively called upon by the most imperious moral considera-

tions to interfere for the preservation of the most precious common good, the eternal foundation of legal and social order, the absolute anarchy which invariably accompanies total violent revolutions would produce the most destructive consequences to the general interest of the confederacy; because the state which is a prey to general disorder, as long as this disorder lasts, has lost all its political functions, and is incapacitated from acting as a substantive member of the league; likewise because it is uncertain when it may be enabled to resume a place which it is essential to the interests of the whole not to permit to remain vacant.[1] But even in this extraordinary case – and such a one we were destined to experience – the interference in the internal relations of the state takes place, not because a fear is entertained for an unnatural growth of its power from revolution (which is often indeed the consequence of political revolutions), but on the other hand because a too great debility, or an entire annihilation, is apprehended to follow.

But as soon as a regular government is established in a state, however it may be constituted, whether it has been founded in justice or violence, whether it is moderate or tyrannical, destructive or beneficial, weak or strong – the state confederacy, as such,

---

[1] When Burke said in the year 1791 that France was 'a chasm in the map of Europe'; this great man well knew that in this chasm might exist not only all the infernal apparatus of bloody anarchy, but that a monstrous tyrannical government which would make Europe tremble, might arise out of it; and he even foresaw, with wonderful sagacity, that things would take this turn when all the imaginary wise-heads of the time held such a result to be absurd, and even sometimes ridiculed the prediction. But *at the period* when he used this expression, France had really disappeared.

No opportunity must therefore be neglected of repeating, even should half a world-full of philosophers, and (should it please God) of philosophical writers die of chagrin in consequence of it – that it was *not* fear for the preponderance of France – for this first unfolded itself in the course of the war – that it was not a wish to profit from France's misfortunes, but that it was compassion for the helplessness of France, the dread lest its splendour, so necessary for Europe, should be eternally eclipsed, and the purest maxims of high and genuine state policy, which dictated the war against the French Revolution. That this war afterwards not only failed of its object but degenerated even from its character, and produced misfortune on the back of misfortune; that we are far from disputing, that we are desirous even deeply to impress on the minds of contemporaries. But the original motives of the sovereigns were doubtless beneficent and just, and they who now maintain that the object of the war was to mutilate, to lame, to destroy and divide France, can, if they are sincere, best explain why it so miserably failed; they know the most about it.

has no longer any title to interfere in its domestic concerns. And yet, however little we are disposed to restrict on any side this incontrovertible position, the nature of the thing here presses upon us one consideration which cannot be neglected without the utmost danger. The internal constitution of a state which, from its geographical situation, its natural or acquired advantages, its relation to the neighbouring states, or from the general situation of Europe, has a visible tendency to aggrandizement and over-poise, or which has already attained a degree of overpoise, will, on this very account, be a fair object of anxiety, of sedulous enquiry and the most attentive observation. For whether the external preponderance of a state, which has arrived at such a pitch of greatness, be facilitated and favoured, or restrained and discouraged, by its internal relations, is manifestly a question of the utmost importance for the whole. We are, therefore, in quality of representatives of the great commonwealth, fully entitled and justified in examining into a subject in some respects foreign to us, not with a view to bring what passes in the interior of another state immediately before our tribunal, but with a view to trace the connection which subsists between its constitutions and our own interests, our own cares and dangers, our own wants and the measures of precaution they may dictate.

RICHARD COBDEN

The extract from Cobden's essay on Russia illustrates a position held consistently by this author (1804-1865). It is a view situated between that which links the erosion of the state with the gradual appearance of international harmony, and the view of those who place their trust in the efficient working of the established order through a 'balance of power'.

Cobden's approach to international relations was not dissimilar to his view of economic policy. Non-intervention was the political counterpart of 'laissez-faire'. He attacks writers like Lord Brougham and Gentz, the 'balance of power' theorists, in this chapter, on the grounds that such a notion was inappropriate for the peaceful ordering of international affairs. Cobden argued that if states devote themselves to trade these contacts would bring peace. For this reason he hoped to see Britain remain out of embroilments in China, the Crimea and Denmark.

Cobden, more a polemicist than a philosopher, can be criticized for failing to examine the arguments of Gentz and Vattel with great care. He too readily exaggerates their arguments, accusing them of seeing a 'union' of European states where this is not precisely the point made by the earlier writers. Their 'balance' is a more complex conception than the one criticized by Cobden. This does not, however, detract from the importance of Cobden's essay. This, and the essay *England, Ireland and America*, of 1835, represents a typical nineteenth-century position, typical in England at least, and sceptical of those who saw international relations in a delicate 'balance' requiring constant vigilance and involvement, in one another's affairs. International relations, in Cobden's opinion, were best conducted between *nations* and not governments, confined, that is, to commerce (and culture) and not to the politics of the 'states' system'.

The chapter on the balance of power is reproduced from *The Political Writings of Richard Cobden*, London, 1867, Vol. 1, pp. 253-283.

Suggested Reading

A. J. P. Taylor, *The Troublemakers; dissent over foreign policy*, 1964.

CHAPTER III

THE BALANCE OF POWER

Our object has not only been to deprecate war as the greatest evil that can befall a people, but to show that we have no interest in maintaining the *status quo* of Turkey; and, consequently, that the armaments which, in a time of peace, are maintained, at an enormous cost, for the purpose of making demonstrations in favour of that country, and against Russia, might be reduced, and their expense spared to the tax-payers of the British empire.

We shall here be encountered with a very general prepossession in favour of our maintaining what is termed a rank amongst the states of the Continent – which means, not that we should be free from debt, or that our nation should be an example to all others for the wealth, education, and virtues of its people, but that England shall be consulted before any other countries presume to quarrel or fight; and that she shall be ready, and shall be called upon, to take a part in every contention, either as mediator, second or principal. So prevalent and so little questioned has this egotistical spirit become, that, when an honourable member rises in Parliament, to call upon a minister of the crown to account for some political changes in Spain, Portugal, or Turkey – instead of the question encountering the laughter of the House (as such an inquiry would probably do from the homely representatives who meet to attend to their constituents' affairs at Washington), or the questioner being put down by the functionary, with something after Cain's answer, 'Am I the Spaniard's keeper?' – the latter offers grave explanations and excuses, whilst the audience looks on with silent attention, as though every word of our foreign secretary were pregnant with the fate of nations bowing to his sway.

If we go back through the Parliamentary debates of the last few reigns, we shall find this singular feature in our national character – the passion for meddling with the affairs of foreigners – more strikingly prominent in every succeeding session; and, at the breaking out of the French Revolution, the reader is astonished to see that the characters of the leaders of the mobs of Paris, Marseilles, and Lyons, and the conduct of the government of France, became the constant subjects of discussion in the House of Commons, almost to the exclusion of matters of domestic interest – Pitt and Burke on one side, and Fox, Grey, and Sheridan on the other, attacking and defending the champions of the Revolution, with the same ardour as if the British legislature were a responsible tribunal, erected over the whole of Christendom, and endowed with powers to decide, without appeal, the destinies of all the potentates and public men of Europe.[1] Unhappily, the same passion had impregnated the minds of the public generally (as it continues to do down to our own day), and the result was, as everybody knows, the Bourbon crusade. But England, in taking upon herself to make war with the spirit of the age, encountered the Fates; and, instead of destroying that infant freedom which, however monstrous and hideous at its birth, was destined to throw off its bloody swathes, and, in spite of the enmity of the world, to dispense the first taste of liberty to Europe – *she was herself the nurse that, by her opposition, rocked the French Revolution into vigorous maturity.*

Our history during the last century may be called the tragedy

---

[1] That this spirit still survives in full vigour, may be shown by the motion recently made in the House of Commons, by Mr T. Duncombe, for interceding with the French Government on behalf of the state prisoners at Ham. Prince Polignac and his confederates attempted, by their *coup d'état*, to deprive France of law, place the whole country in the hands of despots, and reduce it to the monkish ignorance of the Middle Ages, by giving again to priests and bigots the absolute power over the printing press. In this attempt they failed; but freedom conquered at the cost of hundreds of victims. *In England, or any other country but France, those ministers would have suffered death.* Yet, after five years of confinement, behold us interfering with the course of justice, in an empire with whose internal concerns we are no more entitled to mix than with those of China.

Within a week of this display, a lad was transported from Macclesfield for fourteen years, *for stealing a pair of stockings!* We recommend this to our facetious Gallic neighbours, as a fit opportunity for intervention: the mother should be induced to write her case to M. Odillon Barrot, or some other popular member of the Chamber of Deputies.

307

of 'British intervention in the politics of Europe'; in which princes, diplomatists, peers, and generals, have been the authors and actors – the people the victims; and the moral will be exhibited to the latest posterity in 800 millions of debt.

We have said that our proposal to reduce our armaments will be opposed, upon the plea of maintaining a proper attitude, as it is called, amongst the nations of Europe. British intervention in the State policy of the Continent has been usually excused under the two stock pretences of maintaining the balance of power in Europe, and of protecting our commerce; upon which two subjects, as they bear indirectly on the question in hand, we shall next offer a few observations.

The first instance in which we find the 'balance of power' alluded to in a king's speech, is on the occasion of the last address of William III to his parliament, December 31, 1701, where he concludes by saying: 'I will only add this – if you do in good earnest desire to see England *hold the balance of Europe*, it will appear by your right improving the present opportunity.' From this period, down almost to our own time (latterly, indeed, the phrase has become, like many other cant terms, nearly obsolete), there will be found, in almost every successive King's speech, a constant recurrence to the 'balance of Europe'; by which, we may rest assured, was always meant, however it might be concealed under pretended alarm for the 'equilibrium of power' or the 'safety of the Continent', the desire to see England 'hold the balance'. The phrase was found to please the public ear; it implied something of equity; whilst England, holding the balance of Europe in her hand, sounded like filling the office of Justice herself to one-half of the globe. Of course, such a post of honour could not be maintained, or its dignity asserted, without a proper attendance of guards and officers; and we consequently find that, at about this period of our history, large standing armies began to be called for; and not only were the supplies solicited by the government, from time to time, under the plea of preserving the liberties of Europe, but, in the annual mutiny bill (*the same in form as is now passed every year*) the preamble stated, amongst other motives, that the annual army was voted for the purpose of *preserving the balance of power in Europe*. The 'balance of power', then, becomes an important practical subject for investigation; it appeals directly to the business and bosoms of our readers, since it is implicated with an expenditure of more than a dozen millions of money per annum, every farthing of which goes, in the shape of taxation, from the pockets of the public.

Such of our readers as have not investigated this subject, will not be a little astonished to find a great discrepancy in the several definitions of what is actually meant by the 'balance of power'. The theory – for it has never yet been applied to practice – appears, after upwards of a century of acknowledged existence, to be less understood now than ever. Latterly, indeed, many intelligent and practical-minded politicians have thrown the question overboard, along with that of the balance of trade – of which number, without participating in their favoured attributes, we claim to be ranked as one. The balance of power – which has, for a hundred years, been the burden of King's speeches, the theme of statesmen, the ground of solemn treaties, and the cause of wars – which has served, down to the very year in which we write, and which will, no doubt continue to serve, for years to come, as a pretence for maintaining enormous standing armaments, by land and sea, at a cost of many hundreds of millions of treasure – the balance of power is a chimera! It is not a fallacy, a mistake, an imposture – it is an undescribed, indescribable, incomprehensible nothing; mere words, conveying to the mind not ideas, but sounds like those equally barren syllables which our ancestors put together for the purpose of puzzling themselves about words, in the shape of *Prester John*, or the *philosopher's stone*! We are bound, however, to see what are the best definitions of this theory.

'By this balance,' says Vattel, 'is to be understood such a disposition of things as that no one potentate or state shall be able, absolutely, to predominate and prescribe laws to the others.' (*Law of Nations*, book 3, Chap. 3, § 47.)

'What is usually termed a balance of power,' says Gentz, 'is that constitution subsisting among neighbouring states, more or less connected with one another, by virtue of which no one among them can injure the independence or essential rights of another without meeting with effectual resistance on some side, and, consequently, exposing itself to danger.' (*Fragments on the Political Balance*, Chap. I.)

'The grand and distinguishing feature of the balancing system,' says Brougham, 'is the perpetual attention to foreign affairs which it inculcates; the constant watchfulness over every nation which it prescribes; the subjection in which it places all national passions and antipathies to the fine and delicate view of remote expediency; the unceasing care which it dictates of nations most remotely situated, and apparently unconnected with ourselves; the general union which it has effected of all European powers, obeying certain laws, and actuated in general by a common principle; in fine, the right of mutual inspection, universally recognized, among civilized states, in the rights of public envoys and residents.' (*Brougham's Colonial Policy*, Book 3, § 1.)

These are the best definitions we have been able to discover of the system denominated the balance of power. In the first place, it must be remarked that, taking any one of these descriptions separately, it is so vague as to impart no knowledge even of the writer's meaning; whilst, if taken together, one confuses and contradicts another, Gentz describing it to be ' a constitution subsisting among neighbouring states more or less connected with each other'; whilst Brougham defines it as 'dictating a care of nations most remotely situated, and apparently unconnected with ourselves'. Then it would really appear, from the laudatory tone applied to the system by Vattel, who says that it is 'such a disposition of things as that no one potentate or state *shall be able* absolutely to predominate and prescribe laws to the others'; as well as from the complacent manner in which Brougham states 'the general *union which it has effected* of all the European powers, obeying certain laws, and actuated in general by a common principle' – it would seem, from such assurances as these, that there was no necessity for that 'perpetual attention to foreign affairs', or that 'constant watchfulness over every nation', which the latter authority tells us, the system 'prescribes and inculcates'. The only point on which these writers, in common with many other authors and speakers in favour of the balance of power, agree, is in the fundamental delusion that such a system was ever acceded to by the nations of Europe. To judge from the assumption, by Brougham, of a 'general *union* among all the European powers;' from the allusion made by Gentz to that '*constitution* subsisting among neighbouring states'; or from Vattel's reference to 'a disposition of things', etc. – one might be justified in inferring that a kind of federal union had existed for the last century throughout Europe, in which the several kingdoms had found, like the States of America, uninterrupted peace and prosperity. But we should like to know at what period of history such a compact amongst the nations of the Continent was entered into? Was it previously to the peace of Utrecht? Was it antecedent to the Austrian war of succession? Was it prior to the seven years' war, or to the American war? Or did it exist during the French revolutionary wars? Nay, what period of the centuries during which Europe has (with only just sufficient intervals to enable the combatants to recruit their wasted energies) been one vast and continued battle-field, will Lord Brougham fix upon, to illustrate the salutary working of that 'balancing system' which 'places all national passions and antipathies in subjection to the fine and delicate view of remote expediency'?

Again, at what epoch did the nations of the Continent subscribe to that constitution, 'by virtue of which', according to Gentz, 'no one among them can injure the independence or essential rights of another'? Did this constitution exist, whilst Britain was spoiling the Dutch at the Cape, or in the East? – or when she dispossessed France of Canada? – or (worse outrage by far) did it exist when England violated the 'essential rights' of Spain, by taking forcible and felonious possession of a portion of her native soil?[1] Had this constitution been subscribed by Russia, Prussia, and Austria, at the moment when they signed the partition of Poland? – or by France, when she amalgamated with a portion of Switzerland? – by Austria, at the acquisition of Lombardy? – by Russia, when dismembering Sweden, Turkey, and Persia? – or by Prussia, before incorporating Silesia?

---

[1] The conquests of colonies have been regarded with some complacency, because they are merely, in most instances, reprisals for previous depredations by the parent state: but England for fifty years at Gibraltar, is a spectacle of brute violence, unmitigated by any such excuses. Upon no principle of morality can this unique outrage upon the integrity of an ancient, powerful and reknowned nation – placed at a remote distance from our shores – be justified: the example, if imitated, instead of being shunned, universally, would throw all the nations of the earth into barbarous anarchy, and deprive mankind of the blessings of law, justice, and religion. It is time not only to think, but to speak, of those things in a spirit of honest truth. The people of this country – the middling and working classes – have no interest, as we shall by and by have to show, in these acts of unjust aggression and foreign violence. Alas for the cause of morals, if they had!

So far from any such confederation having ever been, by written, verbal, or implied agreement, entered into by the 'European powers, obeying certain laws, and actuated in general by a common principle'; the theory of the balance of power has, we believe, generally been interpreted, by those who, from age to age, have, parrot-like, used the phrase, to be a system invented for the very purpose of supplying the want of such a combination. Regarding it for a moment in this point of view, we should still expect to find that the 'balancing system' had, at some period of modern history, been recognized and agreed to by all the Continental states; and that it had created a spirit of mutual concession and guarantee, by which the weaker and more powerful empires were placed upon a footing of equal security, and by which any one potentate or state was absolutely unable 'to predominate over the others'. But, instead of any such self-denial, we discover that the balance of Europe has merely meant (if it has had a meaning) that which our blunt Dutch king openly avowed as his aim to his parliament – a desire, on the part of the great powers, to *hold the balance of Europe*. England has, for nearly a century, held the European scales – not with the blindness of the goddess of justice herself, or with a view to the equilibrium of opposite interests, but with a Cyclopean eye to her own aggrandizement. The same lust of conquest has actuated, up to the measure of their abilities, the other great powers; and, if we find the smaller states still, in the majority of instances, preserving their independent existence, it is owing, not to the watchful guardianship of the 'balancing system', but to the limits which nature herself has set to the undue extension of territorial dominion – not only by the physical boundaries of different countries, but in those still more formidable moral impediments to the invader – the unity of language, laws, customs, and traditions; the instinct of patriotism and freedom; the hereditary rights of rulers; and, though last not least, that homage to the restraints of justice which nations and public bodies[1] have in all ages avowed, however they may have found excuses for evading it.

So far, then, as we can understand the subject, the theory of a balance of power is a mere chimera – a creation of the politician's

[1] 'Mankind, although reprobates in detail, are always moralists in the gross.' Montesquieu.

brain — a phantasm, without definite form or tangible existence –
a mere conjunction of syllables, forming words which convey
sound without meaning. Yet these words have been echoed by the
greatest orators and statesmen of England; they gingled successively from the lips of Bolingbroke, Chatham, Pitt, Burke, Fox,
Sheridan, Grey, and Brougham; ay, even whilst we were in the
act of stripping the maritime nations of the Continent of their
colonies, then regarded as the sole source of commercial greatness;
whilst we stood sword in hand upon the neck of Spain, or planted
our standard on the rock of Malta; and even when England
usurped the dominion of the ocean, and attempted to extend the
sphere of human despotism over another element, by insolently
putting barriers upon that highway of nations – even then, the
tongues of our orators resounded most loudly with the praises of
the 'balance of power!'[1] There would be something peculiarly
humiliating in connection with this subject in beholding the greatest
minds of successive ages, instead of exercising the faculty of
thought, become the mere automata of authority, and retail, with
less examination than the haberdasher bestows upon the length,
breadth, and quality of his wares, the sentiments bequeathed from
former generations of writers and speakers – but that, unhappily,
the annals of philosophy and of past religions, afford too many
examples of the triumph of mere imitativeness over the higher
faculties of the human intellect.

We must not, however, pass over the 'balance of power', without
at least endeavouring to discover the meaning of a phrase which
still enters into the preamble of an annual act of Parliament, for
raising and maintaining a standing army of ninety thousand men.
The theory, according to the historian Robertson, was first invented
by the Machiavellian statesmen of Italy during the prosperous era
of the Florentine (miscalled) republic; and it was imported into

---

[1] The phrase was actually adopted by Napoleon! who told O'Meara, at
St Helena, that he refused to permit the Emperor Alexander to occupy the
Dardanelles, because, if Russia were in possession of Turkey, the 'balance of
power' in Europe would be destroyed! Lord Dudley Stuart sees much to admire
in this regard for the balance of power, by one who had himself been in military
occupation of all the principal states of Europe: 'But the profound views of that
great man, Napoleon, told him not to accede to either the demand or entreaties
of Alexander; and, on that occasion, though he had invaded the Turkish empire
himself, he saved it by refusing the passage of the Dardanelles to Russia; nay,
he saved Europe itself.' Lord Stuart's Speech, February 19th [1836].

Western Europe in the early part of the sixteenth century, and became 'fashionable', to use the very word of the historian of Charles V, along with many other modes borrowed, about the same time, from that commercial and civilized people. This explanation of its origin does not meet with the concurrence of some other writers; for it is singular but still consistent with the ignisfatuus character of the 'balance of power', that scarcely two authors agree, either as to the nature or the precise period of invention of the system. Lord Brougham claims for the theory an origin as remote as the time of the Athenians; and Hume describes Demosthenes to have been the first advocate of the 'balancing system' – very recommendatory, remembering that ancient history is little else than a calendar of savage wars! There can be little doubt, however, that the idea, by whomsoever or at whatever epoch conceived, sprang from that first instinct of our nature, fear, and originally meant at least some scheme for preventing the dangerous growth of the power of any particular state; *that power being always regarded, be it well remembered, as solely the offspring of conquest and aggrandizement*: notwithstanding, as we have had occasion to show in a former page of this pamphlet, in the case of England and the United States, that labour, improvements, and discoveries, confer the greatest strength upon a people; and that, by these alone, and not by the sword of the conqueror, can nations, in modern and all future times, hope to rise to supreme power and grandeur. And it must be obvious that a system professing to observe a 'balance of power' – by which, says Vattel, 'no one potentate or state shall be able absolutely to predominate'; or, according to Gentz, 'to injure the independence or essential rights of another'; by which, says Brougham, 'a perpetual attention to foreign affairs is inculcated, and a constant watchfulness over every nation is prescribed': it must be obvious that such a 'balancing system' – if it disregards those swiftest strides towards power which are making by nations excelling in mechanical and chemical science, industry, education, morality, and freedom – must be altogether chimerical.

Lord Bacon, indeed, took a broader and more comprehensive view of this question when he wrote, in his essay on empire: '*First*, for their neighbours, there can no general rule be given (the occasions are so variable) save one, which ever holdeth; which is, that princes do keep due sentinel, that none of their neighbours do overgrow so (by increase of territory, by *embracing of trade*, by approaches, *or the like*), as they become more able to annoy them than they were: and this is generally the work of standing councils, to see and *to hinder it*'. This appears to us to be the only sound and correct view of such a principle as is generally understood by the phrase 'the balance of power'. It involves, however, such a dereliction of justice and utter absence of conscientiousness, that subsequent writers upon the subject have not dared to follow out the principle of hindering the growth of trade, and the like (which includes all advance in civilization); although, to treat it in any other manner than that in which it is handled by this 'wisest, greatest, meanest of mankind', is to abandon the whole system to contempt, as unsound, insufficient, and illusory.[1] As for the *rule* of Lord Bacon; were the great Enemy of mankind himself to summon a council, to devise a law of nations which should convert this fair earth, with all its capacity for life, enjoyment, and goodness, into one vast theatre of death and misery, more dismal than his own dark Pandemonium, the very words of the philosopher would compose that law! It would reduce us even below the level of the brute animals. *They* do not make war against their own instincts; but this 'rule' would, if acted upon universally, plunge us into a war of annihilation with that instinct of progression which is the distinguishing nature of intellectual man. It would forbid all increase in knowledge, which, by the great writer's own authority, is power. It would interdict the growth of morality and freedom, which are power. Were Lord Bacon's 'rule' enforced, not only would the uninstructed Russians commence a crusade against our steam-engines and our skilful artisans; the still more barbarous Turk would be called upon to destroy the civilization and commerce of Petersburgh; the savage African would be warranted,

---

[1] Lord Bacon's political maxims are full of moral turpitude. 'Nobody can,' says he, speaking of kingdoms and estates, 'be healthful without exercise – neither natural body nor politic; and certainly to a kingdom or estate, a just and honourable war is the true exercise.' Accordingly, just wars are necessary; and, as there must be an opposite party to a just war, *ergo*, unjust wars are necessary! In speaking of kings, he calls them 'mortal gods on earth'. And, in his chapter on seditions and troubles, he gives many rules for governing and restraining, but not one for instructing the people. We speak of the moral sentiments of this great man, distinctly from his intellectual powers.

nay, compelled to reduce the turbaned Osmanli to his own naked-
ness and a wigwam; nor would the leveling strife cease until either
the 'rule' were abrogated, or mankind has been reduced to the only
pristine possessions – teeth and nails![1]

The balance of power, then, might, in the first place, be very
well dismissed as *chimera*, because no state of things, such as the
'disposition', 'constitution', or 'union', of European powers
referred to as the basis of their system, by Vattel, Gentz, and
Brougham, ever did exist; and secondly, the theory could, on
other grounds, be discarded as *fallacious*, since it gives no definition
– whether by breadth of territory, number of inhabitants, or
extent of wealth – according to which, in balancing the respective
powers, each state shall be estimated; whilst, lastly, it would be
altogether incomplete and inoperative, from neglecting, or refusing
to provide against, the silent and peaceful aggrandizements which
spring from improvement and labour. Upon these triple grounds,

---

[1] There appears to be one honourable member of the British legislature,
and only one, who is an advocate of this policy. Sir Harry Verney, in speaking
after Mr T. Attwood, upon the subject of Russia (see *Mirror of Parliament*,
1833, p. 2878), said: 'The honourable gentleman has represented Russia as a
state sunk in barbarism and ignorance, and hostile to every species of liberty.
I would to God that such a description of Russia were correct!!! I believe the
reverse to be the fact. I believe there is no power on earth which resorts to such
effectual means of propagating her power, civilizing her country, promoting
commerce, manufactures, the acquirement of useful information, and the
propagation of every useful institution, as Russia. Does the honourable gentleman know that at this moment steam-boats navigate the Volga; and that you may
travel in all parts of Russia in the same way as you may through the United
States? Does the honourable gentleman know that the Emperor of Russia sends
abroad agents in whom he can confide, to obtain information relative to improvements and inventions which may be useful to himself? . . . I am quite
sure that, if this country would maintain the balance of power, we must oppose
the encroachments of Russia.'

A Yankee punster would exclaim! 'Sir Harry goes the whole *hog* with *Bacon*
upon the "balance of power"!'

Yes, Sir Harry is right. He and the noble author of the *Novum Organum*,
are the only two philosophers who have taken a true and consistent view of the
question. We are far, however, from including them both under one rule of
inculpation. The honourable member for Buckinghamshire errs, perhaps,
intellectually, and not morally. His chief fault, or rather misfortune, is that he
lives in Buckingham. Let him and the Marquis of Chandos go through a
course of Adam Smith and the economists, beginning with Harriet Martineau;
and they will then be convinced that we cannot profit by the barbarism of another
people, or be injured by their progress in civilization, *any more than the British
nation can gain by the corn laws.*

the question of the balance of power might be dismissed from further consideration. We shall, however, assume, merely for the sake of argument, that such an equilibrium existed in complete efficiency; and the first inquiry that suggests itself is: Upon what principle is Turkey made a member of this European system? The Turks, at least, will be admitted, by everybody, to form no party to this 'union'; nor do they give that 'perpetual attention to foreign affairs which it inculcates'; or that 'constant watchfulness over every nation which it prescribes'. They never read of the balance of power in the Koran; Turkey cannot enter into the political system of Europe; for the Turks are not Europeans. . . .

Down to within a few years of the present time, the Turks were viewed only as the scourge of Christian Europe. When, about a century and a half ago, Louis XIV entered into an alliance with the Sublime Porte, the whole civilized world rung with indignation at the infamous and unnatural combination. And when, more than a century later, on the occasion of the capture of Ockzakow by the Russians, our most powerful minister (Pitt) proposed to forward succours to the aid of Turkey, such was the spirit of opposition manifested by the country, that the armaments already prepared by the government, under the sanction of a servile majority in the Parliament, were reluctantly countermanded. On that occasion, both Burke and Grey, although advocates of the balancing system, refused to acknowledge that the Turks formed parties to it. 'He had never before heard it set forth',[1] said the former, 'that the Turkish Empire was considered as a part of the balance of power in Europe. They had nothing to do with European power; they considered themselves as wholly Asiatic. Where was the Turkish resident at our court, the court of Prussia, or of Holland? They despised and condemned all Christian princes as infidels, and only wished to subdue and exterminate them and their people. What had these worse than savages to do with the powers of Europe, but to spread war, destruction, and pestilence amongst them? All that was holy in religion, all that was moral and humane, demanded an abhorrence of everything that tended to extend the power of that cruel and wasteful empire. Any Christian power was to be preferred to these destructive savages. He had heard, with horror, that the

[1] Burke's Speech, House of Commons, March 29th, 1791. See *Hansard's Parliamentary History*, vol. xxix., pp. 76, 77.

Emperor had been obliged to give up to this abominable power, those charming countries which border upon the Danube, to devastation and pestilence.' . . .

Does Christianity or public virtue call upon us, in 1836, more than they did in 1791, to arm ourselves on behalf of Turkey? . . .

There remains one, and but one, other point from which to view the question of the balance of power; and we may then bid adieu to this monument of the credulity and facility of the human intellect for ever; or, at least, until we happen, perchance, to meet with it in next year's mutiny bill, supplying the '*whereas*' of an act of parliament, with a pretence for maintaining a standing army of upwards of 90,000 men!

Russia, in possession of Constantinople, say the alarmists, would possess a port open at all seasons; the materials for constructing ships; vast tracts of fertile land, capable of producing cotton, silk, wool, etc.; and she would be placed in a situation of easy access to our shores – all of which would tend to destroy the balance of power, and put in danger the interests of the British commerce, in particular. But New York, a port far more commodious than Constantinople, is open at all seasons; the United States possess materials without end for ship-building; their boundless territory of fertile land is adapted for the growth of cotton, silk, wool, etc.; and New York is next door to Liverpool; for – thanks to Providence! – there is no land intervening between the American continent and the shores of this United Kingdom. Yet, we have never heard that the North American continent forms any part of the balance of power! Twenty-four sovereign, free, and independent states, altogether forgotten in a 'balancing system, which dictates an increasing care even of nations most remotely situated, and apparently unconnected with ourselves!' We doubt the equilibrium can hardly be maintained. This is not all. There is the entire southern continent, from the Isthmus of Panama to the point of Cape Horn, likewise entirely omitted. Mercy on us, one scale will certainly kick the beam! Twelve separate empires of South America, bounded on one extremity by Mexico, and on the other by Patagonia; and the vast expanse of territory, settled and unsettled, under the dominion of the Government of Washington, and, altogether, comprising one-third of the habitable globe – have been quite forgotten in a balance of power!

Not having been supplied by the authors of the theory with any rule by which to judge of their mode of estimating or weighing the powers of the respective parties to the balancing system; and being equally uninformed as to the qualifications required from those states which aspired to the union, it would be presumptuous to guess upon what principle Turkey is admitted to a connection with England, from which Brazil is excluded; or why, in forming a balance of the civilized powers, the United States are rejected, in order to give room to admit Russia into one of the scales. It cannot be from proximity that Turkey is preferred to the Brazils. A voyage from Rio Janeiro to Liverpool will average about forty days; whilst the time taken in going from England to Constantinople usually reaches double that period. Nor can it arise from a comparison of our commerce with the two countries, which is four times as valuable with the American as the European state. Then a wise and provident regard to the future cannot be the guiding motive, since the prospect is altogether in favour of the transatlantic empire, which embraces within its bounds a territory equalling in extent the whole of Russia in Europe, and forming the finest, and destined in all probability to be, both as respects vegetable and mineral riches, the most productive amongst all the countries in the world. Religion, language, national character, and the plague, all oppose the claim of the Turk to this preference over the Christian rival; and we can only suspend our conjectures, and entreat that some advocate of the 'balancing system' will inform the world upon what *principle*, commercial, social, or political – in short, upon what ground, consistent with common sense – does the foreign secretary involve Great Britain in the barbarian politics of the Ottoman Government, to the manifest risk of future wars, and the present pecuniary sacrifice attending standing armaments; whilst, with another state, with which we are more deeply interested as traders, more identified as men, and from which we are, navally speaking, less distant, no political intercourse is found necessary? The same argument applies, with more or less force, to the other eleven South American States, with each of which our commerce averages probably more in amount than with Turkey; yet, although they are Christian communities, all but universally at peace,[1] and notwithstanding the future influence which they are inevitably destined to exercise over the interests of the entire world – these countries have not been thought worthy of admission into that system of civilized nations which is now agitated from one extremity to the other with the fate of Mahometan Turkey! However impossible it may be to speculate successfully upon the intended operation of a system which, in reality, never existed except in the precincts of the politician's brain, still it must be remembered that at the time the theory was first invented, it proposed to give to the European powers owning American colonies, a weight proportioned to the extent of those possessions; and the question then arises – which we shall merely propound, and leave in despair, for the solution of such of our readers as may wish to pursue this chimerical inquiry still farther. By what ingenious process was the balance of power preserved, when England, Spain, and Portugal were deprived of their transatlantic territories? Canning, indeed, once talked of 'calling into existence a new world, to adjust the balance of the old'; but, as in many other oratorical flourishes of our state-rhetorician, he meant quite a different practical object: in other and more homely language, that statesman proposed to acknowledge the independence of South America – ten years after every private individual of judgment had predicted the freedom of that Continent. To this day those states which once formed so important a part of the balancing system, as appendages

[1] We add an extract from a letter, dated January 26th, 1836, addressed to the author by a friend – a gallant officer, and an enlightened and amiable man, who, himself, holds an official rank at the British Court from one of the States of South America. 'You, who are so strong an advocate for peace and freedom will be glad to hear of the tranquillity of America, and that our systems of government are at last working well. Of the thirteen transatlantic republics, ten are now in a perfect state of order and prosperity. The capture of Puerto Cabello from a banditti who are in possession of it, will restore that of Venezuela; and the next news from Peru will give us that of the peaceable settlement of its government. Mexico, therefore, will alone remain an exception to this peaceful state; and I am afraid she will long remain so: yet in spite of the troubles of Mexico, she last year raised from her mines (according to the official report of the minister of finance, and without including what was smuggled) thirty millions of dollars, in gold and silver, being three millions more than was ever produced under the most flourishing year of the old Spanish government. As to the national debts of America, the bonds of the United States were used to be sold by basketful, in the first years of their independence, yet they have now paid off the whole. You have about fourteen principal nations in Europe, and you know two or three of them have internal dissensions.'

to the mother countries, are wanting in the scales of Europe; and by what arts, *whether by false weights or the legerdemain of the nation still holding the balance,* the equilibrium can be preserved without them, constituting as they do nearly one third of the terrestrial globe, is a mystery beyond the reach of our powers of divination.

We glanced at the comparative claims of Russia and the United States, to be included in this imaginary States-union: a very few words, upon this point, are all that we shall add to our probably already too extended notice of the 'balance of power'. Upon whatever principle the theory under consideration may have been at first devised – whether, according to Gentz, for the purpose of uniting neighbouring states, or, as Brougham asserts, with a view to the union of all the European powers – it is certain that it would have been held fatal to the success of the balancing system for any one power, and that one among the most civilized, wealthy, and commercial, to have refused to subscribe to its constitution. Yet the United States (for the number of its inhabitants,) the richest, the most commercial, and, for either attack or defence, the most powerful of modern empires; a country which possesses a wider surface of fertile land than Russia could boast even with the accession of Turkey; and, instead of being imprisoned, like Russia, by the Dardanelles and the Sound, owning five thousand miles of coast, washed by two oceans, and open to the whole world: *the United States are not parties to the balance of power!* Ignorant as we are of the rule of admission to and exclusion from this balancing system, it would be vain to conjecture why Russia should be entitled, not only to be a member of this union, but to engross its exclusive attention, whilst North America is unknown or not recognized as of any weight in the balance of power. It cannot be, on our part, from closer neighbourhood; for Russia, even at Constantinople, would – commercially and navally speaking – be three times as distant[1] as New York, from Great Britain. Nor on account of the greater amount of the European commerce transacted by Russia. The commerce of the United States with the countries of Europe, is nearly as great in amount as that of the British empire with the Continent; twice as large as the trade of France with some quarters; and three times that of Russia.

---

[1] The average time of the passage from New York to Liverpool, by the line of packet-ships, is twenty-five days.

It cannot be because of the more important nature of the trade which we carry on with Russia as compared with that with America; since the cotton of the latter gives employment and subsistence to more than a million of our people, and is actually indispensable to our commercial and political existence. Here are cogent reasons why the transatlantic power should form a party to the union of states – why, at least, it should, in place of an empire situated upon the Baltic or Black Sea, be united in political bands with Great Britain. And wherefore is this rich, commercial, and this contiguous country – with a population more entirely enlightened than any besides, and whose improvements and institutions, England and all Europe are eager to emulate – an alien to the 'balancing system', of which Turkey, Spain, and Persia, are members? It would be difficult to find any other satisfactory answer than that which we are able to give as the reason of this exclusion: *America, with infinite wisdom, refuses to be a party to the 'balance of power'.*

Washington (who could remember when the national debt of England was under fifty-five millions; who saw it augmented, by the Austrian war of succession, to seventy-eight millions; and, again increased, by the Seven Years' War, to one hundred and forty-six millions; and who lived to behold the first fruits of the French Revolutionary wars, with probably a presentiment of the harvest of debt and oppression that was to follow – whose paternal eye looked abroad only with the patriotic hope of finding, in the conduct of other nations, example or warning for the instruction of his countrymen) seeing the chimerical objects for which England, *although an island*, plunged into the contentions of the Continent, with no other result to her suffering people but an enduring and increasing debt – bequeathed, as a legacy to his fellow-citizens, the injunction, that they should never be tempted, by any inducements or provocations, to become parties to the States' system of Europe. And faithfully, zealously, and happily has that testament been obeyed! Down even to our day, the feeling and conviction of the people, and consequently of the Government and the authors[1] of the United States, have constantly increased

---

[1] Washington Irving has good-humouredly satirized this national propensity for foreign politics, in the well-known sketch of 'John Bull'. 'He is,' says that exquisite writer, 'a busy-minded personage, who thinks, not merely for himself and family, but for all the country around, and is most generously disposed to be

in favour of a policy from which so much wealth, prosperity, and moral greatness have sprung. America, for fifty years at peace, with the exception of two years of defensive war, is a spectacle of the beneficent effects of that policy which may be comprised in the maxim: As little intercourse as possible betwixt the *Governments*, as much connection as possible between the *nations*, of the world. And when England (*without being a republic*) shall be governed upon the same principles of regard for the interests of the people, and a like common sense view of the advantages of its position, we shall adopt a similar motto for our policy; and then we shall hear no more mention of that costly chimera, the balance of power.

everybody's champion. He is continually volunteering his services to settle his neighbour's affairs, and takes it in great dudgeon if they engage in any matter of consequence without asking his advice; though he seldom engages in any friendly office of the kind without finishing by getting into a squabble with all parties, and then railing bitterly at their ingratitude. He unluckily took lessons in his youth in the noble science of defence; and having accomplished himself in the use of his limbs and weapons, (i.e. standing armies and navies,) and become a perfect master at boxing and cudgel-play, he has had a troublesome life of it ever since. He cannot hear of a quarrel between the most distant of his neighbours, but he begins incontinently to fumble with the head of his cudgel, and consider whether interest or honour does not require that he should meddle in their broils. Indeed he has expended his relations of pride and policy so completely over the whole country, (i.e. *quadripartite treaties and quintrupal alliances,*) that no event can take place without infringing some of his finely-spun rights and dignities. Couched in his little domain, with those filaments stretching forth in every direction, he is like some choleric, bottle-bellied old spider, who has woven his web over a whole chamber, so that a fly cannot buzz, nor a breeze blow, without startling his repose and causing him to sally forth wrathfully from his den. Though really a good-tempered, good-hearted old fellow at bottom, yet he is singularly fond of being in the midst of contention. It is one of his peculiarities, however, that he only relishes the beginning of an affray; he always goes into a fight with alacrity, but comes out of it grumbling even when victorious; and, though no one fights with more obstinacy to carry a contested point, yet, when the battle is over, and he comes to a reconciliation, he is so much taken up with the mere shaking of hands, (*Lord Castlereagh at the Treaty of Vienna,*) that he is apt to let his antagonists pocket all they have been grumbling about. It is not, therefore, fighting that he ought to be so much on his guard against as making friends. . . . All that I wish is, that John's present troubles may teach him more prudence in future; (*nothing of the kind: look at him now, fifteen years after this was written, playing the fool again, ten times worse than ever, in Spain;*) that he may cease to distress his mind about other people's affairs; that he may give up the fruitless attempt to promote the good of his neighbours, and the peace and happiness of the world, by dint of the cudgel; that he may remain quietly at home; gradually get his house into repair; cultivate his rich estate according to his fancy; husband his income – if he thinks proper; bring his unruly children into order – if he can.' *Sketch Book.*

HEINRICH VON TREITSCHKE

Treitschke's robust lectures on all aspects of politics were given at Berlin from 1874. They have received a hostile reception in England. He has been accused of justifying Bismarck, of exaggerated devotion to the nation-state, and of inciting the Germans to militarism in the years before 1914. Thus he was attacked in England during the First World War. The study of Treitschke (1834-1896) by H. W. C. Davis, published in 1914, was a refreshing new approach, looking at his strong Protestant background and the development of his thought as a German nineteenth-century liberal.

Treitschke's style is provocative. His central theme is the necessity for a strong state. He had argued consistently for the strong, unified state, the *Einheitstaat*, which many Germans of the last century favoured. The theme appears in the lectures on politics and it had appeared in his important review of J. S. Mill's essay on *Liberty*, in 1861. Yet in this early work, in *Die Freiheit*, he stressed that there were areas of human activity that should remain beyond the compass of the state. He was to remain 'liberal' in this sense in criticizing Bismarck's harsh control of opinion, especially of the press. He was a supporter of 'liberalism' also in his advocacy of government with the consent of a free people and his association of liberalism and nationalism. He attacked cosmopolitanism. International relations revolved always around the interplay of the nation-states, and these political units were at the centre of Treitschke's consideration of politics. His analysis of the nature and aims of the state is therefore of great importance. The strong would survive and the weak would disappear in this interstate political situation, and war would inevitably play a necessary part. Indeed it was war which created nations, tested their strength and made men into patriots. The very conflict of interstate politics formed part of 'the civilizing mission of mankind'.

The extracts below were translated by Blanche Dugdale and Torben de Bille, with an introduction by the Rt. Hon. Arthur Balfour, London, 1916. The first extract from Vol. I, pp. 19-22 and 28-30, the second from Vol. II, pp. 336-337, and the third from Vol. II, pp. 587-620.

Suggested Reading

H. W. C. Davis, *The Political Thought of Heinrich von Treitschke*, 1914.

Book I

CHAPTER I

THE STATE IDEA

Treat the State as a person, and the necessary and rational multiplicity of States follows. Just as in individual life the ego implies the existence of the non-ego, so it does in the State. The State is power, precisely in order to assert itself as against other equally independent powers. War and the administration of justice are the chief tasks of even the most barbaric States. But these tasks are only conceivable where a plurality of States are found existing side by side. Thus the idea of one universal empire is odious – the ideal of a State co-extensive with humanity is no ideal at all. In a single State the whole range of culture could never be fully spanned; no single people could unite the virtues of aristocracy and democracy. All nations, like all individuals, have their limitations, but it is exactly in the abundance of these limited qualities that the genius of humanity is exhibited. The rays of the Divine light are manifested, broken by countless facets among the separate peoples, each one exhibiting another picture and another idea of the whole. Every person has a right to believe that certain attributes of the Divine reason are exhibited in it to their fullest perfection. No people ever attains to national consciousness without overrating itself. The Germans are always in danger of enervating their nationality through possessing too little of this rugged pride. . . .

The daily life of nations is founded upon mutual give and take, and since Christianity has brought this fact to universal recognition we may lay down that modern civilizations will not perish in the same sense as those of the ancient world, which lacked this knowledge. But it is no merely kindly interchange which takes place; the supreme need is to preserve what has been won. Historical greatness depends less on the first discovery or invention than on forming and keeping. The terrible saying, *Sic vos non vobis*, is once more vindicated . . . . Brave peoples alone have an existence, an evolution or a future; the weak and cowardly perish, and perish justly. The grandeur of history lies in the perpetual conflict of nations, and it is simply foolish to desire the suppression of their rivalry. Mankind has ever found it to be so. The Kingdoms of the Diadochi and the hellenized nations of the East were the natural reaction from the world-empire of Alexander. The extreme one-sidedness of the idea of nationality which has been formed during our century by countries big and small is nothing but the natural revulsion against the world-empire of Napoleon. The unhappy attempt to transform the multiplicity of European life into the arid uniformity of universal sovereignty has produced the exclusive sway of nationality as the dominant political idea. Cosmopolitanism has receded too far.

These examples show clearly that there is no prospect of a settlement of international contradictions. The civilization of nations as well as of individuals tends to specialization. The subtleties of personal character assert themselves proportionately to increase of culture, and with its growth even the differences between nations become more sharply defined. In spite of the increased facilities of communications between different countries, no blending of their peculiarities has taken place; on the contrary, the more delicate distinctions of national character are far more marked to-day than in the Middle Ages. Then the clergy of Europe, united by Latin speech and culture, felt itself to be one body, as against the several peoples . . . . In short, the Middle Ages present a greater uniformity of class feeling and intellectual standards than is perceptible today . . . . The rational task of a legally constituted people, conscious of a destiny, is to assert its rank in the world's hierarchy and in its measure to participate in the great civilizing mission of mankind.

For the notion of sovereignty must not be rigid, but flexible and relative, like all political conceptions. Every State, in treaty-making, will limit its power in certain directions for its own sake. States which conclude treaties with each other thereby curtail their absolute authority to some extent. But the rule still stands, for every treaty is a voluntary curb upon the power of each, and all international agreements are prefaced by the clause '*Rebus sic stantibus*'. No State can pledge its future to another. It knows no arbiter, and draws up all its treaties with this implied reservation. This is supported by the axiom that so long as international law exists all treaties lose their force at the very moment when war is declared between the contracting parties; moreover, every sovereign State has the undoubted right to declare war at its pleasure, and is consequently entitled to repudiate its treaties. Upon this constantly recurring alteration of treaties the progress of history depends; every State must take care that its treaties do not survive their effective value, lest another Power should denounce them by a declaration of war; for antiquated treaties must necessarily be denounced and replaced by others more consonant with circumstances.

It is clear that the international agreements which limit the power of a State are not absolute, but voluntary self-restrictions. Hence, it follows that the establishment of a permanent international Arbitration Court is incompatible with the nature of the State, which could at all events only accept the decision of such a tribunal in cases of second- or third-rate importance. When a nation's existence is at stake there is no outside Power whose impartiality can be trusted. Were we to commit the folly of treating the Alsace-Lorraine problem as an open question, by submitting it to arbitration, who would seriously believe that the award could be impartial? It is, moreover, a point of honour for a State to solve such difficulties for itself. International treaties may indeed become more frequent, but a finally decisive tribunal of the nations is an impossibility. The appeal to arms will be valid until the end of history, and therein lies the sacredness of war.

However flexible the conception of Sovereignty may be we are not to infer from that any self-contradiction, but rather a necessity to establish in what its pith and kernal consists. Legally it lies in the competence to define the limits of its own authority, and politically in the appeal to arms. An unarmed State, incapable of drawing the sword when it sees fit, is subject to one which wields the power of declaring war. To speak of a military suzerainty in time of peace obviously implies a *contradictio in adjecto*. A defence-less State may still be termed a Kingdom for conventional or courtly reasons, but science, whose first duty is accuracy, must boldly declare that in point of fact such a country no longer takes rank as a State.

Book III

CHAPTER XXI

STATE CONFEDERATIONS AND FEDERATED STATES

A Confederation of States, as we have seen it in Switzerland up to 1848, in the Republic of the United Netherlands, and in the North American Union from 1778 to 1787, is recognized by international law as an association of sovereign States, who have bound themselves together, without resigning their independence, to further certain common ends, the chief of which is to provide for defence against a foreign enemy by means of contributions levied from all members of the association. Since all these retain their sovereignty the central authority must be divided, both legally and actually, among the individual members of the Confederation, and this has always been done. A Parliament or Federal Diet assembles, a Congress of ambassadors, who express no will of their own, but are merely the mouthpieces of their Governments, whose desires they have of course helped to frame.

A Confederation of this kind is distinguished from an international alliance pure and simple chiefly by its long continuance. It is devised to last for ever in the human sense of the word, and is either on a living consciousness of national comradeship, or upon common historical traditions. The allied States feel their need of each other in war, and they express it in their political forms. Thus arose Switzerland, which serves us as a general type of confederate Federations. Its members were pledged not only to mutual support against the foreign enemy, but also to bear each other's burdens at home by consent or arbitration. This may lead on to a further series of established institutions, but the sovereignty of each individual State is guaranteed through them all. Consequently the members of a Confederation exercise their natural *liberum veto*. No sovereign can be called on to obey, and therefore each individual must be given the right to object to the decision of the majority.

Book IV

CHAPTER XXVIII

INTERNATIONAL LAW AND INTERNATIONAL INTERCOURSE

When we ask, does an international law exist at all? we are met by two extreme and contradictory conceptions, both alike untenable, of the international life of States. The first, the naturalistic, whose chief champion we already know to be Machiavelli, starts from the principle that the State is absolute power, and may do anything which serves its ends, consequently it can bind itself by no law in its relations with other States, which are determined by purely mechanical considerations of proportionate strength. This is an idea which can only be disproved by its own arguments. We must admit that the State is absolute physical power, but if it insists upon being that, and nothing else, unrestrained by conscience or reason, it will no longer be able to maintain itself in a position of security. Even the naturalistic school will allow that the State aims at producing order within its own boundaries, but how can it do so if it will be pledged to no law beyond those boundaries? A State which went upon the principle of despising faith and loyalty would be constantly threatened by enemies, and would consequently be unable to fulfil its purpose of being physical power. This is borne out by the experience of history, and we see how Cesare Borgia, Machiavelli's own ideal of a Prince, fell finally into the pit which he had digged for others. The State does not identify itself with physical power for its own sake; it is Power, in order to protect and to further the highest welfare of the human race. Taken without qualification, the doctrine of Power, as such, is quite empty of meaning, and unmoral as well, because it can find no justification within itself.

It is opposed by another, as false as itself, the moralizing doctrine of Liberal theorists. Here we find the State regarded as if it were a good little boy, who should be washed, and brushed, and sent to school, who should have his ears pulled to keep him obedient; he, on his side, is expected to be grateful and good, and God knows how much else. All this is German doctrinairism once again, working mischief in this direction also. All our political transgressions have been caused by the idea which comes so naturally to a highly educated people, that a scientifically incontrovertible principle is in itself sufficient to give a new direction to the world of historical fact. To this belief the Germans owe, not merely their spirit of scientific research, but also their manifold errors of practice. Our doctrinaire professors of international law think they have only to formulate a few axioms, and the nations, as reasonable beings, will be bound to agree to them; it is again and again forgotten that stupidity and passion have been among the great powers in history. Yet who can fail to see what a real force the passions of nationality have once more become in the nineteenth century? By what authority do individual men, such as Rotteck, Bluntschli, or Heffter, arrogate to themselves to utter such a 'Thou shalt!' to the State? No human being stands in a position to place positive binding commands upon all governments alike; he must realize that the reasons on which his precepts are based are liable to be modified and overcome by life as it is lived. This deals the death-blow to the false conception of some imaginary law. Only a positive law, then, remains, and no amount of theorizing can lay down principles for it, unconditionally and without more ado. All the labour of science can only prepare the way, until the truth and reason in certain principles of law become a living conviction in the nation. The abstract conception of the State, if it is to be carried to its logical conclusion, requires the existence of some supreme power on earth, endowed with external authority. Thus we are inevitably led to St Peter's Chair, for this supreme authority cannot be vested in any earthly body, but only in the Representative of Christ, who claims to speak in the name of God. No such power, however, ought to exist here below, for our world of beauty ought to be a world of liberty as well. It is evident that this effeminate sentimental conception of the law of nations has only been logically formularized by ultramontane

333

thinkers. The great Code of the Jesuits has carried it to its correct conclusion; the world is there seen as an Ethnarchy and the nations therein as an ideal community, presided over by an Ethnarch, the Pope, who, by his spiritual exhortations and influence, can coerce the individual States, and set limits to the sphere of each, and thus uphold the law among them all. There can be no other logical practical conclusion to an argument which regards the State as a personality acting upon orders. There can never be an international law which will impose itself upon the Great Powers as a practical restraint, by the mere fact of its theoretic scientific existence.

We must recognize, then, that these extreme views are both of them untenable, but we need not despair of establishing a doctrine of international law which is workable, because based upon the facts of history. In doing so it is above all important not to make greater demands upon human nature than its frailty can satisfy. The idealist who loses sight of this principle may all too easily become a disappointed enthusiast. One may be sure that any one who declaims that brute force is the only arbiter in the rivalries of nations is one of the sentimentalists undeceived who once smoked the Pipe of Peace, and who now, having seen that his dreams cannot be realized in this world, has rushed to the other extreme, and sees a crude cynicism in everything. It is true that all the really great political thinkers do cherish a cynical contempt for mankind in general, and with justice, provided it is not carried too far. Those who do not ask too much of human nature are the most successful in calling forth the really great gifts which it possesses amidst all its bestiality and liability to err. Therefore we must start from the historical standpoint, and take the State as it really is; physical power indeed, but also an institution designed to co-operate in the education of the human race. As physical power, its natural inclination will be to seize as many of the necessaries of life as it thinks useful to itself; it is acquisitive by nature. Every State, however, will of its own accord pay a certain respect to the neighbouring Powers. A more definite feeling of law will be evolved by time out of the dictates of reason and a mutual recognition of personal advantage. Every State will realize that it is an integral part of the community of other States in which it finds itself placed, and that it must live with them on some kind of terms, bad or good, as the case may be. These reflections will arise from very real considerations or reciprocity, and not from love to mankind.

The formal side of international law, dealing with such matters as the inviolability of the person of Ambassadors, and the ceremonial therewith connected, was fixed comparatively early, and in modern Europe diplomatic rights are absolutely settled. It is safe to say that this department of the law of nations is much less often infringed than the internal legal ordinances of the average State. Nevertheless the existence of international law must always be precarious, and it cannot cease to be a *lex imperfecta*, because no power higher than the States themselves can be called upon to arbitrate. Everything has to depend upon a mutual give-and-take, and, since the supreme compelling authority is lacking, the co-operation of science, and above all, the force of public opinion, will have an important influence. Savigny declared that international law was no *strictum ius*, but continually in process of development. But this is a long way from asserting the impotence of the law of nations, for changeful as it is, its influence is palpable, and we can follow its consequences step by step at the present day. There is no doubt that the development of modern international law has been quite particularly modified by Christianity, and the cosmopolitanism, in the noble sense of the word, which Christianity has introduced, and which goes beyond and above the State. It was therefore quite reasonable and logical to exclude the Porte, for many hundreds of years, from the scope of European international law. The government of the Sultan had no claim to a full share in its benefits so long as the Porte was dominated by a Mohammedan civilization. Only in later times, when Christianity had gained strength enough in the Balkan Peninsula to drive Mohammedanism somewhat into the background, was Turkey included in the international negotiations of Europe.

History shows us how great States spring to life from the ashes of their smaller brethren. These great States finally attain to a measure of strength which enables them to stand upon their own feet and to become sufficient for themselves. When they have reached this point they are anxious to secure peace, for the safety of their own existence and the civilization of which they are the guardians. Thus an organized comity of nations, or so-called

335

system of States, arises out of the mutual guarantee of law. This necessarily presupposes the existence of at least an approximate balance of power between the States. We have seen how very mechanical this idea became at one time in its application to European polities, but nevertheless it contains a kernel of truth. We cannot think of it as a *trutina gentium* with its scales exactly suspended, but any organized system of States must assume that no one State is so powerful as to be able to permit itself any licence without danger to itself. Here the superiority of Europe to the unripe political world of America at once becomes apparent. Nothing obliges the Union to place any restraint upon its actions, and the small South American Republics have only been spared a direct interference with their affairs because the connexion between them and their greater neighbour is still slight.

Gortschakoff was perfectly right when he said that the last International Congress would promote the interests neither of the nations which always fear attack, nor of those unduly powerful countries which believe themselves strong enough to take the offensive. The observation hit the mark, as may be proved by an actual example. Countries like Belgium and Holland, which, to the great detriment of that science, have unfortunately so long been the home of international jurisprudence, adopted a sentimental view of it, because they lived in constant fear of aggression. In the name of humanity, demands were made upon the victor which were unnatural, and unreasonable, and irreconcilable with the power of the State. The Peace Treaties of Nymegen and Ryswyk both show how Holland was regarded in the seventeenth century as the arena of *la haute politique*. Switzerland held the same position later, and few persons nowadays reflect how ludicrous it is for Belgium to look upon herself as the chosen centre for the science of international law. As it is certain that all such law must be grounded upon practice, so it is equally certain that a State whose position is abnormal will also be the occasion for an abnormal misconstruction of the principles which should govern it. Belgium is a neutral State, therefore incomplete by its very nature; how is it possible to expect a sound and healthy law of nations to proceed from such a source? I must ask you all to keep this in mind when in time to come you are confronted with the voluminous Belgian literature on this subject.

There is, on the other hand, a State in our midst today which believes itself to be always in the position of the assailant, and which is consequently the fountain-head of barbarism in international law. It is the fault of England and of England only, that in time of war the maritime law of nations continues on the level of privileged piracy. Thus we see that, between nations, all law is grounded upon mutual give-and-take, and that it is useless to hold up the phrases and doctrines of a vaguely general humanity for the edification of the countries concerned. In this matter theory must be rooted in practice, and practice presupposes a real reciprocity, or, in other words, a real balance of power.

In order to make no mistake as to the real meaning of international law, we must always remember that it must not run counter to the nature of the State. No State can reasonably be asked to adopt a course which would lead it to destroy itself. Likewise every State in the comity of nations must retain the attributes of sovereignty whose defence is its highest duty even in its international relations. We find the principles of international law most secure in that department of it which does not trench upon questions of sovereignty; that is in the domain of etiquette and of international civil law.

In times of peace these agreements are seldom encroached upon, or if they are, the offence is expiated at once. Any insult offered, even if only outwardly, to the honour of a State, casts doubt upon the nature of the State. We mistake the moral laws of politics if we reproach any State with having an over-sensitive sense of honour, for this instinct must be highly developed in each one of them if it is to be true to its own essence. The State is no violet, to bloom unseen; its power should stand proudly, for all the world to see, and it cannot allow even the symbols of it to be contested. If the flag is insulted, the State must claim reparation; should this not be forthcoming, war must follow, however small the occasion may seem; for the State has never any choice but to maintain the respect in which it is held among its fellows.

From this it follows that all the restraints to which States bind themselves by treaty are voluntary, and that all treaties are concluded on the tacit understanding *rebus sic stantibus*. No State has, or ever will exist, which is willing to hold to all eternity to the agreements which it signs. No state will ever be or ever will be in a position to pledge its whole hereafter to a treaty, which cannot fail to be a limitation of its sovereignty; it always intends that the contract shall eventually be annulled, and shall only apply so long as the present circumstances are not totally altered. This principle is often called inhumane, but its logical conclusion shows it to be the contrary. Only if the State is aware that all its treaties only apply conditionally will it go to work prudently in the making of them. History is not meant to be looked at from the point of view of a judge hearing a civil suit. According to that standard, Prussia, having signed the Treaty of Tilsit, would have been wrong in attacking Napoleon in 1813. But this treaty, like others, had been concluded *rebus sic stantibus*, and, thank God, those *res* had been radically altered some years before. A noble nation was given the chance of shaking off an intolerable yoke, and as soon as a people is aware that their time is come, they have the right to make the attempt.

Politics must never discount the free moral forces in the national life. No State in the world may renounce the 'I' in its sovereignty. If conditions are imposed upon it which impinge upon this, and which it is unable to prevent, then 'the breach is more honoured than the observance'. It is one of the fine things about history that we see nations more easily consoled for their material losses than for injuries to their honour.

The loss of a province can always be accepted as an inward necessity, but a brave people feels continually insulted when it has to endure a servitude, so called. By keeping his troops perpetually upon Prussian soil, Napoleon I filled the most patient hearts with burning hatred. When a State has been hurt in its honour, the breaking of its treaties is only a question of time, as England and France discovered in 1870, when in their Crimean arrogance they closed the Black Sea to the warships of exhausted Russia. Russia was fully justified in using the favourable opportunity of the Franco-Prussian War to set aside this agreement with the tacit consent of Germany.

When a State recognizes that existing treaties no longer express the actual political conditions, and when it cannot persuade the other Powers to give way by peaceful negotiation, the moment has come when the nations proceed to the ordeal by battle. A State thus situated is conscious when it declares war that it is performing an inevitable duty. The combatant countries are moved by no incentives of personal greed, but they feel that the real position of power is not expressed by existing treaties and that they must be determined afresh by the judgment of the nations, since no peaceful agreement can be reached. The righteousness of war depends simply and solely upon the consciousness of a moral necessity. War is justified because the great national personalities can suffer no compelling force superior to themselves, and because history must always be in constant flux; war therefore must be taken as part of the divinely appointed order. Of course it is possible for a Government to be mistaken about the necessity which drives them to declare it; 'War creates no right which was not already existing', as Niebuhr truly said, and, for this very reason, isolated deeds of violence are justified by their successful accomplishment, witness the achievement of German and Italian unity. On the other hand, since not every war is caused by an inward necessity, the historian must keep his vision clear, and remember that the life of States is counted in centuries. The proud saying of the defeated Piedmontese, 'We are beginning again', will always have its place in the chronicles of noble nations.

No Courts of Arbitration will ever succeed in banishing war from the world. It is absolutely impossible for the other members of the group of nations to take an impartial view of any question vitally affecting one of their number. Parties there must be, if only because the nations are bound together, or driven apart by living interests of the most various kinds. What European country could have taken a totally unbiassed attitude towards the question of Alsace and Lorraine, supposing that Germany had been foolish enough to submit it to an Arbitration Court? The wildest imagination cannot picture a detached Tribunal in this instance. Here we have the explanation of the well-known fact, that international Congresses are quite capable of finding legal formulae for the results of a war, but that they can never avert the outbreak of it. A foreign State can only pronounce impartial judgment on matters of third-rate importance.

We have already seen that war is both justifiable and moral, and that the ideal of perpetual peace is not only impossible but immoral as well. It is unworthy of man's reason to regard the impracticable as feasible, but a life of pure intellect is all too often enervating to the reasoning faculty. War cannot vanish from the earth as long as human and passion remain what they are. It is delightful to observe how the feeling of patriotism breaks involuntarily through the cosmopolitan phrases even of the apostles of perpetual peace. The prophet Joel prayed that before its day should dawn Israel might call all the heathen to a bloody reckoning in the valley of Jehoshaphat, and Victor Hugo likewise demanded that the Germans should get their drubbing first. Yet again we must repeat – the arbitrament of forces is the logical outcome of the nature of the State. The mere fact of the existence of many States involves the necessity of war. The dream of eternal peace – said Frederick the Great – is a phantom, which each man rejects when the call of war rings in his own ear. It is impossible to imagine – he went on to say – any balance of power which can last.

War, however, is the very sphere in which we can most clearly trace the triumph of human reason. All noble nations have felt that the physical forces which war unchains require to be regulated, and thus an international military law has been developed, based upon mutual interests. This department of international jurisprudence, which fools dismiss as unworthy of a civilized people, is where the science has achieved the most; in modern days we rarely see crude violations of the laws of war. There is nothing in international law more beautiful, or showing more unmistakably the continual progress of mankind, than a whole series of principles, grounded only upon *universalis consensus* and yet as firmly established as those of the Common Law of any given country. It is evident that the law of nations must always lag a few steps behind the law of the individual States, for certain principles of civilization and law must first be developed at home before they can be put in practice in intercourse abroad. Thus it was impossible to have international legislation against slavery until respect for the individual had become as universal as our century has made it. In the course of centuries the instinct for justice between countries has become so strong, that at any rate the formal side of international law may be looked upon as quite secured. The publicity of modern public life has done much towards this end. The days of the English Blue-books are indeed at an end; Blue, Green, or Yellow, they are all alike intended to befog the Philistine in a cloud of incense; nor is it ever difficult for an adroit diplomat thus to throw dust in the eyes of Parliament. Still, the whole trend of political life has come into the open to such a degree that any gross breach of international law immediately causes great irritation in every civilized country.

We will now examine a few of the fundamental principles which have been legally defined primarily by the peaceful intercourse of nations. Every people without exception must nowadays be allowed to pursue uninterruptedly the trade and commerce, the arts and sciences, which are such a bond between different countries. The races of antiquity sometimes forbade other nations to practise some particular industry, whose secrets they looked upon as their own private possession. Even in the time of the later Roman Empire it was forbidden to instruct the barbarians in the art of shipbuilding, and similar monopolies were practically enforced at the date of the Hanseatic League. In modern days this could no longer happen. No State may deny free competition in trade to its fellows, and this principle is guarded by a system of treaties.

In ancient times, moreover, almost every nation laid claim to some sort of monopoly with regard to the navigation of sea. In later days it was still held that particular seas, which were not exactly the ocean itself, belonged to certain States, as the Adriatic to the Venetian Republic, the Ligurian Sea to Venice, the Gulf of Bothnia to Sweden, and so forth. Now the sea is only the property of the countries upon its shores as far as their military domination of it extends, that is, within cannon range from the shore, and this limit has been altered again quite recently by the advance of technical science. All such questions are finally decided, however, by the realities of power; if a State is in a position to dominate any sea, no amount of well-meant theorizing will make that sea free. The Caspian is nominally controlled by two States which border it, Russia and Persia, but the power of the former is such that we may call the Caspian a Russian Sea. If a Government were established in Constantinople which was really able to shut the Bosphorus against every Navy, it could mock at all the declamations which might be hurled against it. For the rest, the ocean is free to every ship sailing under legitimate colours. The policing of the high seas is provided by the Navies of every country, for every ship of war has the right to stop a merchant vessel and inspect her papers. This is the result of an endlessly long and difficult process of development, but all the Powers are now agreed that an occasional inconvenience to their merchantmen is a lesser evil than sea piracy.

All international rights are guaranteed by treaties between States. It is clear that these must differ in many ways from the contracts of civil law.

The first distinction is that they can only be concluded upon a basis of faith and loyalty, as there is no judge who can enforce their observance. The Athenians were guided by a true instinct when they contracted their agreements only for a limited time. Christian nations think otherwise, and make their treaties for eternity, but, as we have seen, they are made on the understanding that they are only to endure while the conditions of power between the contracting parties are not totally altered. The more this is insisted upon, and the more soberly each State reflects upon it, the more secure will their treaties be.

There are, furthermore, such things as compulsory treaties. No agreement made by sovereign States in time of peace can ever be so described – little Switzerland, for instance, is perfectly at liberty to make or to refuse a peaceful treaty with ourselves – but, on the other hand, every peace imposed by the victor on the vanquished must be compulsory. Here again we are confronted with the question of who can be arbiter endowed with legal authority to pronounce whether a treaty is freely made. Neither does the law of nations admit of lapse by superannuation, for this is the nature of a juridical make-shift. For instance, when the law decrees twenty years to be the prescriptive period for theft, the legislator is acting a pretence for the practical reason that it does not pay to go on inquiring into trivial matters after so great a lapse of time. The life of nations, however, is counted by centuries, so that a prescriptive period can only enter into it after long ages have gone by. Frederick the Great was absolutely within his rights when he claimed the four Silesian Duchies for his State, although the treaties which secured them to his House had been made more than two hundred years before.

In international treaties great stress should be laid upon the cautious use of terms, and in this respect also we can trace a great progress in the course of history. In former times it sometimes happened that a treaty which was apparently concluded got no recognition because the plenipotentiaries had ostensibly exceeded their powers. Ancient States got out of the difficulty by delivering up the plenipotentiaries, but today this is no longer possible. The contracting States are now not only obliged to bind themselves specifically, but a definite period is also laid down for the ratification of all treaties by the supreme authorities concerned, and until this ratification is accomplished the contract is not completed. As a secondary point, States are now bound by their treaties, no matter in whom the supreme authority is vested. The French Republic is pledged to the treaties made by the French Empire. It is therefore important that contracts should be worded as clearly as possible, and, as a general rule, should contain no secret clauses, for these confuse the legal issue by leading the nations, which are ignorant of their contents, to form a false estimate of the obligations for which they are mutually responsible; and they may in consequence become a danger to their own Government.

Old-fashioned Cabinets thought that secret clauses gave them an opportunity of tripping up a rival State, but the weapon was double-edged. Exceptions, of course, there are. When Prussia made terms of peace with the conquered States of South Germany in 1866, an offensive and defensive alliance was secretly contracted, which was kept dark for a time. There were good reasons for this, for when France, in the following year, made her desire for war evident it was publicly announced that North and South Germany would stand together.

There is one subject above all others in which international law may be set upon a firm footing, namely, international civil law, the treatment which a State metes out to aliens. An immeasurable step in advance was made when the foreigner was made absolutely secure of the protection of the law in every civilized country. It is an insult to the human race to say that the law of nations still rests upon mere force. This is untrue, but still men must not demand the impossible of one another. The difficulties spring to light the moment the subject of international civil law is closely studied, for we are faced again with the reservation which all these obligations contain, and we see them subject to each nation's care for its own security. Let us make as many treaties as we like about international civil law, but they must all presuppose that the alien is not troublesome to ourselves. Should he become so, the State must have power to expel him without giving reasons, even if it has signed a treaty which, as a rule, ensures security of residence to the subjects of another Government. It is thus that persons are got rid of who are suspected of being spies or unauthorized agents; discussions of such cases would usually be very unpleasant and injurious to the friendly relations between the countries. It is therefore a perfectly reasonable principle that every foreigner may be immediately driven out with no explanation beyond that his presence is not desired. There must be no tampering with this right, for otherwise honest dwellers in a foreign land will not be left free from annoyance, and consequently what seems harsh at first sight turns out to be the truest kindness. It is impossible, on the other hand, for the State to be legally empowered to banish its own subjects. If we were to expel the Jesuits, we might at least be sure that they would find an asylum everywhere; but if the State tried to do the same by ordinary criminals, it would simply have to blow them into the air, for no other country would receive them. Strictly speaking, the right of banishment is inconsistent with an organized political society.

The process of time has connected a reciprocal support in the prosecution of criminals with the mutual defence of civil law, and with it a whole series of the most difficult problems have come into being. It is easy enough to state the theory that the whole human race is concerned in prosecuting crime, and among noble nations this principle presents no difficulties until we come to the definition of what crime is. The distinction between ordinary and political crime at once becomes of primary importance. Every State must make the prosecution of persons accused of high treason by another Government dependent upon its own interests. A state of war may be latent between two countries who are outwardly friendly, as is the case with France and Germany at the present time. Again, it may often happen that a man whom the law of his own country regards as a political traitor may be the welcome guest of another nation, and it would be unreasonable to require that they should deliver him up. Agreements can be made in respect of the extradiction of common offenders though no State will engage itself to refuse its protection to political criminals, but will always reserve the right of judgment for each case. This applies to political offences in general, although there are certain bomb-throwing Anarchists pure and simple about whom a mutual arrangement might be possible.

The exact degree of ordinary crime which involves extradition can, of course, only be settled by positive treaties; but it should in any case be limited to really serious offences. The great differences of legal procedure in the various countries make it imperatively necessary to try offenders as much as possible by their own laws, and experience has shown that this expansion of the powers of courts, as far as can be managed, has had good results.

Out of the joint maintenance of law has sprung an ordered comity of nations, or system of States, which has also received its settled outward forms. The disputes over etiquette in the seventeenth century which seem so ludicrous to us now had the right idea at the back of them in spite of their lack of good taste. Even today a difference exists between royal majesty and petty princes, and nonetheless because unwritten, between the Great Powers and second- or third-rate States. A State may be defined as a Great Power if its total destruction would require a coalition of other States to accomplish. The preponderance of Great Powers is felt on all hands today, yet it has been the very means of ensuring a certain security in international traffic. The Congress of Aix-la-Chapelle in 1818 set diplomatic relations on so firm a footing that all civilized countries now differentiate exactly between the various classes of diplomats. Another result of the undue preponderance of the leading European Powers in modern history has been to exclude the smaller States from taking part in Congresses unless they are directly concerned in a disputed point. If, however, one of these small countries is consulted, its opinion is given the same weight as that of one of the Great Powers. Moreover, a Congress is not ruled by a majority but by the *liberum veto* of natural Law. I have spoken already about the unreasonableness of deciding by the vote of a majority, when the question at issue is not one of power in which physical strength supports the decision by the many against the few. It is not logical to proceed on this basis in a Congress which is not waging war, but is formulating the results of war, and of whom unanimity must consequently be demanded.

345

It is not possible to lay down any fixed principles for international policy, for, as we have seen, the unconditional doctrine of intervention is as false as its antithesis. Every State may be placed in a position where the party strifes of another country are a menace to its own freedom. Thus we may find that a cosmopolitan party at the helm of a neighbouring State may lead to consequences so important for ourselves that we are bound for our own sake to interfere. Such intervention is always fraught with danger, for the worship of national independence has waxed so strong in our own day that any meddling with it will produce a strong reaction in other countries beyond the one directly concerned. Stern experience has taught modern States to hold themselves aloof as much as possible from the private affairs of their neighbours. No dogmas can decide these problems, but when its own safety is at stake a State should, and will, take action.

When a war is actually in progress its guiding political idea is to bring about new conditions of international law which will express the real relative strength of the contending parties and be recognized by both of them. It is, therefore, perfectly equitable to wage war in the most effective manner possible, so that its goal of peace may be reached as quickly as may be. For this reason the blow must be aimed at the enemy's heart, and the use of the most formidable weapons is absolutely justifiable, provided that they do not inflict needless suffering on the wounded. Philanthropists may declaim as much as they like against explosive shells fired into the powder magazines of wooden battle-ships, but still facts remain unchanged. States in conclave have decided what weapons are to be forbidden; the use of explosive bullets for small arms was prohibited at the instance of Russia. It is permissible to take advantage of all the enemy's weak points, and a State may turn treason and mutiny within its enemy's borders to serve its own ends. Nothing but the rapid march of events prevented us in Prussia from making a compact with Hungary in 1866.

It is equally impossible to deny to a belligerent State the right of employing all its troops in the field, whether they be savages or civilized men. It is important to take an unbiassed view of ourselves in this question, in order to guard against prejudice in respect of other nations. The Germans raised a fearful outcry against the French for letting loose the Turcos against a civilized nation in the last war. It was a natural accusation in the passion of the moment, but our calmer judgment can find no violation of international law in what was done. The principle stands that a belligerent State may, and must, throw all its troops and all its physical resources into the struggle. Where is it possible to draw the line? Which of the charming races which make up its Empire is Russia to withhold from the field? A State is obliged to make the fullest use of all its material strength, but it must do so in accordance with the honourable usages which have been settled by the long experience of war. Yet with all this, the employment of the Turcos places the claim of France to be the leader of civilization in a peculiar light. Thus a whole series of complaints arises because demands are made upon a State which it cannot possibly satisfy. In the national wars of the present day every honest subject is a spy, and therefore the banishment of 80,000 Germans from France is 1870 was not in itself a violation of the law, but was only indefensible because it was carried out with a certain brutality.

There is one rule of humanity in war which is theoretically of universal application, although it is only practically recognized in land campaigns; namely, that it is States who are fighting, and not their individual citizens. Certain definite signs there must be, therefore, to distinguish those persons who are entitled to fight by authority of the State, and who are to be treated as soldiers. It is an ugly gap in international law that no universal agreement has as yet been reached on this point, although it is the foundation of all humanity in war. A soldier must feel that he has no foe but the soldiers of the enemy, and that he need not fear that the peasant who has met him in peaceful fashion will be shooting at him half an hour later from behind a bush. The behaviour of soldiery in an enemy's country is sure to be unfeeling and cruel if they do not know who they should treat as soldiers like themselves, and who as highway robbers. No one can be recognized as a soldier unless he has taken the oath of allegiance, stands under the Articles of War, and wears some kind of badge which need not be exactly a full uniform. It goes without saying that the irregular levies who hover around the enemy, and do not stand under the Articles of War, should be treated with unrelenting severity. It is urgently necessary that an international agreement should be

347

come to over the forms which make an armed person a real member of a lawful army. The question was discussed in Brussels in 1874, when the difference of interests at once became apparent. Small States like Switzerland had no desire to bind themselves by any obligations.

For the time being every State continues to decide for itself alone which of its opponents it will consider as belonging to the enemy's army, and which are to be regarded merely as robbers. Many of the *francs-tireurs* of 1870–71 deserve our moral respect by their despairing efforts to save their country, but from the point of view of international law they were highway thieves. As such, Napoleon justly treated Schill and his companions. Schill was a Prussian staff-officer who deserted, who tempted his men to do the same, and who then began a war against France as chief of a band of robbers in the eye of the law. The King's anger against his action knew no bounds, for it was the end of all political cohesion if every staff-officer were at liberty to collect a little army and fight upon his own account. Nevertheless when Napoleon held to the letter of international law he perpetrated an unexampled piece of cruelty, and did a very imprudent thing into the bargain. Every noble feeling was naturally on Schill's side, even as Schenkendorf made him prophesy:

> Und mein König selbst wird sagen:
> Ruh in Frieden, treuer Schill!
> (For my king himself will tell me,
> 'Sleep in peace, true-hearted Schill.')

Yet with all this the action of the enemy was absolutely in accordance with the law of nations.

When it is quite clearly defined who is part of the army, and who may claim honourable treatment as a prisoner of war, it becomes possible to spare the private property of a hostile country to a very great extent. But here again it is important to understand that national pride must not be insulted in the name of humanity. At the same Congress in Brussels, Prussia proposed that a conquered hostile province should be administered *ipso jure* by the military authorities of the enemy. This would in many ways be an advantage for material existence. When a general knows that he will have the support of international law in requiring the obedience of the enemy's officials he will impose stricter discipline upon his own troops, and altogether he will be able to act more humanely. Nevertheless there are more important things to be considered than trade and commerce. The German proposal expressed the confidence of a nation accustomed to conquer, but could we seriously desire that Prussian officials should be legally compelled to obey the orders of a Russian general? Such an excess of humanity would not only lead to dishonour but would also be inhumane. We expect our countrymen to resist the enemy by every means allowed. Let us call to mind our experiences in the past. No East Prussian subject can forget how President Dohna wrought against the enemy, and during the Russian occupation, collected the taxes for the rightful king. Are such acts to be forbidden in the name of philanthropy, and does not patriotism count for more? It matters more that a nation should keep its honour unsullied than that a Russian, incensed by such opposition from the sturdy men of Prussia, should burn a couple of villages which he had meant to rule over with his knout. International law must not meddle in kindness' name with the moral possessions of a people.

Private property may be respected to the widest extent, even when the enemy is in actual and purely military possession, so long as the limits of the hostile army are clearly defined. Requisitions are permitted, and it is a universal practice to give *bons* in exchange; the business of getting these repaid is naturally the concern of the conquered party. The wanton burning of villages, and attack upon property as such, of which the devastation of the Palatinate by Melac is such a terrible example, is looked upon by all modern civilized States as a breach of international law. Private property may only be injured to the extent rendered inevitable by the exigencies of war. It is mere mockery, however, to apply these principles to warfare against savages. A Negro tribe must be punished by the burning of their villages, for it is the only kind of example which will avail. If the German Empire has abandoned this principle today it has done so out of disgraceful weakness, and for no reasons of humanity or high respect for law.[1]

The standard of forbearance expected even of civilized nations should not be higher than the feeling for law which is common to

[1] Lecture delivered in the winter of 1891-92.

349

all nations, and the State should not be used for experiments in philanthropy. We had a striking example of this truth in the Franco-Prussian War, when, in an access of false kindness, we undertook to respect the private property of France upon the seas. The impulse was noble and humane, but we forgot that among the other States stood England, turning a deaf ear on principle to generous ideas, and moreover we never reckoned that France would not pay us back in our own coin. Our unreciprocated generosity relieved France of the necessity of protecting her commerce against our ships of war, and enabled her to keep her whole fleet free for the war. Her marines, and her first-class naval artillery were all brought ashore, and in the course of the winter we constantly had to fight against these naval troops. Thus our action only put weapons into the enemy's hands. Every forward step in international humanity must be founded upon reciprocity.

We must now consider a number of cases in which doubt arises whether the property in question belongs to the State or to private owners. It goes without saying that all the property of the State is the spoil of the victor, and this applies first and foremost to military stores in the widest sense, as State railways, etc. A more difficult question arises with regard to the depots of the railways owned by private companies, but nevertheless accorded a practical monopoly by the State. There is no doubt that the enemy may make use of the rolling stock during the war, but may he keep the waggons besides? The nature of the French railways fully justified our decision in the last war: they were State-owned, and we kept the waggons we had taken, in order, when the settlement came, to return them in part payment. The problem of Banks is still harder to decide. There are Banks, such as our own Reichsbank, in which a Board of bankers have an interest as well as the State. Commercially this is an advantage, for it brings the Bank more in touch with the big business, and places it in the front rank of contemporary commercial life. It is, however, an illusion to suppose that it thus secured from confiscation at the hands of a foreign conqueror. An enemy must undoubtedly treat it as a State Bank, and will not consider the smaller share in it held by private persons. Modern international law lays down that those great treasures of a State which serve the ends of Science and Art are to be regarded as the common property of all mankind and immune from the hand of the spoiler. Formerly this principle was systematically trampled upon.

As regards treatment of the standing army, and of all persons connected with national defence, each individual can claim honourable treatment as a prisoner of war, and all attempts to place such persons in the ranks of their enemy's army is contrary to international law. It is doubtful, however, whether this principle applied to past centuries, for it is one which depends entirely upon the sense of justice of a given age. The mercenary system showed so total a disregard of the finer feelings at the beginning of the eighteenth century that one French Regiment, of German nationality, was taken from the French by the Saxons at Hochstadt, and again later from the Saxons by the Swedes; from the Swedes it passed over to the Prussians at Stralsund, and finally remained with them as the 'Young Anhalt' Regiment. Nevertheless, when Frederick the Great put the captive Saxons in the Prussian ranks at Pirna, it was felt that a proceeding which had once been undisputed was now no longer possible. The Saxons deserted in herds, and a repetition of the experiment in modern days would palpably be madness, as well as a breach of law.

No one contests the right of every State not only to make war, but to declare itself neutral in the wars of others, in so far as material conditions allow. It is mere boasting when a State declares a neutrality which it is not in a position to uphold, for neutrality needs defence as much as does participation with one of the belligerents. The neutral State must disarm every soldier who crosses its frontier, and should it fail to do so the belligerents are justified under some circumstances in refusing to recognize its neutrality, even if it has only permitted the armed enemy to enter a single one of its villages.

Unhappily the laws of war are still very differently interpreted on land and on the seas, and it is here that the mischievous influence of English power over civilization and universal law cannot fail to strike any one who chooses to see it. The melancholy saying of Schiller still holds good:

> Auf den Wellen ist alles Welle,
> Auf dem Meer ist kein Eigentum.
> (There is nothing stable among the waves,
> Where no man calls anything his own.)

Deeply mortifying as this is to our pride, it is true, because even today there is no balance of power at sea, and for this we have no one to blame but England. Her superiority is so immeasurable that she can do whatever she pleases. A balance of naval power must be brought to pass before the ideals of humanity and international law can hope to be realized upon the seas. The modern infatuation of public opinion is often astonishing; again and again countries are belauded which are following false paths; again and again the sentimentalities of Belgian teachers of international law and the barbarisms of the English maritime code are held up to admiration. Every other State would be ready, under certain conditions, to respect merchant shipping in time of war, but England alone holds by the principle that at sea there is no distinction to be made between the property of the State and the property of the individual. So long as one State takes its stand upon this all the others must imitate its barbarism. Of course maritime conditions cannot be quite the same as those on land, because there are many commodities which serve the purposes of war. Therefore freedom for private property cannot be so widely extended at sea, but this is no reason why ocean warfare should to all eternity remain ocean piracy, or why belligerents should be authorized to despoil one another of all merchandise without distinctions made.

Up till now all progress in maritime law has been brought about by the second-class navies. Again and again we see how the Powers are driven for their own sakes to make humane regulations, and in this we have the explanation of the efforts made by the smaller countries to soften the maritime law. We must not suppose that the English are worse individually than anybody else, and if we were in their position we might perhaps act as they do. In the League of armed neutrality in 1780 the second-class navies laid down, firstly, that the flag should cover the goods and the enemy's non-military merchandise should pass free in neutral bottoms; and secondly, that all blockades must be effective, and no Power be given the right to declare a blockade of a whole coast which was not actually closed by hostile warships. Treaty after treaty tried to give effect to these principles. England has now at last acknowledged that the flag covers the goods, a concession forced from her by the rise of American sea-power. If it had depended upon Germany, the question of freedom for private property at sea would have been settled long ago by international discussion; but theory has no influence over the law of nations, unless it expresses to some extent the actual relative power of the different States.

From whatever angle we view political science we find that its proper function lies in dealing with that only true humanity which is rooted in the actual facts of history, and that the dreams of fancy are beyond its scope. The destinies of States are accomplished by processes of attraction and repulsion whose final consummation is hidden from mortal eyes, and whose tendencies can only be dimly guessed at. There is no need for us to become critics of history, for the real point is to understand how the Divine plan has unfolded itself little by little in all the variety of actual existence. A practical politician is great if he can read the signs of the times, and foresee more or less the trend of history at a given moment. No quality beseems him better than modesty. He must not stray with blind uncertainty among the many complex circumstances which he has to handle, but he must concentrate upon the attainable and keep his goal clearly before him. It is my hope that you may have learned from these lectures how many factors go to the making of history and how carefully considered all our political judgments should therefore be. If what I have said has taught you this modesty of true science. I shall be well content.